WILLIAM SHA

✳

LOVE'S LABOUR'S LOST

EDITED WITH AN INTRODUCTION AND A COMMENTARY BY JOHN KERRIGAN

THE PLAY IN PERFORMANCE BY NICHOLAS WALTON

PENGUIN BOOKS

PENGUIN BOOKS

Published by the Penguin Group
Penguin Books Ltd, 80 Strand, London WC2R ORL, England
Penguin Group (USA) Inc., 375 Hudson Street, New York, New York 10014, USA
Penguin Group (Canada), 10 Alcorn Avenue, Toronto, Ontario, Canada M4V 3B2
(a division of Pearson Penguin Canada Inc.)
Penguin Ireland, 25 St Stephen's Green, Dublin 2, Ireland
(a division of Penguin Books Ltd)
Penguin Group (Australia), 250 Camberwell Road, Camberwell, Victoria 3124, Australia
(a division of Pearson Australia Group Pty Ltd)
Penguin Books India Pvt Ltd, 11 Community Centre, Panchsheel Park,
New Delhi – 110 017, India
Penguin Group (NZ), cnr Airborne and Rosedale Roads, Albany, Auckland 1310, New Zealand
(a division of Pearson New Zealand Ltd)
Penguin Books (South Africa) (Pty) Ltd, 24 Sturdee Avenue, Rosebank 2196, South Africa

Penguin Books Ltd, Registered Offices: 80 Strand, London WC2R ORL, England

www.penguin.com

This edition first published in Penguin Books 1982
Reissued in the Penguin Shakespeare series 2005

005

This edition copyright © Penguin Books, 1982, 1996
Introduction, Commentary and Account of the Text copyright © John Kerrigan, 1982
General Introduction and Chronology copyright © Stanley Wells, 2005
The Play in Performance and Further Reading copyright © Nicholas Walton, 2005

All rights reserved

The moral right of the editors has been asserted

Set in Monophoto Ehrhardt
Printed in England by Clays Ltd, St Ives plc

ISBN-13: 978–0–141–02055–6

www.greenpenguin.co.uk

Penguin Books is committed to a sustainable
future for our business, our readers and our planet.
This book is made from Forest Stewardship
Council™ certified paper.

ALWAYS LEARNING   PEARSON

CONTENTS

CONTENTS

GENERAL INTRODUCTION

Every play by Shakespeare is unique. This is part of his greatness. A restless and indefatigable experimenter, he moved with a rare amalgamation of artistic integrity and dedicated professionalism from one kind of drama to another. Never shackled by convention, he offered his actors the alternation between serious and comic modes from play to play, and often also within the plays themselves, that the repertory system within which he worked demanded, and which provided an invaluable stimulus to his imagination. Introductions to individual works in this series attempt to define their individuality. But there are common factors that underpin Shakespeare's career.

Nothing in his heredity offers clues to the origins of his genius. His upbringing in Stratford-upon-Avon, where he was born in 1564, was unexceptional. His mother, born Mary Arden, came from a prosperous farming family. Her father chose her as his executor over her eight sisters and his four stepchildren when she was only in her late teens, which suggests that she was of more than average practical ability. Her husband John, a glover, apparently unable to write, was nevertheless a capable businessman and loyal townsfellow, who seems to have fallen on relatively hard times in later life. He would have been brought up as a Catholic, and may have retained Catholic sympathies, but his son subscribed publicly to Anglicanism throughout his life.

The most important formative influence on Shakespeare was his school. As the son of an alderman who became bailiff (or mayor) in 1568, he had the right to attend the town's grammar school. Here he would have received an education grounded in classical rhetoric and oratory, studying authors such as Ovid, Cicero and Quintilian, and would have been required to read, speak, write and even think in Latin from his early years. This classical education permeates Shakespeare's work from the beginning to the end of his career. It is apparent in the self-conscious classicism of plays of the early 1590s such as the tragedy of *Titus Andronicus*, *The Comedy of Errors*, and the narrative poems *Venus and Adonis* (1592–3) and *The Rape of Lucrece* (1593–4), and is still evident in his latest plays, informing the dream visions of *Pericles* and *Cymbeline* and the masque in *The Tempest*, written between 1607 and 1611. It inflects his literary style throughout his career. In his earliest writings the verse, based on the ten-syllabled, five-beat iambic pentameter, is highly patterned. Rhetorical devices deriving from classical literature, such as alliteration and antithesis, extended similes and elaborate wordplay, abound. Often, as in *Love's Labour's Lost* and *A Midsummer Night's Dream*, he uses rhyming patterns associated with lyric poetry, each line self-contained in sense, the prose as well as the verse employing elaborate figures of speech. Writing at a time of linguistic ferment, Shakespeare frequently imports Latinisms into English, coining words such as abstemious, addiction, incarnadine and adjunct. He was also heavily influenced by the eloquent translations of the Bible in both the Bishops' and the Geneva versions. As his experience grows, his verse and prose become more supple, the patterning less apparent, more ready to accommodate the rhythms of ordinary speech, more colloquial in diction, as in the speeches of the Nurse in *Romeo and Juliet*, the characterful prose of Falstaff and Hamlet's soliloquies. The effect is of increasing psychological realism, reaching its greatest heights in *Hamlet*, *Othello*, *King Lear*, *Macbeth* and *Antony and Cleopatra*. Gradually he discovered ways of adapting the regular beat of the pentameter to make it an infinitely flexible instrument for matching thought with feeling. Towards the end of his career, in plays such as *The Winter's Tale*, *Cymbeline* and *The Tempest*, he adopts a more highly mannered style, in keeping with the more overtly symbolical and emblematical mode in which he is writing.

So far as we know, Shakespeare lived in Stratford till after his marriage to Anne Hathaway, eight years his senior, in 1582. They had three children: a daughter, Susanna, born in 1583 within six months of their marriage, and twins, Hamnet and Judith, born in 1585. The next seven years of Shakespeare's life are virtually a blank. Theories that he may have been, for instance, a schoolmaster, or a lawyer, or a soldier, or a sailor, lack evidence to support them. The first reference to him in print, in Robert Greene's pamphlet *Greene's Groatsworth of Wit* of 1592, parodies a line from *Henry VI, Part III*, implying that Shakespeare was already an established playwright. It seems likely that at some unknown point after the birth of his twins he joined a theatre company and gained experience as both actor and writer in the provinces and London. The London theatres closed because of plague in 1593 and 1594; and during these years, perhaps recognizing the need for an alternative career, he wrote and published the narrative poems *Venus and Adonis* and *The Rape of Lucrece*. These are the only works we can be certain that Shakespeare himself was responsible for putting into print. Each bears the author's dedication to Henry Wriothesley, Earl of Southampton (1573–1624), the second in warmer terms than the first. Southampton, younger than Shakespeare by ten years, is the only person to whom he personally dedicated works. The Earl may have been a close friend, perhaps even the beautiful and adored young man whom Shakespeare celebrates in his *Sonnets*.

The resumption of playing after the plague years saw the founding of the Lord Chamberlain's Men, a company to which Shakespeare was to belong for the rest of his career, as actor, shareholder and playwright. No other dramatist of the period had so stable a relationship with a single company. Shakespeare knew the actors for whom he was writing and the conditions in which they performed. The permanent company was made up of around twelve to fourteen players, but one actor often played more than one role in a play and additional actors were hired as needed. Led by the tragedian Richard Burbage (1568–1619) and, initially, the comic actor Will Kemp (d. 1603), they rapidly achieved a high reputation, and when King James I succeeded Queen Elizabeth I in 1603 they were renamed as the King's Men. All the women's parts were played by boys; there is no evidence that any female role was ever played by a male actor over the age of about eighteen. Shakespeare had enough confidence in his boys to write for them long and demanding roles such as Rosalind (who, like other heroines of the romantic comedies, is disguised as a boy for much of the action) in *As You Like It*, Lady Macbeth and Cleopatra. But there are far more fathers than mothers, sons than daughters, in his plays, few if any of which require more than the company's normal complement of three or four boys.

The company played primarily in London's public playhouses – there were almost none that we know of in the rest of the country – initially in the Theatre, built in Shoreditch in 1576, and from 1599 in the Globe, on Bankside. These were wooden, more or less circular structures, open to the air, with a thrust stage surmounted by a canopy and jutting into the area where spectators who paid one penny stood, and surrounded by galleries where it was possible to be seated on payment of an additional penny. Though properties such as cauldrons, stocks, artificial trees or beds could indicate locality, there was no representational scenery. Sound effects such as flourishes of trumpets, music both martial and amorous, and accompaniments to songs were provided by the company's musicians. Actors entered through doors in the back wall of the stage. Above it was a balconied area that could represent the walls of a town (as in *King John*), or a castle (as in *Richard II*), and indeed a balcony (as in *Romeo and Juliet*). In 1609 the company also acquired the use of the Blackfriars, a smaller, indoor theatre to which admission was more expensive, and which permitted the use of more spectacular stage effects such as the descent of Jupiter on an eagle in *Cymbeline* and of goddesses in *The Tempest*. And they would frequently perform before the court in royal residences and, on their regular tours into the provinces, in non-theatrical spaces such as inns, guildhalls and the great halls of country houses.

Early in his career Shakespeare may have worked in collaboration, perhaps with Thomas Nashe (1567–*c*. 1601) in *Henry VI, Part I* and with George Peele (1556–96) in *Titus Andronicus*. And towards the end he collaborated with George Wilkins (*fl.* 1604–8) in *Pericles*, and with his younger colleagues Thomas Middleton (1580–1627), in *Timon of Athens*, and John Fletcher (1579–1625), in *Henry VIII*, *The Two Noble Kinsmen* and the lost play *Cardenio*. Shakespeare's output dwindled in his last years, and he died in 1616 in Stratford, where he owned a fine house, New Place, and much land. His only son had died at the age of eleven, in 1596, and his last descendant died in 1670. New Place was destroyed in the eighteenth century but the other Stratford houses associated with his life are maintained and displayed to the public by the Shakespeare Birthplace Trust.

One of the most remarkable features of Shakespeare's plays is their intellectual and emotional scope. They span a great range from the lightest of comedies, such as *The Two Gentlemen of Verona* and *The Comedy of Errors*, to the profoundest of tragedies, such as *King Lear* and *Macbeth*. He maintained an output of around two plays a year, ringing the changes between comic and serious. All his comedies have serious elements: Shylock, in *The Merchant of Venice*, almost reaches tragic dimensions, and *Measure for Measure* is profoundly serious in its examination of moral problems. Equally, none of his tragedies is without humour: Hamlet is as witty as any of his comic heroes, *Macbeth* has its Porter, and *King Lear* its Fool. His greatest comic character, Falstaff, inhabits the history plays and *Henry V* ends with a marriage, while *Henry VI, Part III*, *Richard II* and *Richard III* culminate in the tragic deaths of their protagonists.

Although in performance Shakespeare's characters can give the impression of a superabundant reality, he is not a naturalistic dramatist. None of his plays is explicitly set in his own time. The action of few of them (except for the English histories) is set even partly in England (exceptions are *The Merry Wives of Windsor* and the Induction to *The Taming of the Shrew*). Italy is his favoured location. Most of his principal story-lines derive from printed writings; but the structuring and translation of these narratives into dramatic terms is Shakespeare's own, and he invents much additional material. Most of the plays contain elements of myth and legend, and many derive from ancient or more recent history or from romantic tales of ancient times and faraway places. All reflect his reading, often in close detail.

Holinshed's *Chronicles* (1577, revised 1587), a great compendium of English, Scottish and Irish history, provided material for his English history plays. The *Lives of the Noble Grecians and Romans* by the Greek writer Plutarch, finely translated into English from the French by Sir Thomas North in 1579, provided much of the narrative material, and also a mass of verbal detail, for his plays about Roman history. Some plays are closely based on shorter individual works: *As You Like It*, for instance, on the novel *Rosalynde* (1590) by his near-contemporary Thomas Lodge (1558–1625), *The Winter's Tale* on *Pandosto* (1588) by his old rival Robert Greene (1558–92) and *Othello* on a story by the Italian Giraldi Cinthio (1504–73). And the language of his plays is permeated by the Bible, the Book of Common Prayer and the proverbial sayings of his day.

Shakespeare was popular with his contemporaries, but his commitment to the theatre and to the plays in performance is demonstrated by the fact that only about half of his plays appeared in print in his lifetime, in slim paperback volumes known as quartos, so called because they were made from printers' sheets folded twice to form four leaves (eight pages). None of them shows any sign that he was involved in their publication. For him, performance was the primary means of publication. The most frequently reprinted of his works were the non-dramatic poems – the erotic *Venus and Adonis* and the more moralistic *The Rape of Lucrece*. The *Sonnets*, which appeared in 1609, under his name but possibly without his consent, were less successful, perhaps because the vogue for sonnet sequences, which peaked in the 1590s, had passed by then. They were not reprinted until 1640, and then only in garbled form along with poems by other writers. Happily, in 1623, seven years after he died, his colleagues John Heminges

(1556–1630) and Henry Condell (d. 1627) published his collected plays, including eighteen that had not previously appeared in print, in the first Folio, whose name derives from the fact that the printers' sheets were folded only once to produce two leaves (four pages). Some of the quarto editions are badly printed, and the fact that some plays exist in two, or even three, early versions creates problems for editors. These are discussed in the Account of the Text in each volume of this series.

Shakespeare's plays continued in the repertoire until the Puritans closed the theatres in 1642. When performances resumed after the Restoration of the monarchy in 1660 many of the plays were not to the taste of the times, especially because their mingling of genres and failure to meet the requirements of poetic justice offended against the dictates of neoclassicism. Some, such as *The Tempest* (changed by John Dryden and William Davenant in 1667 to suit contemporary taste), *King Lear* (to which Nahum Tate gave a happy ending in 1681) and *Richard III* (heavily adapted by Colley Cibber in 1700 as a vehicle for his own talents), were extensively rewritten; others fell into neglect. Slowly they regained their place in the repertoire, and they continued to be reprinted, but it was not until the great actor David Garrick (1717–79) organized a spectacular jubilee in Stratford in 1769 that Shakespeare began to be regarded as a transcendental genius. Garrick's idolatry prefigured the enthusiasm of critics such as Samuel Taylor Coleridge (1772–1834) and William Hazlitt (1778–1830). Gradually Shakespeare's reputation spread abroad, to Germany, America, France and to other European countries.

During the nineteenth century, though the plays were generally still performed in heavily adapted or abbreviated versions, a large body of scholarship and criticism began to amass. Partly as a result of a general swing in education away from the teaching of Greek and Roman texts and towards literature written in English, Shakespeare became the object of intensive study in schools and universities. In the theatre, important turning points were the work in England of two theatre directors, William Poel (1852–1934) and his disciple Harley Granville-Barker (1877–1946), who showed that the application of knowledge, some of it newly acquired, of early staging conditions to performance of the plays could render the original texts viable in terms of the modern theatre. During the twentieth century appreciation of Shakespeare's work, encouraged by the availability of audio, film and video versions of the plays, spread around the world to such an extent that he can now be claimed as a global author.

The influence of Shakespeare's works permeates the English language. Phrases from his plays and poems – 'a tower of strength', 'green-eyed jealousy', 'a foregone conclusion' – are on the lips of people who may never have read him. They have inspired composers of songs, orchestral music and operas; painters and sculptors; poets, novelists and film-makers. Allusions to him appear in pop songs, in advertisements and in television shows. Some of his characters – Romeo and Juliet, Falstaff, Shylock and Hamlet – have acquired mythic status. He is valued for his humanity, his psychological insight, his wit and humour, his lyricism, his mastery of language, his ability to excite, surprise, move and, in the widest sense of the word, entertain audiences. He is the greatest of poets, but he is essentially a dramatic poet. Though his plays have much to offer to readers, they exist fully only in performance. In these volumes we offer individual introductions, notes on language and on specific points of the text, suggestions for further reading and information about how each work has been edited. In addition we include accounts of the ways in which successive generations of interpreters and audiences have responded to challenges and rewards offered by the plays. The Penguin Shakespeare series aspires to remove obstacles to understanding and to make pleasurable the reading of the work of the man who has done more than most to make us understand what it is to be human.

Stanley Wells

THE CHRONOLOGY OF
SHAKESPEARE'S WORKS

A few of Shakespeare's writings can be fairly precisely dated. An allusion to the Earl of Essex in the chorus to Act V of *Henry V*, for instance, could only have been written in 1599. But for many of the plays we have only vague information, such as the date of publication, which may have occurred long after composition, the date of a performance, which may not have been the first, or a list in Francis Meres's book *Palladis Tamia*, published in 1598, which tells us only that the plays listed there must have been written by that year. The chronology of the early plays is particularly difficult to establish. Not everyone would agree that the first part of *Henry VI* was written after the third, for instance, or *Romeo and Juliet* before *A Midsummer Night's Dream*. The following table is based on the 'Canon and Chronology' section in *William Shakespeare: A Textual Companion*, by Stanley Wells and Gary Taylor, with John Jowett and William Montgomery (1987), where more detailed information and discussion may be found.

The Two Gentlemen of Verona	1590–91
The Taming of the Shrew	1590–91
Henry VI, Part II	1591
Henry VI, Part III	1591
Henry VI, Part I (perhaps with Thomas Nashe)	1592
Titus Andronicus (perhaps with George Peele)	1592
Richard III	1592–3

INTRODUCTION

Love's Labour's Lost has finally come into its own. After more than three centuries of neglect, it stands today among those Shakespeare plays which can be guaranteed to fill houses, thrill audiences, and – most difficult of all – please actors. Ironically, the play is now popular for precisely those qualities which previously kept it from favour. It has no towering central role, no Hamlet or Falstaff, and in the days of Garrick and the Victorian actor-managers, when audiences demanded star actors playing star parts, this made it theatrically unattractive. Now audiences are prepared to respect the play's sociability, its breadth, its capacity to accommodate on more or less equal dramatic terms a whole community of characters from a king to a constable and clown. Its language, too, has been vindicated. In the past, on stages cluttered with scenery and elaborate costumes, its verbal virtuosity must have seemed odd and irrelevant. On today's bare, or nearly bare, boards, the lines sing, crackle with wit, or creak along with laughable pedantry (each idiom appropriate to its speaker), the language seeming part of the comic action. Which is not to say that the play offers exclusively verbal pleasures. It is full of brilliantly engineered situations in which dialogue is used to express and intensify deep dramatic tensions. The multiple eaves-dropping scene (IV.3) is only the most famous of these contrivances. Here again, modern audiences can enjoy something deplored by their predecessors. Theatrical contrivance no longer repels us; indeed, we rather like it.

We do not now expect plays to be 'realistic'; we simply want them to be dramatically telling. In short, *Love's Labour's Lost* has ceased to seem at once crabbed and juvenile; it is today celebrated as the first work of Shakespeare's genius.

The comedy was composed about 1595, when Shakespeare was in his early thirties. He had already written at least eight plays – including the first tetralogy of English histories, *The Comedy of Errors*, and *Titus Andronicus* – and his creative method had become more or less settled. All his early plays and poems (with the exception of such of the *Sonnets* as were composed in the early 1590s) draw heavily on literary sources. Typically, Shakespeare found a good subject, conscientiously read round it, then turned his reading into theatre. In the case of *Love's Labour's Lost*, he seems to have done something different, and this may explain why the play feels like a new departure, a sudden creative step forward. Although a few echoes of Robert Wilson's *The Cobbler's Prophecy* (*c.* 1590) and Pierre de la Primaudaye's *L'Académie française* (1577, translated in 1586) have been detected, and the earlier plays of John Lyly together with the Italian *commedia dell'arte* have been identified as general influences, no one has ever found a substantial source for *Love's Labour's Lost*. The search has been thorough, but nothing significant has turned up, and it is now thought that, in view of the simplicity of the play's plot, there never was anything to find. Certainly, it is easy to imagine Shakespeare inventing a story in which a King and three lords, shadowed by a clutch of lowlier characters, swear an oath to form an austere academy, break their vows by falling in love with a visiting Princess and her three ladies, and are separated from their women for a year and a day when the Princess hears of her father's death. It is a touching tale; it has charm; and it is packed with dramatic potential.

As it became apparent that the foundations of *Love's Labour's Lost* were not going to be unearthed in Elizabethan literature, scholars began to look for the play's origins among the details of Elizabethan life. Fifty years ago, it was fashionable to take the King's jest about 'the school of night' (IV.3.253) as a pointed allusion to a group of writers, scientists, and freethinkers centred on Sir Walter Raleigh, and to identify that group (by a strange circularity) with the coterie established within the comedy by Navarre. Shakespeare had populated his play – it was said – with satirical versions of Raleigh, George Chapman, Thomas Nashe, John Florio, and other contemporary notables. This theory has recently fallen into disrepute: historians have shown that Raleigh had no clearly defined coterie, and literary critics (observing, no doubt, that the number of candidates for each comic role had multiplied to the point of absurdity) have pointed out that characterization in *Love's Labour's Lost* is more general than specific. Still, the notion that the play is about a group called 'the school of night' persists among readers and theatregoers (largely because it has found its way into popular editions), and it is worth driving another nail into its coffin. The fundamental assumption of the topical-satirical interpreters – that the King's remark at IV.3.253 needs clarification from outside the text – is, I believe, demonstrably false. Hearing Berowne call his black-haired mistress 'fair', Navarre retorts:

> *O paradox! Black is the badge of hell,*
> *The hue of dungeons, and the school of night;*
> *And beauty's crest becomes the heavens well.*
>
> IV.3.252-4

As the comma after 'dungeons' (present in the first edition of the play, derived from Shakespeare's manuscript) makes clear, there are three phrases in parallel here: black is the badge of hell, black is the hue of dungeons, and black is the school where night learns to be black. The lines are perfectly lucid.

Scholars have sought the origins of *Love's Labour's Lost* in sixteenth-century France as well as in Elizabethan England. Encouraged by the fact that Navarre's lords bear the names of real aristocrats, they have tried to find some occasion on which Biron, de Mayenne, and Longueville (Shakespeare's Berowne, Dumaine, and Longaville) were together in the company of Henry of Navarre – preferably reading books. They have not succeeded. Indeed, since de Mayenne was a Catholic leader bitterly opposed to the pro-Huguenot Navarre, success was never very likely. Nor has the search for real-life equivalents of the Princess and her ladies borne fruit. Some have regarded the meeting between Marguerite de Valois and Henry of Navarre at Nérac in 1578 as the historical source of the play's French embassy. But the similarities are not great. Apart from anything else, Henry and Marguerite met as an estranged man and wife, not as a king and princess falling in love at first sight. In so far as *Love's Labour's Lost* can be related to contemporary events – which is hardly at all – it seems to be an oblique response to the unification of France and Navarre under Henry in 1589–94. Like the anonymous *The Trial of Chivalry* (*c.* 1600) – another play which deals with love-affairs between the heirs of France and Navarre in a historically fantastic framework (the Earl of Pembroke, one of its central characters, no more fought in France than de Mayenne was Navarre's fellow-scholar) – *Love's Labour's Lost* offered its Elizabethan audience a reassuringly light-hearted view of an alliance across the Channel which probably seemed in reality rather disturbing. (Despite the defeat of the Armada in 1588, Protestant England lived in fear of invasion by unfriendly Catholic powers.) Where the play uses history, it uses it as something to escape from.

But why would Shakespeare suddenly write a play without a source? After all, his early work – invariably source-secured – had been both artistically and commercially successful. It is not without significance that *Love's Labour's Lost* is, as a play, preoccupied with the making of plays. There is the Masque of Russians prepared for the visiting women by the men (V.2.158–264), and the Pageant of the Nine Worthies prepared by the low characters for the high (V.2.543–711). At the end of the comedy, the contention between Ver and Hiems, spring and winter, provides another inset show (V.2.880–920). And the whole action is betrayed as theatre by Berowne when he says that the year and a day interposed between the lovers and marriage is 'too long for a play' (V.2.867). Interestingly, the two other Shakespearian dramas which can best claim to be sourceless – *A Midsummer Night's Dream* (written shortly after *Love's Labour's Lost*) and *The Tempest* (the last non-collaborative work, *c.* 1611) – are similarly preoccupied. The 'tedious and brief' tragedy of Pyramus and Thisbe, Prospero's masque for Ferdinand and Miranda, Ariel's vanishing banquet: these demand comparison with the shows in *Love's Labour's Lost*. At the threshold of creative maturity and again at the end of his career, Shakespeare seems to have needed to construct plays which – through their investigation of language, disguise, illusion, convention, directed action, and the drama which can be built from them – helped him come to terms with his art.

In *A Midsummer Night's Dream*, drama is magical. When Oberon and Puck make Demetrius Helena's lover by the operation of the love-juice, they frame by magic precisely that process of self-discovery through role-play which Petruchio uses to make his shrewish wife Kate find herself in an imposed obedience. They create, in theatre, theatre. Again, if Bottom plays a lover's part by choice, he is cast as an ass by enchantment; contrariwise, if Puck can 'put a girdle round about the earth | In forty minutes' (II.1.175-6) it is because the dramatic economy, dissolving time, allows his sorcery scope. By the end of the comedy, drama and magic have become so mingled that Puck's last speech, beginning 'If we shadows have offended' (V.1.413-28), registers as an apology both for the fairies and for the actors (often called 'shadows') who have played them. In *The Tempest*, drama is not so much magical as metaphysical. Prospero is a playwright deity: he summons storms as easily as shows; he directs men about his island like actors in a play, submitting them to his tragicomic scenario; he punishes, rewards, and forgives. Significantly, he does not leave his realm, or his play, without a tribute to that greater author, God (Epilogue 13-20). But the link has been forged, in any case, at IV.1.148-58, where Prospero's dismissal of the masque of Iris, Juno, and Ceres is said to foreshadow the end of the world. Stern, loving, potent, baffled by the ingratitude of man, Prospero is a glimpse of God, and in his art we see an image of the Divine Will. Neither magical nor metaphysical, drama in *Love's Labour's Lost* is life itself. Here, more searchingly and single-mindedly than in any other of his plays, Shakespeare explores the theatricality of culture. Songs and sonnets, prose and poetry, masking, masqueing, sighs, formal proposals and more formal rejections: these constitute the comedy. And they are but heightened, courtly forms of those words, disguises, illusions, conventions, and directed actions through which we all live on the world's great stage. So this most private play is also thoroughly public. Not about French politics, and still less about 'the school of night', *Love's Labour's Lost* investigates drama, and, in doing so, it inquires into the character of that sociable, sophisticated, and essentially dramatic animal, man.

*

Almost all Shakespeare's comedies confront death, the bold antagonist of laughter and happy endings. In *The Comedy of Errors*, for example, old Egeon, sentenced in the first scene, is rescued from execution by only the narrowest margin in the last. (Significantly, he is Shakespeare's addition to the source.) Again, in *Twelfth Night*, a play with more than a hint of things violent and sad, the scene chills when Viola describes the death of her imaginary, lovelorn sister – she who 'sat like Patience on a monument, | Smiling at grief' (II.4.113–14). And in the last of the comedies, *Measure for Measure*, not one but two characters face execution: Claudio – who pleads for life in one of the most terrifying speeches in all Shakespeare (III.1.121–35) – and the murderer Barnardine. But *Love's Labour's Lost* engages with death so much more directly than even these plays that it has been suggested (wrongly, I think) that it cannot belong to the same comic genre. Egeon, father of the twin Antipholi, does not die: the Princess's father does. Viola's sister is a fiction, invented to relieve the speaker's sense of her own unhappy inactivity in love: Katharine's sister really was killed by Cupid's cruel arrows (V.2.13–15). *Measure for Measure* threatens two characters with death: *Love's Labour's Lost* begins with a stern reminder that we are all under sentence.

If Navarre can contemplate that truth with assurance, it is not because he welcomes the prospect of a grave. Rather, he believes that he has found a way of evading death's worst consequence:

> *Let fame, that all hunt after in their lives,*
> *Live registered upon our brazen tombs,*
> *And then grace us in the disgrace of death;*
> *When, spite of cormorant devouring Time,*
> *Th'endeavour of this present breath may buy*
> *That honour which shall bate his scythe's keen edge,*
> *And make us heirs of all eternity.*   I.1.1–7

These, the opening lines of the play, have a remarkable affinity with the poems written to the young man in that other almost sourceless and roughly contemporary work, the *Sonnets*. Verbal echoes ring clear: 'Devouring Time, blunt thou the lion's paws' (Sonnet 19), 'Not marble nor the gilded monuments | Of princes shall outlive this pow'rful rhyme' (Sonnet 55), 'Give my love fame faster than Time wastes life; | So thou prevent'st his scythe and crooked knife' (Sonnet 100). Just as striking is the overlap in subject-matter: Navarre, like the poet of the poems, wants death to be defeated by the defeat of Time. However, whereas the poet advises the young man to 'breed', Navarre ushers Berowne, Longaville, and Dumaine towards sexual self-denial. To win 'fame' and outlive life, he says, the lords should study, fast, go without sleep, and absolutely avoid the company of women. They should 'war' against their 'affections' (I.1.9). The proposal is not only (to judge by the *Sonnets*) un-Shakespearian: it is comically anti-comic, radically at odds with the values of the play which it initiates. Comedy has always celebrated cakes, ale, and marriage at the expense of the contemplative life. Orlando and Toby Belch are its heroes, not Jaques and Malvolio. In Comedy, anyone who seeks an immortality as sterile as Navarre's badly needs to learn the virtue of worldly things. 'Nothing 'gainst Time's scythe can make defence', Comedy warns, 'Save breed, to brave him when he takes thee hence' (Sonnet 12). The Princess of France and her three ladies wait in the wings.

At first, *Love's Labour's Lost* unfolds like *King Lear*. When Navarre presents the academic schedule to his lords (I.1.15–23), he comically anticipates Lear with his map; he is another monarch offering foolish but settled policy to his court for approval. Longaville and Dumaine behave like benign versions of Goneril and Regan; they tell the King what he wants to hear. Berowne reacts like Cordelia; he resists. Just as Cordelia criticizes her father's plan to abdicate so that he can crawl towards death unburdened, so Berowne speaks against Navarre's decision to prepare for death by retreating from public duties to the studious quiet of his rural park. And in both plays, those best placed to dissuade the sovereign fail to do so because of the way they express themselves. Lear's favourite daughter, unable to heave her heart into her mouth, makes love sound like grudging duty; and Navarre's most intelligent courtier so compulsively twists wisdom into wit that the King cannot disentangle his good counsel from the sophistry which surrounds it.

Here, of course, the plays start to diverge. No one could be less like Cordelia, with her radiant sincerity, than Berowne. 'Truth', he declares (using the imagery of St John's Gospel to compel the King's assent), is a kind of 'light' (I.1.75). So it follows that scholars get no nearer 'truth' by reading; since it dulls the 'light' which is the eye (Berowne here draws on the common sixteenth-century belief that the eye produces the beams by which it sees), reading can only blur the 'light' which the scholar's eye seeks:

> *Light seeking light doth light of light beguile;*
> *So, ere you find where light in darkness lies,*
> *Your light grows dark by losing of your eyes.*
>
> I.1.77–9

Much the better course, he goes on – how different this is from Cordelia's 'Nothing, my lord' (I.1.87) – is for ocular 'light' to find the 'light' which it looks for in the gleam of a mistress's 'fairer eye' (line 81). Dr Johnson observed in exasperation: 'The whole sense of this gingling declamation ... might have been told with less obscurity in fewer words.' Quite so; but Berowne is the gingler, not Shakespeare. What we are given in the first scene of *Love's Labour's Lost* is a finely controlled sketch of a man whose verbal powers and love of acclaim are together so nearly boundless that he treats language less as a means of communication than as a vehicle for self-congratulatory display. There is much to be said in favour of Cordelia's silence.

Nevertheless, some of Berowne's objections to the King's scheme are weighty. The most striking, perhaps, is his blunt assertion that without heavenly help – without 'special grace' from God – a 'war' against the 'affections' simply cannot be won. Replying to Navarre's claim that 'necessity' compels him to meet the approaching Princess, Berowne says:

> *Necessity will make us all forsworn*
> *Three thousand times within this three years' space;*
> *For every man with his affects is born,*
> *Not by might mastered, but by special grace.*
> *If I break faith, this word shall speak for me:*
> *I am forsworn on mere 'necessity'.*
>
> I.1.147–52

That Shakespeare was in sympathy with this can be deduced from a number of plays, not just *Love's Labour's Lost*. Consider *Measure for Measure*. There we are shown a man who fights Navarre's 'war' so vigorously that his moral constitution weakens, breaks, and finally festers. By struggling too hard for perfection, Angelo falls into sin. He becomes, not the angel which his name implies, but what Isabella calls him at the denouement: a 'devil' (V.1.29). What should he have done? Comedy and St Paul answer – for once – in unison: he should have married. Indeed, his belated acceptance of Mariana falls like a spring sunbeam – tentative but hopeful – across the bleak last act of the play. So when Comedy advances the Princess, it does more than take revenge on Navarre for rejecting sex and festivity: it saves him from spiritual vexation, and protects his kingdom from the kind of tyranny which the harrowed Angelo imposes on Vienna.

King Lear begins with fairy-tale formality, but its symmetries quickly crumble into chaos as the bonds which connect father and child, master and servant, perish. *Love's Labour's Lost* is quite different. Artful, ornate, poised, spacious, a kind of dramatic Fontainebleau fit for noblemen and women to live, love, and be bereft in, it preserves its symmetries throughout. Perhaps as a consequence of this, its genius is dialectical. Speech answers speech and character balances character. The grand design is held together by organized disagreement. Take the Princess's lines near the beginning of Act IV:

> *Glory grows guilty of detested crimes,*
> *When, for fame's sake, for praise, an outward part,*
> *We bend to that the working of the heart;*
> *As I for praise alone now seek to spill*
> *The poor deer's blood, that my heart means no ill.*

IV.1.31–5

In one sense this cannot be a reply to the play's first speech. The Princess did not hear Navarre's ringing oration; and her subject is in any case the death of a deer, not the mortality of man. But there is another sense – the dramatic one – in which her lines clamour to be read as an attack on the academy. If it is a crime for the Princess to hunt the deer for 'fame', against her heart's inclining, it must also be criminal for the King to 'war' against his heart's 'affections' for 'fame, that all hunt after in their lives' (I.1.1). Evidently the Princess would agree with Berowne that the 'affects' should be respected. But her speech is in one way more critical of the academy than anything which that courtier had been able to muster. Berowne's love of acclaim is such that, though he dislikes the King's means to 'fame', he does not object to his end. The Princess, by contrast, sees beyond 'fame' to the 'praise' which it entails, and, like the poet of the *Sonnets* (in 84 and 95, for example), she detects and despises those qualities which the praised man shares with the hypocrite. Navarre wants admiration to create for him an 'outward part' which can then be admired; he seeks acclaim for his apparent, not his real, divided, warring self. But the Princess (as we see at II.1.1–19, where Boyet tries to praise her) regards admiration and acclaim as the thin end of a flattering wedge. It is most appropriate that *Love's Labour's Lost* should end, in the songs of Ver and Hiems, with a debate. We talk, loosely, about a play's action constituting an argument; in *Love's Labour's Lost*, argument often constitutes the action.

It is one of the most delightful ironies of the comedy that when, in Act V, the courtiers actually confront men of renown – or at least their semblances – they do nothing but fleer, mock, and jibe at them. So eager are they to prove to the women that their own show, the abortive

Masque of Russians, was not utterly foolish that they do everything they can to sabotage the Pageant of the Nine Worthies – indifferent, apparently, to the injury which this does to the memory of famous men. They will not join Costard in his celebration of Pompey; they refuse to applaud Nathaniel's Alexander (the curate, they say, lacks the conqueror's wry neck); the baby Hercules in the shape of Armado's page is just tolerated; but Judas Maccabaeus (played by the pedant) is greeted by a torrent of abuse, and his fame rendered infamous, his 'Maccabaeus' turned to 'Iscariot' (V.2.591–7). The women sit by in disapproving silence as their lovers and Boyet triumph over the unfortunate players. They seem to sympathize with Holofernes's rebuke (which doubtless stills audiences because part of every theatregoer has enjoyed the men's mockery and feels implicated): 'This is not generous, not gentle, not humble' (line 626).

Even more striking than the lords' cruelty is their increasing concentration on death. Judas, they say, should 'hang himself'; his countenance is 'A death's face in a ring' and 'The carved bone face on a flask' (lines 601, 609, and 613). Boyet's valediction to the pedant could scarcely be more resonantly ominous: 'A light for Monsieur Judas! It grows dark; he may stumble' (line 627). Death is insistent. Once established in the courtiers' abuse, it begins to infect the players' replies. When Armado, the last Worthy, offers himself as Hector, that 'flower' of chivalry, only to be greeted by 'That mint!' and 'That columbine!' (line 653), he retorts, gravely: 'The sweet war-man is dead and rotten. Sweet chucks, beat not the bones of the buried. When he breathed, he was a man' (lines 658–60). Such is the impact of this speech (it recalls Hamlet's show-stopping remembrance of his father (I.2.187–8): ''A was a man. Take him for all in

xxxiii

all, | I shall not look upon his like again') that it darkens everything which follows. When Armado challenges Costard for revealing Jaquenetta's pregnancy, we cannot believe that the braggart himself poses a threat to the clown. Yet his 'Thou shalt die!' (line 676) is fearful nevertheless: Costard must indeed one day die. Death, here, is not the abstraction of Navarre's first speech. Nor is it the lot of a hunted animal or lost sister. It is the fixed destiny of a known character on stage before us. The Pageant has prepared us for the greatest shock in Shakespeare:

> *Enter a messenger, Monsieur Marcade*
>
> MARCADE
> God save you, madam.
>
> PRINCESS   *Welcome, Marcade,*
> But that thou interruptest our merriment.
>
> MARCADE
> I am sorry, madam, for the news I bring
> Is heavy in my tongue. The King your father –
>
> PRINCESS
> Dead, for my life!
>
> MARCADE   *Even so; my tale is told.*
>
> V.2.712–16

It sounds faintly paradoxical, that suggestion that something 'prepared' can 'shock'. But one's experience both in life and in the theatre is that anticipation, far from reducing the impact of a revelation, may actually increase it. Think of the many strands in *Macbeth* which lead towards 'Macduff was from his mother's womb | Untimely ripped' (V.6.54–5), and then recall the effect of the words on audiences. Think, too, of the shock of bereavement, which always registers when someone close has died, even if the dead person was last seen – as in the

French King's case – 'decrepit, sick, and bedrid'
(I.1.136), and even though we all know that death is
inevitable, always, in a final sense, expected. Significantly, Shakespeare has crafted V.2 in such a way that,
in the theatre, Marcade's actual entry is not noticed. What
happens is that the characters and the audience gradually
become aware that there is something on stage more important that the clown and the braggart, squaring up for
a fight. Marcade seems to emerge from, rather than enter,
the action. Good directors have always co-operated with
this sense of emergence. Thus, in Peter Brook's 1946–7
production, as the stage-lights dimmed slowly over the
Pageant ('It grows dark' indeed) they simultaneously went
up on the black-clad messenger, as though Death himself
were taking shape among the vulnerable mortals. And in
John Barton's superb 1978 *Love's Labour's Lost* shadows
were thick from the start. The action was played under a
fixed set of autumn boughs; leaves fell in elegies; the
costumes were sombre and the lighting restrained;
Armado, far from being a swaggering gallant, was an
ageing Quixote. And the arrival of Marcade was a great
shock.

*

The low characters who inhabit Navarre's park have
always found favour. Even William Hazlitt, who was
generally hostile towards *Love's Labour's Lost*, admired
them. 'If we were to part with any of the author's
comedies, it should be this', he wrote dismissively in his
Characters of Shakespeare's Plays (1817), only to add, in
an affectionately ample qualification: 'Yet we should be
loath to part with Don Adriano de Armado, that mighty
potentate of nonsense, or his page, that handful of wit;
with Nathaniel the curate, or Holofernes the school-

master, and their dispute after dinner on "the golden cadences of poesy"; with Costard the clown, or Dull the constable.' But if the low characters have been long loved, their dramatic function has been until quite recently little understood. Coleridge, Hazlitt's contemporary, noted in his 1818 lectures that Armado and Costard share with the King and his lords a love of argumentative rhetoric; but he did not feel, apparently, that this linguistic overlap helped unify the play. It was left to Walter Pater, in a magnificent but flawed essay first published in 1885, to unite high and low linguistically. In *Love's Labour's Lost*, Pater argued, Shakespeare had set out to analyse and satirize 'that pride of dainty language and curious expression' which was so incident to the high Elizabethan authors, and to himself on occasion – and, it must be added, to Pater. The play shows 'this foppery of delicate language' operating on several levels of sophistication, 'passing from the grotesque and vulgar pedantry of Holofernes, through the extravagant but polished caricature of Armado, to become the peculiar characteristic of a real though still quaint poetry in Biron himself, who is still chargeable even at his best with just a little affectation.'

In one sense Pater did not go far enough, though in another he went too far. If, instead of organizing the play into a pyramid with Berowne at the top, he had conceded the obvious – that the academic oath is both the lynchpin of the action and a recurring centre of dramatic interest – he might have uncovered a more radical and inclusive principle of unity than he actually did. For Shakespeare has put the oath unambiguously into the category of Holofernes's 'vulgar pedantry', Armado's 'extravagant' rhetoric, his page's wordplay, Nathaniel's bad Latin, and Costard's competitive banter with Boyet: all these utterances try to attract the admiration which the King calls 'fame'. *Love's Labour's Lost* needs no scenery because its characters 'hunt' renown across a linguistic landscape. Significantly, Shakespeare records the progress of the chase in his Pageant of the Nine Worthies. Jaquenetta and Dull – rustic taciturnity and illiteracy personified – play no part in the show, except, in Dull's case, for the occasional inarticulate rumble on the tabor (see V.1.146–8). But Costard, who has a rudimentary feeling for rhetoric, qualifies as the first Worthy. He is followed by the eagerly linguistic, if not always competent, Nathaniel. Then comes Mote – so much the epitome of verbal wit that his very name puns on the word 'word' (see the commentary for I.2). Holofernes – that master of fecund sterility, that prolific rhymester and arid quibbler – succeeds him. And the last Worthy, naturally, is the master of Mote and the 'word', Armado:

> *A man in all the world's new fashion planted,*
> *That hath a mint of phrases in his brain;*
> *One who the music of his own vain tongue*
> *Doth ravish like enchanting harmony. . . .*
> *A man of fire-new words, fashion's own knight.*
>
> I.1.162–5, 176

In Elizabethan pronunciation, the show's title sounds suspiciously like 'Pageant of the Nine Wordies'.

In what sense, then, did Pater go too far? He overestimated the unifying power of the language theme, because he was unresponsive to the other integuments which hold the play together. Sex, for instance. Hardly has Berowne delivered his warning about the vigour of the 'affects' than his evidence is brought in by Dull. Costard is in custody because he has – in the words of Armado's lavish and jealous letter – '*Sorted and consorted,*

*contrary to thy proclaimed edict and continent canon . . .
With a child of our grandmother Eve, a female . . . Jaquenetta . . . the weaker vessel*' (I.1.250–61). The clown is
absolutely unrepentant. 'It is the manner of a man to
speak to a woman', he says, and 'Such is the sinplicity of
man to hearken after the flesh' (I.1.206–7, 214–15).
Costard, it could be said, adds practice to Berowne's pre-
cept. But his position in the comic dialectic is more
interesting than that. The mock-biblical idiom of his
excuses rather draws attention to than conceals what he
Freudianly calls his 'sinplicity'. If Berowne is too
theoretical, Costard is too carelessly practical. If the King
is too ascetic, the clown is too sensual. Comedy and St
Paul would tell Costard, like Navarre and Angelo, to
marry.

Not that that places Costard precisely either: he is far
from being a simple sensualist. His very excuses for attempting seduction displace the 'affects' from the sensual
to a linguistic sphere in a way which is highly reminiscent
of the comedy's most sterile couple, Holofernes and Nathaniel. 'Speak to a woman' and 'hearken after the flesh'
(as though sex were conversation) have exactly the same
overtones as the curate's description of Dull – 'he hath
never fed of the dainties that are bred in a book' (IV.2.24)
– and the pedant's account of the origin of his verse:
'begot in the ventricle of memory, nourished in the womb
of *pia mater*, and delivered upon the mellowing of occasion' (IV.2.69–71). Like Holofernes and Nathaniel, Costard knows that words as well as babies breed. Like them,
he knows what it is to 'affect the letter' (IV.2.55). It is
hardly surprising, then, that when he fails to move
Navarre by his appeal to the appetites he proliferates
words instead. To the King's 'It was proclaimed a year's
imprisonment to be taken with a wench', he replies 'I was

taken with none, sir; I was taken with a damsel' (I.1.275–8). Told that a 'damsel' is as illegal as a 'wench', he tries first 'virgin' and then 'maid'; and, when forced to end the exchange by the King's intransigence, he does so with a parting quibble (line 286).

The encounter between Navarre and Costard works superbly in the theatre, and not just because the clown's self-justification and sophistry are beautifully articulated: Shakespeare gradually makes both Navarre and the audience aware that the opposition here is less real than apparent. As Costard tries to wriggle through the proclamation by chopping and changing words, Navarre's recent erasure of the very decree which the clown wants to evade through the power of that mere 'word . . . "necessity" ' inevitably comes to mind. That the King is smitten by the same recollection seems clear: he sentences Costard not to the 'year's imprisonment' required by the law but to a token 'week with bran and water' (I.1.275, 288). The confrontation is a miniature Shakespearian comedy: it moves from distinction to unity; it is corrective, yet ultimately reassuring; Navarre's notion that his oath has raised him above other men is razed, but so gently and by such a beguiling representative of common humanity that his loss is made a kind of gain.

Armado, the play's other seducer, has no such encounter with the King. Although we are told more than once that he is intimate with the nobles (I.1.160–76, V.1.90–103), we do not see him in their company until the Pageant assembles. Nevertheless, Shakespeare forges so many links between the braggart and his superiors that it is difficult to assess one without judging the other. If they swear to 'study three years', so does he (I.2.35–6); and if they escape from school through the loophole of a 'word', he succumbs easily to his page's suggestion that one may 'put "years" to the word "three", and study three years in two words' (I.2.52–4). If Berowne is outwitted in a first encounter with his mistress, Jaquenetta similarly outfaces her admirer (II.1.114–28, I.2.126–39). If love drives Berowne to poetry, it makes Armado brimful of sonnets (IV.3.12–17, I.2.176–8); and if the courtier includes a sample of his work in a letter which goes astray, so does the braggart (IV.2.105–18, IV.1.89–94). When Longaville seeks the 'authority' of Berowne's sophistry to excuse his love for Maria, one cannot help remembering how Armado asked Mote to list the names of great men who have loved so that his affection for the dairymaid could be excused by some show of 'authority' (IV.3.285, I.2.65). And if Berowne, Costard, and the Princess reply to the King's first speech, so does Armado; he makes Navarre's metaphorical 'war' literal, and, as a result, exposes the absurdity of the whole campaign: 'If drawing my sword against the humour of affection would deliver me from the reprobate thought of it, I would take desire prisoner . . .' (I.2.58–60).

For most of the play, then, Armado is a convex mirror held up to the court. He reflects, grotesquely, the folly of the lords. But in the last scene he emerges as an important figure in his own right. It is his argument with Costard which fragments the Pageant. And it is the same ribald wrangle which holds our attention until Marcade arrives. Now, though the clown deals indiscreetly with the braggart here, morals are undoubtedly on his side. Armado was wrong to break his oath to 'study three years', and wrong to get Jaquenetta pregnant outside wedlock. Still, neither wrong is quite irreversible, and once Armado has promised to 'right [himself] like a soldier' by marrying the maid and labouring 'three year' in the fields as penance for his perjury, his honour is restored (V.2.720,

873). Meanwhile, he has made himself the custodian of Comedy. What Costard reveals to the court is that, while the lords and ladies have lingered, Armado has bred to brave Time's scythe. Even as the Princess hears of her father's death, we are aware of new life elsewhere: another braggart 'brags' – a child boasts its parentage – in the dairymaid's 'belly' (V.2.673–4). It is on the strength of his opposition to death and despair, demonstrated by his eagerness to breed new life, that Armado is granted the privilege of introducing the songs of Ver and Hiems.

*

Most Shakespeare criticism is written by academics, and most academics are male. Perhaps this explains why the men who join Navarre's academy have been generally indulged and their mistresses sometimes abused. The following comments (from a usually shrewd scholar) typify this strand in the critical tradition: the Princess 'consistently misjudges the situations in which she finds herself'; 'the genuineness of the men's affections . . . the women fail to perceive'; and, once they do get a glimmering of the lords' intentions, all endorse 'Rosaline's reaction to Berowne's courtship' at V.2.60–68 – 'arrogant and spiteful' though it is. I believe, on the contrary, that Shakespeare has made the women much more sensible, sensitive, and generous than the men.

Certainly the lords are misunderstood; they are even, towards the end of the play, misunderstood deliberately. But this is perfectly natural. To the wooed, wooing is always at least potentially ambiguous. So stylized is the language of courtship, and so careful is the lover making his first hesitant advances to seem more ideal than real, that his sincerity is necessarily difficult to gauge. Deceit cloaks easily under sonnets, jewelled favours, and masks.

In love, as in the theatre, feigned passion can be very convincing. (Shakespeare makes this point eloquently at III.1.10–23 by having Mote – who can hardly have loved a mistress yet – tell Armado how to win a wench by singing, sighing, and striking postures.) What is more, the dangers of deception increase greatly if the wooed woman wants to be won; and there is no doubt that the 'girls of France' (IV.3.347) are attracted to the King and his lords. Rosaline, Katharine, and Maria have lost their hearts before the play even begins (the Princess's question at II.1.77–9 is rhetorical), and their mistress quickly gives hers away. Aware of their vulnerability, all four cultivate a protective scepticism. They are, as the Princess says when introducing Rosaline's 'arrogant and spiteful' speech about Berowne, 'wise girls to mock [their] lovers so' (V.2.58).

But if – by some act of God – the ladies had shared our privileged access to the lords and had seen them sigh and groan in private, would they have reacted differently to the proposals made late in V.2? Would they, instead of delaying, have married at once? I think not. The passion which the men display in III.1, IV.3, and the first part of V.2, although deeply felt and delightful, is immature. Anyone who has known adolescent love will recognize the heady mixture: on the one hand, the mistress is ideal, out of reach, 'holy' (V.2.160); on the other, a short cut to sensual pleasure:

> *love, first learnèd in a lady's eyes,*
> *Lives not alone immurèd in the brain,*
> *But with the motion of all elements*
> *Courses as swift as thought in every power,*
> *And gives to every power a double power,*
> *Above their functions and their offices.*

xlii

It adds a precious seeing to the eye:
A lover's eyes will gaze an eagle blind.
A lover's ear will hear the lowest sound
When the suspicious head of theft is stopped.
Love's feeling is more soft and sensible
Than are the tender horns of cockled snails.
Love's tongue proves dainty Bacchus gross in taste.
For valour, is not Love a Hercules,
Still climbing trees in the Hesperides?
Subtle as Sphinx; as sweet and musical
As bright Apollo's lute, strung with his hair.
And when Love speaks, the voice of all the gods
Make heaven drowsy with the harmony.

IV.3.303–21

This is exquisite, but as a Definition of Love decidedly inadequate. It persuades by provocation, not argument. Although less paradoxical than *Ovid's Banquet of Sense* (1595) – that extraordinary poem of Chapman's in which each sense is roused in turn so that the reader may be purged of desire – it nevertheless invites a reaction against itself. 'Berowne,' one wants to say, 'this Love of yours sounds most appealing; but what of the woman who creates it?'

Perhaps understandably, the young dramatist praised by Henry Chettle in 1592 for having a 'demeanour no less civil than he excellent in the quality he professes' paid great attention in his comedies to the incivility which love rouses in lovers. In *The Two Gentlemen of Verona*, for example, Valentine's crying-up of Sylvia over Julia – his mistress, he says, is a 'heavenly saint', a 'Sovereign to all the creatures on the earth' (II.4.143, 151) – not only contrasts tellingly with Sylvia's generosity towards her: it marks that decisive and destructive point in the play at which Proteus's thoughts begin to drift away from the woman he has promised to love. The nobles of Navarre are even more competitive than the Veronese gentry. When Berowne calls his mistress (like Sylvia) 'heavenly', the King replies that beside the Princess she is but 'an attending star' (IV.3.219, 229). And when Berowne, stung by this, declares 'O, but for my love, day would turn to night!', Navarre deflates his hyperbole by observing that Rosaline's favour is dark, not light (lines 231, 245). Round abuse follows on both sides, until the banter declines into bawdry:

BEROWNE

   O, if the streets were pavèd with thine eyes,
     Her feet were much too dainty for such tread.

DUMAINE

   O, vile! Then, as she goes, what upward lies
     The street should see as she walked overhead.

                         IV.3.276–9

What is – since this is so clearly not – the proper way to praise a mistress? Berowne and his fellows could learn from Shakespeare's most famous sonnet to the dark lady. 'My mistress' eyes are nothing like the sun' not only scrupulously avoids exaggeration (far from being 'heavenly', the poet's love 'treads on the ground') but refuses to exalt the lady above those admired by others. Its moving final couplet is a model of modesty and decorum: 'And yet, by heaven, I think my love *as* rare | As any she belied with false compare' (Sonnet 130).

   That there is some connexion between Berowne's dark-haired and black-eyed mistress, the dark lady of the *Sonnets*, and, more distantly, that other Rosaline, abandoned for the sake of Juliet by Romeo – the 'pale hard-hearted wench' with a 'black eye' (II.4.4, 14) – is indisputable. What to make of it is the critical problem. Evidently, Berowne's most ferocious attack on his mistress overlaps with the bitter poems written to the dark lady by the poet after he discovers that she has betrayed him sexually with the young man (Sonnets 131–52):

> *What? I love? I sue? I seek a wife?*
> *A woman, that is like a German clock,*
> *Still a-repairing, ever out of frame,*
> *And never going aright, being a watch,*
> *But being watched that it may still go right!*
> *Nay, to be perjured, which is worst of all;*
> *And among three to love the worst of all –*
> *A whitely wanton with a velvet brow,*
> *With two pitch-balls stuck in her face for eyes;*
> *Ay, and, by heaven, one that will do the deed*
> *Though Argus were her eunuch and her guard!*
>
> III.1.186–96

But Berowne's rage is not motivated by the facts, as the poet's is. He has no evidence – indeed, no reasonable grounds for assuming – that Rosaline is unchaste. Has Shakespeare perhaps let his own feelings about a woman (she who became the dark lady of the *Sonnets*) invade those of Berowne? Many have thought so. Serenus Zeitblom, the narrator of Thomas Mann's *Dr Faustus*, for example, says this:

> *There can be no doubt that the strangely insistent and even unnecessary, dramatically little justified character-ization of Rosaline as a faithless, wanton, dangerous piece of female flesh – a description given to her only in Biron's speeches, whereas in the actual setting of the comedy she is no more than pert and witty – there can be no doubt that this characterization springs from a compulsion, heedless*

xlv

> *of artistic indiscrepancies, on the poet's part, an urge to bring in his own experiences and, whether it fits or not, to take poetic revenge for them. Rosaline, as the lover never tires of portraying her, is the dark lady of the second sonnet sequence, Elizabeth's maid of honour, Shakespeare's love, who betrayed him with the lovely youth.*
>
> (Chapter 24; translated by H. T. Lowe-Porter)

My own view is that if Berowne's contempt for Rosaline has been fuelled by Shakespeare's feelings towards a real, treacherous mistress (and I suspect that it has) the private emotions have in no way distorted the drama. Berowne's outburst may not be motivated by the facts, but it fits his character well for all that. It is an aspect of his immaturity that he should groundlessly abuse his mistress for doing the very 'deed' which his own 'affects' urge. Like his dramatic descendant, Benedick, Berowne enjoys being a mocker of love, 'A very beadle to a humorous sigh' (III. 1.172); and, like Benedick, he is aggressive towards the woman he loves because he wants to defend the detachment which allows him to mock. It may not be a worthy reaction, but it is understandable.

Less forgivable, perhaps, is the male insensitivity which declares itself in the Pageant of the Nine Worthies and which surfaces for a second time in the belated pressing of the marriage suits. Hardly has Marcade delivered his sad message than Navarre advises the Princess to 'rejoice at friends but newly found' rather than 'wail friends lost' (V.2.744–6). Is it any wonder that she – unable to follow his twisted syntax yet gathering enough to find his attitude inconceivable – should say: 'I understand you not' (line 747)? True, comedies often end with the displacement of Age by Youth, and in the Plautine tradition to which Shakespeare owes so much this displacement is

xlvi

commonly enshrined in a marriage which disregards the
views of a parent. But even Comedy refuses to dance on
dead men's graves. Navarre wants his marriage to follow
so hard upon a royal funeral that the baked meats served
to the mourners could feed the wedding guests: he wants
to create in his kingdom precisely the kind of disorder
which makes Claudius's Denmark the natural habitat not
of Comedy but of Tragedy. It is indeed a tribute to the
perceptiveness and generosity of the women that, even
with this conspicuous example of male inadequacy before
them, they agree in principle to marry. The year of
divorce which they ask their lovers to respect is quite
unlike the month required of Courtall and Freeman by
Ariana and Gatty at the end of Etherege's *She Would If
She Could* or the open-ended delay demanded by Ara-
minta from Congreve's Vainlove: it is not even marginally
coquettish. Recognizing that the men have no faults
which experience cannot amend, the Princess, Rosaline,
Katharine, and Maria simply ask their lovers to submit to
the trying complexity of life outside Navarre's park, and
to the power of Time.

*

On three separate occasions, *Love's Labour's Lost* stalls,
reaches deadlock, and apparently denies itself a comic
conclusion, only to recover. After the collapse of the
Russian Masque, Berowne's abuse of Boyet becomes so
vituperative that Costard's arrival pulls the scene back
from the brink of a brawl (V.2.459–84). Still more spectacular is the confrontation between Costard and Armado
after the disintegration of the Pageant. Here, a character
new to the play, Marcade, is needed to restore – at a cost
– order (V.2.669–712). The third and most serious discord
comes when the Princess and her ladies offer delayed

rather than immediate marriage. Berowne and the King deliver in response what sounds like the play's epilogue, a regretful farewell to the longed-for comic conclusion:

BEROWNE

> *Our wooing doth not end like an old play;*
> *Jack hath not Jill. These ladies' courtesy*
> *Might well have made our sport a comedy.*

KING

> *Come, sir, it wants a twelvemonth and a day,*
> *And then 'twill end.*

BEROWNE   *That's too long for a play.*

V.2.863–7

But this, of course, is no more an epilogue than that seemingly final speech with which Theseus dispatches the newly-weds 'to bed' some seventy lines from the end of *A Midsummer Night's Dream* (V.1.353–60). At what Navarre calls 'the latest minute of the hour' (V.2.782), both *Love's Labour's Lost* and its successor blossom into the unexpected.

The last speeches of Puck, Oberon, and Titania stop their play's drift towards fantasy. We have been charmed into thinking that life is all love, festivity, and pantomime lions, and then we hear Puck say:

> *Now the hungry lion roars*
> *And the wolf behowls the moon,*
> *Whilst the heavy ploughman snores*
> *All with weary task foredone.*
> *Now the wasted brands do glow*
> *Whilst the screech-owl, screeching loud,*
> *Puts the wretch that lies in woe*
> *In remembrance of a shroud. . . .*

V.1.361–8

Oberon is less threatening: he promises to protect the lovers' children from scars and harelips. And Titania speaks only of blessing. Nevertheless, the fairies' lines add up to a clear warning that beyond the still centre of Theseus's great house – even 'Now . . . Whilst' we listen – life is at best a mingled yarn. It may begin with blemishes, and it must end in a 'shroud'.

The songs of Ver and Hiems, like the fairies' last speeches, open a window on the wide world. They remind us that, beyond the King's enclosed park, 'lady-smocks all silver white', shepherds playing 'on oaten straws', 'merry larks', 'rooks', 'daws', and the chanting 'cuckoo', 'icicles', 'Dick', 'Tom', and 'greasy Joan', 'coughing', 'brooding', 'roasted crabs' and the 'staring owl' proliferate multitudinously. And they warn us that life is mingled: spring is a season of 'delight', but not for the man mocked as a cuckold by the cuckoo; winter is icy, harbouring no bright 'lady-smocks', yet it has fresh milk, log fires, piping hot apples, and an oddly 'merry' owl. But the songs differ from the speeches in one crucial respect: life is heaped around the Athenian lovers; it spreads along the axis of Time for those who gather to hear the owl and the cuckoo. 'Now' and 'Whilst' are replaced, in *Love's Labour's Lost*, by that structure so common in the early sonnets, 'When . . . Then'.

Winter and summer, spring and autumn, these are more obvious opposites than spring and winter; and spring is both logically and chronologically winter's successor, not its precursor. Why, then, did Shakespeare make Ver and Hiems contend, and why in that order? No doubt he wanted to echo in his songs the main movement of the play, from youthful 'delight' to cold death and divorce. (The spring song, like the life lived in the park, is full of pleasant artifice; winter is more harshly actual.)

But there is another, more hopeful, rationale, and it registers very strongly in the theatre. From spring to winter is the King's 'twelvemonth and a day'. As the songs are sung, Time seems to pass and the future is grappled to the instant. A show is at last heard through in peace and civility, a kingdom forms on stage – the low with the high, headed by a King and the new Queen – and, as the seasons change, the lovers prove inseparable. Armado's last words, 'You that way; we this way' (V.2.920), announce, then, only a qualified separation, for his show has already conducted the stage and theatre audiences through a year and a day to the true, comic end of the action. The owl and the cuckoo assure us that the labour of love will not be very long lost.

John Kerrigan

THE PLAY IN PERFORMANCE

Love's Labour's Lost's rich and varied vocabulary spans the range of Shakespeare's poetic invention, giving performers the chance to voice the dramatist's 'sharp wit' (V.2.398), as well as some of his 'honey-tongued' 'silken terms' (334, 406). With roles ranging from a king to a constable, a schoolmaster to a Spanish braggart, a princess to a dairymaid, *Love's Labour's Lost* invites contrasting characterizations, and lends itself to a wide array of acting styles. It contains memorable cameo roles, and some of Shakespeare's most innovative and poetic dramatic writing. As a script for performance it possesses the power to charm and disarm audiences simultaneously.

Love's Labour's Lost shares many similarities with *A Midsummer Night's Dream* at a structural level; polite decorum in the opening scenes gives way to playful merriment in the 'park' and in the Athenian woods respectively. Set designers have often created contrasts between the King's court and the 'park' in which he lodges the Princess and her companions. In the King's 'little academe' (I.1.13) there is much solemn talk of 'statutes' (17), 'oaths' (19), and 'philosophy' (32), while in the park the Princess and her ladies unreservedly gossip and banter under 'the cool shade of a sycamore' (V.2.89). Throughout the nineteenth and twentieth centuries the park setting inspired elaborate stage pictures: Laurence Olivier created an impressive backdrop of tree-lined pathways for his production at the National Theatre in 1968, and in 1990 at the RSC Terry Hands covered the stage floor with shining coloured leaves.

Though the King's court has traditionally been presented as a stuffy and closeted space reflective of his personality, some directors, including Terry Hands (RSC, 1990) and Ian Judge (RSC, 1993), have pictured the lords in more luxurious surroundings. Actors and directors must decide whether the King's decree is motivated by his own desire to make Navarre 'the wonder of the world' (I.1.12), or whether it is an honourable, and perhaps timely attempt to curtail his appetite for some of the unruly pleasures enjoyed during the 'kingly state of youth' (IV.3.291).

Set designers have commonly evoked an autumnal, elegiac atmosphere. Peter Brook took inspiration from paintings by the French Rococo artist Jean-Antoine Watteau (1684–1721) for his production at Stratford-upon-Avon in 1946, and John Barton's autumnal park setting in 1978 at the RSC resembled paintings by the English painter John Everett Millais (1829–96). Trevor Nunn (National, 2003) used the First World War, and Kenneth Branagh the Second World War, as the backdrop for their stage and screen productions. Other settings have helped emphasize the play's status as a comedy of youth. A rock score accompanied Michael Kahn's 1968 production at the American Shakespeare Theatre, Connecticut. In this production, the King and his men were dressed as hippies, while the Princess and her ladies dressed in miniskirts. Shakespeare emphasizes his characters' youthful exuberance above any restrictive sense of their royal demeanour, and the play can be adapted to suit most historical settings.

Music has often proved a key element in evoking atmosphere. The play calls for three songs (III.1.3, IV.1.126–9 and V.2.883–918), but some directors have added more. Ian Judge had his lords sing their love sonnets, and Kenneth Branagh went one step further for his film adaptation, turning the play itself into a musical reminiscent of the Hollywood Golden Age of cinema. At their most passionate, Branagh's characters break into songs by Irving Berlin, Cole Porter and George Gershwin. David Garrick had commissioned a full musical version as early as 1771, but it never reached the stage.

The dramatis personae are neatly divided into different generations. Young actors have traditionally portrayed the love-struck lords and ladies, while the roles of Don Armado and Holofernes have customarily fallen to more mature performers. The French lord Boyet's age has proved more open to interpretation. While jests about his being 'Cupid's grandfather' (II.1.241) may indicate advanced maturity, his behaviour at times suggests a younger spirit, if not a younger man. Similarly, Mote's 'tenderness of years' (III.1.4) has been portrayed by actors of different ages, and, like Puck in *A Midsummer Night's Dream*, the role has occasionally been portrayed by child performers, or by women cross-dressed.

Love's Labour's Lost's spry spirit stems primarily from the entertaining interactions between the lords and ladies when together, and when apart. Though the characters at the centre of the drama are a king and a princess, directors have not always chosen to emphasize their royal status. The King and his attendants in Ian Judge's RSC production dressed and behaved like university undergraduates. Though the King can, and perhaps should be played in the opening scene as a solemn aesthete, Richard Griffiths (RSC, 1978) and Simon Russell Beale (RSC, 1990) have shown that he can become the focus of much of the play's comedy. Of the four men, the King's hypocritical abandonment of his own decree that the men should not see women for a period of three years is arguably the most astonishing, and his ensuing embarrassment has often been met by audiences with a mixture of delight, compassion and commiseration. Any sense of the King's stateliness is challenged by his readiness to dress as a Muscovite, and to adopt a thick Russian accent, to court the French ladies in V.2. Along with the eavesdropping scene in IV.3, this scene has long been considered one of the comic highlights in performance. Boyet describes the lords' appearance in their 'shapeless gear' as 'ridiculous' (V.2.303, 306). While the lords simply wear white masks in Elijah Moshinsky's 1984 BBC television production, in the theatre actors have often worn false beards, danced Cossack jigs, and worn other pieces of distinctive Russian costume. To add to the absurdity and hilarity of the scenario, one of the lords in Terry Hands's 1990 RSC production dressed as a bear.

Berowne's passionate renunciation of the King's decree ('Have at you then, affection's men-at-arms!' (IV.3.288)) has often singled him out as the play's natural romantic and comic lead, and the part has been played by actors of glamorous presence. His sceptical voice dominates the opening scene, and his immediate objection to the King's unsociable decree is certain to amuse. Like Mercutio in *Romeo and Juliet*, Berowne jests at his friends' solemnity, and is always ready to 'whip hypocrisy' (149), yet actors must decide whether his lengthy speeches are driven by his fierce intelligence or by a competitive desire to be the virtuoso performer of the group. Joseph Fiennes, in Trevor Nunn's National Theatre production, portrayed Berowne as a sensitive and serious poetic figure, lacking the aggressive, chauvinist bravado of other portrayals, including Mike Gwilym's in the BBC television production.

The King describes Berowne as a man who habitually 'leap[s]' and 'laugh[s]' (IV.3.146) when displaying his wit, but he has often been presented as a more tranquil and enigmatic character. In John Barton's 1978 RSC production, Michael Pennington emphasized Berowne's contemplative nature. Pennington's Berowne did not speak for the love of hearing his own voice, but out of a compulsive need to communicate his opinions. Kenneth Branagh's Berowne is noticeably older (and implicitly more experienced in the art of love) than his companions in his film version, and like Pennington's Berowne, he has more in common with the bitingly sagacious Jaques from *As You Like It* than with a hot-blooded and feisty Mercutio figure. An actor's success in the role will depend not only upon his ability to charm and amuse, but also upon his ability to convey Berowne's passion, and disarming frankness.

Much of the lords' comedy is visual. One of its highlights, IV.3, is the episode in which the lords eavesdrop upon one another. Each subtly 'stands aside' as another lord enters the scene, giving the audience multiple perspectives from which to watch and enjoy the action. The stage-picture is given further depth through Berowne's positioning; his line 'Like a demi-god here sit I in the sky' (IV.3.77) suggests that he finds a raised position from which he can 'o'er-eye' the proceedings, while remaining clearly visible to the spectators. In the open-roofed playhouses of the sixteenth century the performers may have hidden behind one of the two pillars on stage, but as scenery has become more grand and spectacular, actors have found ever more inventive and unusual locations in which to conceal themselves. Over the years actors have posed as statues, accidentally dropped books, sneezed and battled hard to suppress their character's glee during this scene.

While the women's roles allow for comic characterization they all call for a maturity that is only truly found in Berowne among the men. From the start, the women have an understanding of life's sorrows as well as of its joys.

The Princess comes to Navarre in the knowledge that her father is 'decrepit, sick, and bedrid' (I.1.136), and Katharine has lost a sister who 'might ha' been a grandam ere she died' (V.2.17). Virginia Grainger, who played Katharine in Ian Judge's production, thought of her as older and more sophisticated than 'The young Dumaine' (II.1.56), and Jenny Quayle, who played the Princess in the same production, discovered a philosophical and moral side to her personality, which is noticeably absent among the men (RSC Production Pack, 1993). Actors must judge for themselves the point at which, and the extent to which, their characters fall in love with their suitors. It may even be debated in the rehearsal room whether the women fall in love at all.

The Princess and Rosaline delight in mocking the men of Navarre. Both roles anticipate qualities in Beatrice from *Much Ado About Nothing*, but it is Berowne's amour, Rosaline, who has traditionally been regarded as possessing the more caustic and roguish wit. There is a danger that the two women can seem too similar, as both are articulate, witty and wise. Rosaline has often been portrayed as a cool and self-confident woman, while the Princess has been presented as more capricious. Actresses must negotiate the dynamics of their relationship and decide how to differentiate between their sharp wits. Costume has often proved useful in drawing marked differences between the two women. In John Barton's 1978 RSC production, Carmen Du Sautoy's Princess was intentionally far less glamorous than Jane Lapotaire's Rosaline. Du Sautoy's wig of tightly coiled red ringlets and eye-glasses framed her as a bookish intellectual figure, in contrast to Lapotaire's Rosaline, who appeared more sexually alluring and sassy. Spatial arrangements can also help separate the characters. In Elijah Moshinsky's BBC television production, for example, Maureen Lipman's Princess is often positioned at the centre of the group of women, which draws attention to her royal status, and also sets her apart from Rosaline, who is quite literally manoeuvred into a supporting role. The ladies listen intently to the Princess's words, framing her, rather than Rosaline, as the wittiest and most engaging character.

As the Princess's only male companion, Boyet is readily identifiable, but the nature of his relationship with the ladies is not absolutely clear. He is simultaneously their chaperone, confidante and playfellow: he flirts and enjoys bawdy banter with Rosaline (IV.1.109–129), and tries unsuccessfully to kiss Katharine (II.1.208–10). Boyet has often been presented as an old-fashioned diplomat who enjoys a comfortable relationship with the women, but the text also allows for him to be interpreted as a more spirited and amorous figure. How, for example, should he respond as he watches the lords and ladies court one another? He may observe it all with pleasure and amusement, or alternatively, like Don Pedro at the close of *Much Ado About Nothing*, their happiness may provoke sadness.

Together, Don Armado and his page Mote make a wonderful double act, and their quick-fire repartee is both amusing and endearing. At twenty-five years of age, Paul Scofield was one of the youngest professional actors to be cast in the role in Peter Brook's production in 1946. Don Adriano de Armado shares both human and comedic qualities with characters such as Bottom in *A Midsummer Night's Dream* and Malvolio in *Twelfth Night*. As with Malvolio, his idiosyncrasies of behaviour and expression make him a source of constant amusement and 'recreation' (I.1.159) for the courtly lords, but his amorous feelings for Jaquenetta and his enthusiasm for the 'theatricals' performed at court link him more closely with Bottom.

Armado's dramatic voice and 'vain tongue' (I.1.164) are instantly recognizable because of his elaborate and arcane speech patterns: 'I do affect the very ground, which is base, where her shoe, which is baser, guided by her foot which is basest, doth tread' (I.2.161–3). In Ian Judge's RSC production, Daniel Massey spoke Armado's lines with a subtle Spanish accent, but in Kenneth Branagh's film, Timothy Spall adopts a wildly exaggerated Spanish inflection, adding further Spanish flavour to the role through his resemblance to the Surrealist painter Salvador Dali. While Spall's caricature clearly presents Armado as a figure of fun to be mocked and laughed at, Massey's more subtle portrayal focused on Don Armado's gentility and humanity, and any mockery of such a figure emphasized his identity and placement as an outsider to the King's court. In Clive Brill's dramatized audio-recording (Arkangel, 1998), Alan Howard performs Armado's lines with a sharp lisp, which readily distinguishes his voice for the audio listener. In this recording, as in some stage productions, both the King and Boyet imitate Armado's accent to great comic affect when they read his letters aloud in I.1.216–65 and IV.1.63–88 respectively.

While the role of Don Armado allows for moments of high comedy, the actor must also deliver some of the play's most profound and moving speeches. As the lords mock Hector's reputation during the performance of the Nine Worthies, Armado steps forward and redirects their thoughts toward their own mortality: 'The sweet war-man is dead and rotten. Sweet chucks, beat not the bones of the buried. When he breathed, he was a man' (V.2.658–60). Armado's lines look forward to the announcement of the King of France's death, and their delivery at this point draws a sharp contrast between the foolish yet honourable braggart and the distinguished yet thoughtless lords. In

Moshinsky's television production, David Warner's lugubrious Don Armado sounds a mournful note throughout, helping prepare the audience for his acute sensitivity in the final act.

Costard was probably written originally for the leading comic actor in Shakespeare's company, Will Kemp, who is known to have played Dogberry in *Much Ado About Nothing*. Where Armado's speech amuses through its ostentation, Costard's entertains through its down-to-earth quality: ' "Remuneration" '! O, | that's the Latin word for three farthings' (III.1.134–5). The role requires the talents of accomplished comedians: in Branagh's film the Broadway comic actor Nathan Lane brought a vaudevillian quality to the role, both in costume and physicality. Costard will not be silenced and part of his charm is his impish and mischievous quality.

The erudite and scholarly discussions between Holofernes and Nathaniel have often been shortened. While the Elizabethan topical references and Latinate words in these scenes may deter directors from including them in their entirety, the scenes have often proved a comic highlight despite, even sometimes because of, their apparent impenetrability. The very structure of Holofernes's speeches is ploddingly, comically pedantic, and an actor may savour his words and deliver his schoolmasterly condemnations of Dull's 'monster Ignorance' (IV.2.23) with a haughty flourish. Dull's delayed and perfectly timed confession that he has not understood a word spoken by the two learned men (V.1.144) is assured a laugh, and it serves further to align audience sympathies with these comic characters, whose innate dignity and decency is juxtaposed with the lords' immaturity at the end. The lords' rude mockery of these characters during the performance of the Nine Worthies is discomforting and shameful; the performers leave the stage 'dismayed' (V.2.565) and 'out of countenance' (618). Holofernes criticizes the lords' behaviour as 'not generous, not gentle, not humble' (626), and spectators are likely to agree.

Along with the multiple eavesdropping scene from IV.3, and the appearance of the visored lords dressed as Muscovites in V.2, the performance of the Nine Worthies at the close has often proved another of the play's highlights, inviting comic invention from actors and designers alike. The structure of the scene is reminiscent of the Mechanicals' performance of 'Pyramus and Thisbe' at Theseus and Hippolyta's wedding ceremony in *A Midsummer Night's Dream* where the audience pass cruel judgement upon the rustic performers' acting abilities. The lords' interjections are juvenile, bordering upon the malicious, and the tone in which these lines are delivered will influence the audience's reaction to the men at the close. Boyet's participation in ridiculing the players may prove problematic for an actor who has portrayed him as noble and dignified up to this point; again, tone is paramount in determining how the character's conduct should be interpreted.

The festive merriment is brought to an abrupt end with Marcade's appearance. In an instant Shakespeare moves from comedy to tragedy, and as Berowne suggests 'the scene begins to cloud' (V.2.717). It has become customary to dress Marcade in black mourning clothes, and some directors, following Peter Brook's lead, have prolonged his entrance to heighten the sense of fearful anticipation. Brook slowly dimmed the lights, and had the news of the King's death met with a lengthy silence. Marcade has come to embody the figure of Death itself in many late-twentieth-century productions.

The ladies' final speeches can prove problematic because the demands they make upon the men require a significant change in tone. After the lovers' stylish wit, the seriousness of these speeches can come as something of a shock, and performers must convince spectators of their newfound solemnity. The Princess's demand that the King 'go with speed | To some forlorn and naked hermitage, | Remote from all the pleasures of the world' (V.2.789–91) voices her own sense of grief and sadness, yet Rosaline's decree that Berowne should 'enforce the painèd impotent to smile' (843) momentarily re-establishes a lightness of tone. Faced with these dramatic changes in tone, directors are confronted with the challenge of how to end this play that seems to fight against the conventions of comedy. In his production for the National Theatre in 1968, Laurence Olivier concluded the play on a romantic note with the lovers standing together under a starlit sky as snowflakes began to fall. In contrast with this sentimental ending, Ian Judge ended his production with the sound of gunfire heralding the war that would part the lovers once more, perhaps for ever.

Love's Labour's Lost continues to inspire fresh approaches from directors and actors alike. No matter whether the play is presented as 'some delightful ostentation, or show, or pageant, or antic' (V.1.106), it is sure to elicit 'sudden breaking out of mirth' (108–9) and 'eruptions' (108) of applause.

Nicholas Walton

FURTHER READING

The Arden Shakespeare *Love's Labour's Lost*, edited by
H. R. Woudhuysen (1998), provides a detailed discussion
of the play's date, sources, structure and literary and social
contexts. It also provides a thorough examination of the
play's stage history, looking at some of its challenges and
rewards as well as notable productions and individual
performances. The Oxford Shakespeare *Love's Labour's
Lost*, edited by G. R. Hibbard (1990), also offers a detailed
introduction, with an appendix in which John Caldwell
provides the musical score for Rosaline's song 'Thou canst
not hit it' (IV.1.126–9). The BBC TV Shakespeare edition
(1984) notes the emendations and cuts made to the text
for this production, and also includes an essay by Henry
Fenwick about the filming process. In his preface to the
play for *The Norton Shakespeare* complete works (1997),
Walter Cohen considers the social dynamics at play in the
drama, as well as gender and racial issues raised by the
work. A brief account of what is presumed to be a lost
Shakespearian drama – *Love's Labour's Won* – appears in
the Oxford Shakespeare *Complete Works* (ed. Stanley Wells
and Gary Taylor, 1986), and editorial problems are listed
and discussed in the *Textual Companion* published to
accompany that edition. Discussions of the play's possible
sources and influences appear in volume I of Geoffrey
Bullough's *Narrative and Dramatic Sources of Shakespeare*
(1957) and Leo Salingar's *Shakespeare and the Traditions
of Comedy* (1974).

A comprehensive overview of the play's critical and

performance history can be gleaned from a selection of anthologies, which reprint noteworthy essays and theatrical reviews. *'Love's Labour's Lost': Critical Essays*, edited by Felicia Hardison Londré (1997), is a particularly valuable anthology, gathering together extracts from lectures, essays, reviews, theatregoer's notes, and interviews with actors and directors. The material ranges from works written in 1598 through to important twentieth-century works on the play's textual difficulties and editorial problems. *'Love's Labour's Lost': A Guide to the Play*, edited by John S. Pendergast (2002), explores the play's critical history, and compares critical approaches; Pendergast discusses many of the works that are reviewed in brief in D. J. Palmer's essay included in *Shakespeare: A Bibliographical Guide* (ed. Stanley Wells, 1990) and those works listed in *'Love's Labour's Lost': An Annotated Bibliography* (ed. Nancy Lenz Harvey and Anna Kirwan Carey, 1984). *Shakespeare: Early Comedies*, edited by Pamela Mason (1995), also reprints important works by critics ranging from Samuel Johnson and George Bernard Shaw to Anne Barton and James Calderwood. Further overviews of the play can be read in Harold Bloom's *Shakespeare: The Invention of the Human* (1999) and Stanley Wells's *Shakespeare: The Poet and his Plays* (1997). William C. Carroll's *The Great Feast of Language in 'Love's Labour's Lost'* (1976) provides a more detailed book-length study of the work.

Love's Labour's Lost's peculiarity among Shakespeare's comedies, and the challenges that it presents to conventional understandings of genre and gender roles have received much critical attention. Shakespeare's manipulation of comic conventions is discussed in Robert Ornstein's *Shakespeare's Comedies* (1986) and Alexander Leggatt's *Shakespeare's Comedy of Love* (1974). Further studies on this topic include: Cyrus Hoy's *'Love's Labour's*

Lost and the Nature of Comedy' (*Shakespeare Quarterly* 13, 1962, pp. 31–40), Keir Elam's *Shakespeare's Universe of Discourse: Language-Games in the Comedies* (1984) and C. L. Barber's *Shakespeare's Festive Comedy* (1959). The play's sexual and gender dynamics are considered from a variety of perspectives in Mark Breitenberg's *Anxious Masculinity in Early Modern England* (1996), Irene Dash's *Wooing, Wedding and Power: Women in Shakespeare's Plays* (1981) and Coppélia Kahn's *Man's Estate: Masculine Identity in Shakespeare* (1981). Katharine Eisamann Maus's essay 'Transfer of Title in *Love's Labour's Lost*: Language, Individualism, Gender', printed in *Shakespeare Left and Right* (ed. Ivo Kamps, 1991), explores similar concerns. Both M. M. Mahood's *Shakespeare's Wordplay* (1957) and David and Ben Crystal's *Shakespeare's Words* (2002) are valuable reference works that help elucidate some of Shakespeare's elaborate wordplay in this drama.

While *Love's Labour's Lost*'s performance history is discussed in editions and anthologies, Miriam Gilbert's study *Shakespeare in Performance: 'Love's Labour's Lost'* (1993) is the most thorough and detailed discussion of the play's theatrical afterlife. Gilbert focuses her discussion on four major RSC productions, but makes reference to other performances throughout the nineteenth and twentieth centuries. This study provides a wealth of information about the play in performance, including theatrical anecdotes alongside detailed descriptions of the productions. The Royal Shakespeare Company produced an instructive education pack to accompany Ian Judge's 1993 RSC production; the pack includes costume sketches and pictures of the set design, along with interviews with the director and some of the cast members. Edward Petherbridge writes of his experience of playing Don Armado in Barry Kyle's 1984 RSC production in *Players of Shakespeare 2* (ed.

Russell Jackson and Robert Smallwood, 1988), and Janet Clare gives an account of four twentieth-century productions in *Shakespeare in Performance* (ed. Keith Parsons and Pamela Mason, 1995, pp. 119–24). Kenneth Branagh's film version is examined by Samuel Crowl in *The Cambridge Companion to Shakespeare on Film* (ed. Russell Jackson, 2000, pp. 222–41), by Katherine Eggert in *Shakespeare The Movie II* (ed. Richard Burt and Lynda E. Boose, 2003, pp. 72–89) and by Kenneth S. Rothwell in *A History of Shakespeare on Screen: A Century of Film and Television* (2004, pp. 249–51).

Nicholas Walton

LOVE'S LABOUR'S LOST

THE CHARACTERS IN THE PLAY

KING FERDINAND OF NAVARRE
BEROWNE
LONGAVILLE } lords attending the King
DUMAINE

DON ADRIANO DE ARMADO, a Spanish braggart
MOTE, his page
HOLOFERNES, a schoolmaster
NATHANIEL, a curate
DULL, a constable
COSTARD, a swain
JAQUENETTA, a dairymaid
A FORESTER

THE PRINCESS OF FRANCE
ROSALINE
MARIA } ladies attending the Princess
KATHARINE
BOYET, a French lord
TWO LORDS
MARCADE, a messenger

Lords and attendants

Enter Ferdinand, King of Navarre, Berowne, Longa-
ville, and Dumaine

KING

Let fame, that all hunt after in their lives,
Live registered upon our brazen tombs,
And then grace us in the disgrace of death;
When, spite of cormorant devouring Time,
Th'endeavour of this present breath may buy
That honour which shall bate his scythe's keen edge,
And make us heirs of all eternity.
Therefore, brave conquerors – for so you are,
That war against your own affections
And the huge army of the world's desires –   10
Our late edict shall strongly stand in force:
Navarre shall be the wonder of the world;
Our court shall be a little academe,
Still and contemplative in living art.
You three, Berowne, Dumaine, and Longaville,
Have sworn for three years' term to live with me,
My fellow-scholars, and to keep those statutes
That are recorded in this schedule here.
Your oaths are passed; and now subscribe your names,
That his own hand may strike his honour down   20
That violates the smallest branch herein.
If you are armed to do as sworn to do,
Subscribe to your deep oaths, and keep it too.

LONGAVILLE

I am resolved. 'Tis but a three years' fast.

The mind shall banquet though the body pine.
Fat paunches have lean pates, and dainty bits
Make rich the ribs but bankrupt quite the wits.

He signs

DUMAINE

My loving lord, Dumaine is mortified.
The grosser manner of these world's delights
30   He throws upon the gross world's baser slaves.
To love, to wealth, to pomp, I pine and die,
With all these living in philosophy.

He signs

BEROWNE

I can but say their protestation over.
So much, dear liege, I have already sworn,
That is, to live and study here three years.
But there are other strict observances:
As not to see a woman in that term —
Which I hope well is not enrollèd there;
And one day in a week to touch no food,
40   And but one meal on every day beside —
The which I hope is not enrollèd there;
And then to sleep but three hours in the night,
And not be seen to wink of all the day,
When I was wont to think no harm all night,
And make a dark night too of half the day —
Which I hope well is not enrollèd there.
O, these are barren tasks, too hard to keep,
Not to see ladies, study, fast, not sleep.

KING

Your oath is passed, to pass away from these.

BEROWNE

50   Let me say no, my liege, an if you please.
I only swore to study with your grace,
And stay here in your court for three years' space.

LONGAVILLE

You swore to that, Berowne, and to the rest.

BEROWNE

By yea and nay, sir, then I swore in jest.
What is the end of study, let me know?

KING

Why, that to know which else we should not know.

BEROWNE

Things hid and barred, you mean, from common
                sense?

KING

Ay, that is study's god-like recompense.

BEROWNE

Com'on then, I will swear to study so,
To know the thing I am forbid to know: 60
As thus – to study where I well may dine,
When I to feast expressly am forbid;
Or study where to meet some mistress fine,
When mistresses from common sense are hid;
Or, having sworn too hard-a-keeping oath,
Study to break it and not break my troth.
If study's gain be thus, and this be so,
Study knows that which yet it doth not know.
Swear me to this, and I will ne'er say no.

KING

These be the stops that hinder study quite,   70
And train our intellects to vain delight.

BEROWNE

Why, all delights are vain, but that most vain
Which, with pain purchased, doth inherit pain:
As painfully to pore upon a book
   To seek the light of truth, while truth the while
Doth falsely blind the eyesight of his look.
   Light seeking light doth light of light beguile;

So, ere you find where light in darkness lies,
Your light grows dark by losing of your eyes.
80 Study me how to please the eye indeed
    By fixing it upon a fairer eye,
Who dazzling so, that eye shall be his heed,
    And give him light that it was blinded by.
Study is like the heaven's glorious sun,
    That will not be deep-searched with saucy looks.
Small have continual plodders ever won,
    Save base authority from others' books.
These earthly godfathers of heaven's lights,
    That give a name to every fixèd star,
90 Have no more profit of their shining nights
    Than those that walk and wot not what they are.
Too much to know is to know naught but fame,
And every godfather can give a name.

KING
How well he's read, to reason against reading.

DUMAINE
Proceeded well, to stop all good proceeding.

LONGAVILLE
He weeds the corn, and still lets grow the weeding.

BEROWNE
The spring is near when green geese are a-breeding.

DUMAINE
How follows that?

BEROWNE   Fit in his place and time.

DUMAINE
In reason nothing.

BEROWNE   Something then in rhyme.

KING
100 Berowne is like an envious sneaping frost
    That bites the first-born infants of the spring.

BEROWNE
    Well, say I am! Why should proud summer boast

8

Before the birds have any cause to sing?
Why should I joy in an abortive birth?
At Christmas I no more desire a rose
Than wish a snow in May's new-fangled shows,
But like of each thing that in season grows.
So you, to study now it is too late,
Climb o'er the house to unlock the little gate.

KING

Well, sit you out. Go home, Berowne. Adieu!   110

BEROWNE

No, my good lord, I have sworn to stay with you.
And though I have for barbarism spoke more
    Than for that angel knowledge you can say,
Yet, confident, I'll keep what I have sworn,
    And bide the penance of each three years' day.
Give me the paper, let me read the same,
And to the strictest decrees I'll write my name.

KING

How well this yielding rescues thee from shame.

BEROWNE (*reading*) *Item: that no woman shall come within
a mile of my court* – hath this been proclaimed?   120

LONGAVILLE Four days ago.

BEROWNE Let's see the penalty – *on pain of losing her
tongue*. Who devised this penalty?

LONGAVILLE Marry, that did I.

BEROWNE Sweet lord, and why?

LONGAVILLE

To fright them hence with that dread penalty.

BEROWNE

A dangerous law against gentility!
*Item: if any man be seen to talk with a woman within the
term of three years, he shall endure such public shame as
the rest of the court can possibly devise.*   130
This article, my liege, yourself must break;
    For well you know here comes in embassy

9

The French King's daughter with yourself to speak –
    A maid of grace and complete majesty –
About surrender up of Aquitaine
    To her decrepit, sick, and bedrid father.
Therefore this article is made in vain,
    Or vainly comes th'admirèd Princess hither.

KING

What say you, lords? Why, this was quite forgot.

BEROWNE

140 So study evermore is overshot.
While it doth study to have what it would,
It doth forget to do the thing it should;
And when it hath the thing it hunteth most,
'Tis won as towns with fire – so won, so lost.

KING

We must of force dispense with this decree.
She must lie here on mere necessity.

BEROWNE

Necessity will make us all forsworn
    Three thousand times within this three years' space;
For every man with his affects is born,
150   Not by might mastered, but by special grace.
If I break faith, this word shall speak for me:
I am forsworn on mere 'necessity'.
So to the laws at large I write my name,
    And he that breaks them in the least degree
Stands in attainder of eternal shame.
    Suggestions are to other as to me,
But I believe, although I seem so loath,
I am the last that will last keep his oath.

He signs

But is there no quick recreation granted?

KING

160 Ay, that there is. Our court, you know, is haunted

With a refinèd traveller of Spain;
A man in all the world's new fashion planted,
    That hath a mint of phrases in his brain;
One who the music of his own vain tongue
    Doth ravish like enchanting harmony;
A man of compliments, whom right and wrong
    Have chose as umpire of their mutiny.
This child of fancy, that Armado hight,
    For interim to our studies shall relate
In high-born words the worth of many a knight   170
    From tawny Spain, lost in the world's debate.
How you delight, my lords, I know not, I,
But I protest I love to hear him lie,
And I will use him for my minstrelsy.

BEROWNE
Armado is a most illustrious wight,
A man of fire-new words, fashion's own knight.

LONGAVILLE
Costard the swain and he shall be our sport,
And so to study three years is but short.
    Enter Dull with a letter,
    and Costard

DULL Which is the Duke's own person?
BEROWNE This, fellow. What wouldst?   180
DULL I myself reprehend his own person, for I am his
    grace's farborough. But I would see his own person in
    flesh and blood.
BEROWNE This is he.
DULL Signeour Arm–, Arm–, commends you. There's
    villainy abroad. This letter will tell you more.
COSTARD Sir, the contempts thereof are as touching me.
KING A letter from the magnificent Armado.
BEROWNE How low soever the matter, I hope in God for
    high words.   190

LONGAVILLE A high hope for a low heaven. God grant us patience!

BEROWNE To hear, or forbear hearing?

LONGAVILLE To hear meekly, sir, and to laugh moderately; or to forbear both.

BEROWNE Well, sir, be it as the style shall give us cause to climb in the merriness.

COSTARD The matter is to me, sir, as concerning Jaquenetta. The manner of it is, I was taken with the
200 manner.

BEROWNE In what manner?

COSTARD In manner and form following, sir – all those three: I was seen with her 'in' the 'manor'-house, sitting with her upon the 'form', and taken 'following' her into the park; which, put together, is 'in manner and form following'. Now, sir, for the 'manner' – it is the manner of a man to speak to a woman. For the 'form' – in some form.

BEROWNE For the 'following', sir?

210 COSTARD As it shall follow in my correction – and God defend the right!

KING Will you hear this letter with attention?

BEROWNE As we would hear an oracle.

COSTARD Such is the sinplicity of man to hearken after the flesh.

KING (reading) Great deputy, the welkin's vicegerent, and sole dominator of Navarre, my soul's earth's god, and body's fostering patron –

COSTARD Not a word of Costard yet.

220 KING So it is –

COSTARD It may be so; but if he say it is so, he is, in telling true – but so.

KING Peace!

COSTARD Be to me and every man that dares not fight.

KING No words!

COSTARD Of other men's secrets, I beseech you.

KING *So it is, besieged with sable-coloured melancholy, I did* *commend the black oppressing humour to the most whole-* *some physic of thy health-giving air; and, as I am a* *gentleman, betook myself to walk. The time when? About* 230 *the sixth hour; when beasts most graze, birds best peck,* *and men sit down to that nourishment which is called* *supper. So much for the time when. Now for the ground* *which — which, I mean, I walked upon. It is yclept thy* *park. Then for the place where — where, I mean, I did* *encounter that obscene and most preposterous event that* *draweth from my snow-white pen the ebon-coloured ink* *which here thou viewest, beholdest, surveyest, or seest. But* *to the place where. It standeth north-north-east and by* *east from the west corner of thy curious-knotted garden.* 240 *There did I see that low-spirited swain, that base minnow* *of thy mirth —*

COSTARD Me?

KING *That unlettered small-knowing soul —*

COSTARD Me?

KING *That shallow vassal —*

COSTARD Still me?

KING *Which, as I remember, hight Costard —*

COSTARD O, me!

KING *Sorted and consorted, contrary to thy established pro-* 250 *claimed edict and continent canon, which with — O, with —* *but with this I passion to say wherewith —*

COSTARD With a wench.

KING *With a child of our grandmother Eve, a female, or, for* *thy more sweet understanding, a woman. Him I — as my* *ever-esteemed duty pricks me on — have sent to thee, to* *receive the meed of punishment, by thy sweet grace's offi-* *cer, Anthony Dull, a man of good repute, carriage, bear-*

13

ing, and estimation.

260 DULL Me, an't shall please you. I am Anthony Dull.

KING *For Jaquenetta — so is the weaker vessel called — which I apprehended with the aforesaid swain, I keep her as a vessel of thy law's fury, and shall, at the least of thy sweet notice, bring her to trial. Thine in all compliments of devoted and heart-burning heat of duty,*

Don Adriano de Armado

BEROWNE This is not so well as I looked for, but the best that ever I heard.

KING Ay, the best for the worst. But, sirrah, what say you
270 to this?

COSTARD Sir, I confess the wench.

KING Did you hear the proclamation?

COSTARD I do confess much of the hearing it, but little of the marking of it.

KING It was proclaimed a year's imprisonment to be taken with a wench.

COSTARD I was taken with none, sir; I was taken with a damsel.

KING Well, it was proclaimed 'damsel'.

280 COSTARD This was no damsel neither, sir; she was a virgin.

KING It is so varied too, for it was proclaimed 'virgin'.

COSTARD If it were, I deny her virginity. I was taken with a maid.

KING This 'maid' will not serve your turn, sir.

COSTARD This maid will serve my turn, sir.

KING Sir, I will pronounce your sentence: you shall fast a week with bran and water.

COSTARD I had rather pray a month with mutton and
290 porridge.

KING
And Don Armado shall be your keeper.

My Lord Berowne, see him delivered o'er;
And go we, lords, to put in practice that
Which each to other hath so strongly sworn.

Exeunt King, Longaville, and Dumaine

BEROWNE
I'll lay my head to any goodman's hat
These oaths and laws will prove an idle scorn.
Sirrah, come on.
COSTARD I suffer for the truth, sir; for true it is I was
taken with Jaquenetta, and Jaquenetta is a true girl.
And therefore welcome the sour cup of prosperity! 300
Affliction may one day smile again, and till then sit
thee down, sorrow!   *Exeunt*

Enter Armado and Mote, his page   I.2

ARMADO Boy, what sign is it when a man of great spirit
grows melancholy?
MOTE A great sign, sir, that he will look sad.
ARMADO Why, sadness is one and the self-same thing,
dear imp.
MOTE No, no; O Lord, sir, no!
ARMADO How canst thou part sadness and melancholy,
my tender juvenal?
MOTE By a familiar demonstration of the working, my
tough signor.   10
ARMADO Why tough signor? Why tough signor?
MOTE Why tender juvenal? Why tender juvenal?
ARMADO I spoke it, tender juvenal, as a congruent epith-
eton appertaining to thy young days, which we may
nominate tender.
MOTE And I, tough signor, as an appertinent title to your
old time, which we may name tough.
ARMADO Pretty and apt.

15

MOTE How mean you, sir? I pretty and my saying apt, or
20   I apt and my saying pretty?

ARMADO Thou pretty, because little.

MOTE Little pretty, because little. Wherefore apt?

ARMADO And therefore apt, because quick.

MOTE Speak you this in my praise, master?

ARMADO In thy condign praise.

MOTE I will praise an eel with the same praise.

ARMADO What, that an eel is ingenious?

MOTE That an eel is quick.

ARMADO I do say thou art quick in answers. Thou heatest
30   my blood.

MOTE I am answered, sir.

ARMADO I love not to be crossed.

MOTE (*aside*) He speaks the mere contrary – crosses love
    not him.

ARMADO I have promised to study three years with the
    Duke.

MOTE You may do it in an hour, sir.

ARMADO Impossible.

MOTE How many is one thrice told?

40 ARMADO I am ill at reckoning. It fitteth the spirit of a
    tapster.

MOTE You are a gentleman and a gamester, sir.

ARMADO I confess both. They are both the varnish of a
    complete man.

MOTE Then I am sure you know how much the gross sum
    of deuce-ace amounts to.

ARMADO It doth amount to one more than two.

MOTE Which the base vulgar do call three.

ARMADO True.

50 MOTE Why, sir, is this such a piece of study? Now here is
    three studied ere ye'll thrice wink; and how easy it is to
    put 'years' to the word 'three', and study three years in

two words, the dancing horse will tell you.

ARMADO A most fine figure!

MOTE (*aside*) To prove you a cipher.

ARMADO I will hereupon confess I am in love; and as it is
base for a soldier to love, so am I in love with a base
wench. If drawing my sword against the humour of
affection would deliver me from the reprobate thought
of it, I would take desire prisoner, and ransom him to 60
any French courtier for a new-devised curtsy. I think
scorn to sigh: methinks I should outswear Cupid.
Comfort me, boy. What great men have been in love?

MOTE Hercules, master.

ARMADO Most sweet Hercules! More authority, dear boy,
name more; and, sweet my child, let them be men of
good repute and carriage.

MOTE Samson, master: he was a man of good carriage –
great carriage, for he carried the town-gates on his
back like a porter – and he was in love. 70

ARMADO O well-knit Samson! Strong-jointed Samson! I
do excel thee in my rapier as much as thou didst me in
carrying gates. I am in love too. Who was Samson's
love, my dear Mote?

MOTE A woman, master.

ARMADO Of what complexion?

MOTE Of all the four, or the three, or the two, or one of
the four.

ARMADO Tell me precisely of what complexion.

MOTE Of the sea-water green, sir. 80

ARMADO Is that one of the four complexions?

MOTE As I have read, sir; and the best of them too.

ARMADO Green indeed is the colour of lovers; but to have
a love of that colour, methinks Samson had small reason
for it. He surely affected her for her wit.

MOTE It was so, sir, for she had a green wit.

ARMADO My love is most immaculate white and red.

MOTE Most maculate thoughts, master, are masked under
such colours.

90 ARMADO Define, define, well-educated infant.

MOTE My father's wit and my mother's tongue assist me!

ARMADO Sweet invocation of a child – most pretty and
pathetical!

MOTE

> If she be made of white and red,
> Her faults will ne'er be known,
> For blushing cheeks by faults are bred,
> And fears by pale white shown.
> Then if she fear or be to blame,
> By this you shall not know,

100 > For still her cheeks possess the same
> Which native she doth owe.

A dangerous rhyme, master, against the reason of white
and red.

ARMADO Is there not a ballad, boy, of the King and the
Beggar?

MOTE The world was very guilty of such a ballad some
three ages since, but I think now 'tis not to be found;
or, if it were, it would neither serve for the writing nor
the tune.

110 ARMADO I will have that subject newly writ o'er, that I
may example my digression by some mighty precedent.
Boy, I do love that country girl that I took in the park
with the rational hind Costard. She deserves well.

MOTE (aside) To be whipped – and yet a better love than
my master.

ARMADO Sing, boy. My spirit grows heavy in love.

MOTE (aside) And that's great marvel, loving a light
wench.

ARMADO I say, sing.

MOTE Forbear till this company be passed.   120
    Enter Dull, Costard,
    and Jaquenetta

DULL Sir, the Duke's pleasure is that you keep Costard
    safe; and you must suffer him to take no delight, nor
    no penance, but 'a must fast three days a week. For
    this damsel, I must keep her at the park; she is allowed
    for the dey-woman. Fare you well.

ARMADO (*aside*) I do betray myself with blushing. –
    Maid –

JAQUENETTA Man.

ARMADO I will visit thee at the lodge.

JAQUENETTA That's hereby.   130

ARMADO I know where it is situate.

JAQUENETTA Lord, how wise you are!

ARMADO I will tell thee wonders.

JAQUENETTA With that face?

ARMADO I love thee.

JAQUENETTA So I heard you say.

ARMADO And so farewell.

JAQUENETTA Fair weather after you.

DULL Come, Jaquenetta, away!
                      Exeunt Dull and Jaquenetta

ARMADO Villain, thou shalt fast for thy offences ere thou   140
    be pardoned.

COSTARD Well, sir, I hope when I do it I shall do it on a
    full stomach.

ARMADO Thou shalt be heavily punished.

COSTARD I am more bound to you than your fellows, for
    they are but lightly rewarded.

ARMADO Take away this villain. Shut him up.

MOTE Come, you transgressing slave, away!

COSTARD Let me not be pent up, sir. I will fast being
    loose.   150

MOTE No, sir, that were fast and loose. Thou shalt to prison.

COSTARD Well, if ever I do see the merry days of desolation that I have seen, some shall see –

MOTE What shall some see?

COSTARD Nay, nothing, Master Mote, but what they look upon. It is not for prisoners to be too silent in their words, and therefore I say nothing. I thank God I have as little patience as another man, and therefore I can
160   be quiet.   *Exeunt Mote and Costard*

ARMADO I do affect the very ground, which is base, where her shoe, which is baser, guided by her foot, which is basest, doth tread. I shall be forsworn, which is a great argument of falsehood, if I love. And how can that be true love which is falsely attempted? Love is a familiar; Love is a devil; there is no evil angel but Love. Yet was Samson so tempted, and he had an excellent strength; yet was Solomon so seduced, and he had a very good wit. Cupid's butt-shaft is too hard for
170   Hercules' club, and therefore too much odds for a Spaniard's rapier. The first and second cause will not serve my turn; the passado he respects not, the duello he regards not. His disgrace is to be called boy, but his glory is to subdue men. Adieu, valour; rust, rapier; be still, drum; for your manager is in love; yea, he loveth. Assist me, some extemporal god of rhyme, for I am sure I shall turn sonnet. Devise, wit; write, pen; for I am for whole volumes in folio.   *Exit*

                                   *

II.1   *Enter the Princess of France, Rosaline, Maria, and Katharine, with Boyet and two more attendant Lords*

BOYET

    Now, madam, summon up your dearest spirits.
    Consider who the King your father sends,
    To whom he sends, and what's his embassy:
    Yourself, held precious in the world's esteem,
    To parley with the sole inheritor
    Of all perfections that a man may owe,
    Matchless Navarre; the plea of no less weight
    Than Aquitaine, a dowry for a queen.
    Be now as prodigal of all dear grace
    As Nature was in making graces dear   10
    When she did starve the general world beside,
    And prodigally gave them all to you.

PRINCESS

    Good Lord Boyet, my beauty, though but mean,
    Needs not the painted flourish of your praise.
    Beauty is bought by judgement of the eye,
    Not uttered by base sale of chapmen's tongues.
    I am less proud to hear you tell my worth
    Than you much willing to be counted wise
    In spending your wit in the praise of mine.
    But now to task the tasker. Good Boyet,   20
    You are not ignorant all-telling fame
    Doth noise abroad Navarre hath made a vow,
    Till painful study shall outwear three years,
    No woman may approach his silent court.
    Therefore to's seemeth it a needful course,
    Before we enter his forbidden gates,
    To know his pleasure; and in that behalf,
    Bold of your worthiness, we single you
    As our best-moving fair solicitor.
    Tell him the daughter of the King of France,   30
    On serious business craving quick dispatch,
    Importunes personal conference with his grace.

    Haste, signify so much, while we attend,
    Like humble-visaged suitors, his high will.

BOYET

    Proud of employment, willingly I go.

PRINCESS

    All pride is willing pride, and yours is so.

                                Exit Boyet

    Who are the votaries, my loving lords,
    That are vow-fellows with this virtuous Duke?

FIRST LORD

    Lord Longaville is one.

PRINCESS   Know you the man?

MARIA

40   I know him, madam. At a marriage feast
    Between Lord Perigort and the beauteous heir
    Of Jacques Falconbridge, solemnizèd
    In Normandy, saw I this Longaville.
    A man of sovereign parts he is esteemed;
    Well fitted in arts, glorious in arms.
    Nothing becomes him ill that he would well.
    The only soil of his fair virtue's gloss –
    If virtue's gloss will stain with any soil –
    Is a sharp wit matched with too blunt a will,
50   Whose edge hath power to cut, whose will still wills
    It should none spare that come within his power.

PRINCESS

    Some merry mocking lord, belike – is't so?

MARIA

    They say so most that most his humours know.

PRINCESS

    Such short-lived wits do wither as they grow.
    Who are the rest?

KATHARINE

    The young Dumaine, a well-accomplished youth,

Of all that virtue love for virtue loved;
Most power to do most harm, least knowing ill,
For he hath wit to make an ill shape good,
And shape to win grace though he had no wit.   60
I saw him at the Duke Alençon's once;
And much too little of that good I saw
Is my report to his great worthiness.

ROSALINE

Another of these students at that time
Was there with him, if I have heard a truth.
Berowne they call him – but a merrier man,
Within the limit of becoming mirth,
I never spent an hour's talk withal.
His eye begets occasion for his wit,
For every object that the one doth catch   70
The other turns to a mirth-moving jest,
Which his fair tongue – conceit's expositor –
Delivers in such apt and gracious words
That agèd ears play truant at his tales
And younger hearings are quite ravishèd,
So sweet and voluble is his discourse.

PRINCESS

God bless my ladies! Are they all in love,
That every one her own hath garnishèd
With such bedecking ornaments of praise?

FIRST LORD

Here comes Boyet.

Enter Boyet

PRINCESS   Now, what admittance, lord?   80

BOYET

Navarre had notice of your fair approach,
And he and his competitors in oath
Were all addressed to meet you, gentle lady,
Before I came. Marry, thus much I have learned:

23

He rather means to lodge you in the field,
Like one that comes here to besiege his court,
Than seek a dispensation for his oath,
To let you enter his unpeopled house.
Here comes Navarre.

Enter the King, Berowne, Longaville, and Dumaine

KING

90 Fair Princess, welcome to the court of Navarre.

PRINCESS 'Fair' I give you back again, and 'welcome' I
have not yet. The roof of this court is too high to be
yours, and welcome to the wide fields too base to be
mine.

KING

You shall be welcome, madam, to my court.

PRINCESS

I will be welcome, then. Conduct me thither.

KING

Hear me, dear lady. I have sworn an oath –

PRINCESS

Our Lady help my lord! He'll be forsworn.

KING

Not for the world, fair madam, by my will.

PRINCESS

100 Why, will shall break it; will, and nothing else.

KING

Your ladyship is ignorant what it is.

PRINCESS

Were my lord so, his ignorance were wise,
Where now his knowledge must prove ignorance.
I hear your grace hath sworn out house-keeping.
'Tis deadly sin to keep that oath, my lord,
And sin to break it.
But pardon me, I am too sudden-bold;
To teach a teacher ill beseemeth me.

24

Vouchsafe to read the purpose of my coming,
And suddenly resolve me in my suit.   110

She offers the King a paper

KING

Madam, I will, if suddenly I may.

PRINCESS

You will the sooner that I were away,
For you'll prove perjured if you make me stay.

The King reads

Berowne and Rosaline converse apart

BEROWNE Lady, I will commend you to my mine own
heart.

ROSALINE Pray you, do my commendations; I would be
glad to see it.

BEROWNE I would you heard it groan.

ROSALINE Is the fool sick?

BEROWNE Sick at the heart.   120

ROSALINE Alack, let it blood.

BEROWNE Would that do it good?

ROSALINE My physic says ay.

BEROWNE Will you prick't with your eye?

ROSALINE *Non point*, with my knife.

BEROWNE Now God save thy life.

ROSALINE And yours from long living.

BEROWNE I cannot stay thanksgiving.

He leaves her

KING

Madam, your father here doth intimate
The payment of a hundred thousand crowns,   130
Being but the one half of an entire sum
Disbursèd by my father in his wars.
But say that he, or we – as neither have –
Received that sum, yet there remains unpaid
A hundred thousand more, in surety of the which

One part of Aquitaine is bound to us,
Although not valued to the money's worth.
If then the King your father will restore
But that one half which is unsatisfied,
140   We will give up our right in Aquitaine
And hold fair friendship with his majesty.
But that, it seems, he little purposeth,
For here he doth demand to have repaid
A hundred thousand crowns, and not demands,
On payment of a hundred thousand crowns,
To have his title live in Aquitaine –
Which we much rather had depart withal,
And have the money by our father lent,
Than Aquitaine, so gelded as it is.
150   Dear Princess, were not his requests so far
From reason's yielding, your fair self should make
A yielding 'gainst some reason in my breast,
And go well satisfied to France again.

PRINCESS

You do the King my father too much wrong,
And wrong the reputation of your name,
In so unseeming to confess receipt
Of that which hath so faithfully been paid.

KING

I do protest I never heard of it;
And if you prove it, I'll repay it back
Or yield up Aquitaine.

160 **PRINCESS**   We arrest your word.
Boyet, you can produce acquittances
For such a sum from special officers
Of Charles his father.

KING   Satisfy me so.

BOYET

So please your grace, the packet is not come

Where that and other specialties are bound.
Tomorrow you shall have a sight of them.

KING

It shall suffice me; at which interview
All liberal reason I will yield unto.
Meantime, receive such welcome at my hand
As honour, without breach of honour, may   170
Make tender of to thy true worthiness.
You may not come, fair Princess, in my gates;
But here without you shall be so received
As you shall deem yourself lodged in my heart,
Though so denied fair harbour in my house.
Your own good thoughts excuse me, and farewell.
Tomorrow shall we visit you again.

PRINCESS

Sweet health and fair desires consort your grace.

KING

Thy own wish wish I thee in every place.

Exeunt King, Berowne, Longaville,
and Dumaine

Enter Dumaine

DUMAINE

Sir, I pray you, a word. What lady is that same?   180

BOYET

The heir of Alençon, Katharine her name.

DUMAINE

A gallant lady. Monsieur, fare you well.   *Exit*
Enter Longaville

LONGAVILLE

I beseech you a word. What is she in the white?

BOYET

A woman sometimes, an you saw her in the light.

LONGAVILLE

Perchance light in the light. I desire her name.

BOYET
　She hath but one for herself – to desire that were a
　　　shame.

LONGAVILLE
　Pray you, sir: whose daughter?

BOYET
　Her mother's, I have heard.

LONGAVILLE
　God's blessing on your beard!

BOYET
190　Good sir, be not offended.
　She is an heir of Falconbridge.

LONGAVILLE
　Nay, my choler is ended.
　She is a most sweet lady.

BOYET
　Not unlike, sir; that may be.

Exit Longaville

　　Enter Berowne

BEROWNE
　What's her name in the cap?

BOYET
　Rosaline, by good hap.

BEROWNE
　Is she wedded or no?

BOYET
　To her will, sir, or so.

BEROWNE
　You are welcome, sir! Adieu.

BOYET
200　Farewell to me, sir, and welcome to you.

Exit Berowne

MARIA
　That last is Berowne, the merry madcap lord.

Not a word with him but a jest.

BOYET   And every jest but a word.

PRINCESS

It was well done of you to take him at his word.

BOYET

I was as willing to grapple as he was to board.

KATHARINE

Two hot sheeps, marry!

BOYET   And wherefore not 'ships'?

No sheep, sweet lamb, unless we feed on your lips.

KATHARINE

You sheep, and I pasture. Shall that finish the jest?

BOYET

So you grant pasture for me.

           He tries to kiss her

KATHARINE   Not so, gentle beast.

My lips are no common, though several they be.

BOYET

Belonging to whom?

KATHARINE   To my fortunes and me.   210

PRINCESS

Good wits will be jangling; but, gentles, agree.

This civil war of wits were much better used

On Navarre and his book-men, for here 'tis abused.

BOYET

If my observation, which very seldom lies,

By the heart's still rhetoric disclosèd with eyes

Deceive me not now, Navarre is infected.

PRINCESS

With what?

BOYET

With that which we lovers entitle 'affected'.

PRINCESS

Your reason?

29

BOYET

220   Why, all his behaviours did make their retire
   To the court of his eye, peeping thorough desire.
   His heart, like an agate with your print impressed,
   Proud with his form, in his eye pride expressed.
   His tongue, all impatient to speak and not see,
   Did stumble with haste in his eyesight to be.
   All senses to that sense did make their repair,
   To feel only looking on fairest of fair.
   Methought all his senses were locked in his eye,
   As jewels in crystal for some prince to buy;
   Who, tendering their own worth from where they were
230   glassed,
   Did point you to buy them along as you passed.
   His face's own margin did quote such amazes
   That all eyes saw his eyes enchanted with gazes.
   I'll give you Aquitaine, and all that is his,
   An you give him for my sake but one loving kiss.

PRINCESS

   Come, to our pavilion. Boyet is disposed.

BOYET

   But to speak that in words which his eye hath dis-
       closed.
   I only have made a mouth of his eye
   By adding a tongue which I know will not lie.

MARIA

240   Thou art an old love-monger, and speakest skilfully.

KATHARINE

   He is Cupid's grandfather, and learns news of him.

ROSALINE

   Then was Venus like her mother, for her father is but
       grim.

BOYET

   Do you hear, my mad wenches?

MARIA   No.

BOYET   What then, do you see?

MARIA

  Ay, our way to be gone.

BOYET   You are too hard for me.

                              Exeunt

*

Enter Armado and Mote   III.1

ARMADO Warble, child: make passionate my sense of
   hearing.

MOTE (*singing*) Concolinel.

ARMADO Sweet air! Go, tenderness of years, take this key,
   give enlargement to the swain, bring him festinately
   hither. I must employ him in a letter to my love.

MOTE Master, will you win your love with a French
   brawl?

ARMADO How meanest thou? Brawling in French?

MOTE No, my complete master; but to jig off a tune at 10
   the tongue's end, canary to it with your feet, humour it
   with turning up your eyelids, sigh a note and sing a
   note, sometime through the throat as if you swallowed
   love with singing love, sometime through the nose as if
   you snuffed up love by smelling love, with your hat
   penthouse-like o'er the shop of your eyes, with your
   arms crossed on your thin-belly doublet like a rabbit
   on a spit, or your hands in your pocket like a man after
   the old painting; and keep not long in one tune, but a
   snip and away. These are compliments, these are hum- 20
   ours, these betray nice wenches, that would be betrayed
   without these; and make them men of note – do you
   note me? – that most are affected to these.

ARMADO How hast thou purchased this experience?

MOTE By my penny of observation.

ARMADO But O – but O –

MOTE 'The hobby-horse is forgot.'

ARMADO Callest thou my love 'hobby-horse'?

MOTE No, master. The hobby-horse is but a colt, (*aside*)
30 and your love perhaps a hackney. (*To him*) But have
you forgot your love?

ARMADO Almost I had.

MOTE Negligent student! Learn her by heart.

ARMADO By heart and in heart, boy.

MOTE And out of heart, master. All those three I will
prove.

ARMADO What wilt thou prove?

MOTE A man, if I live; and this 'by', 'in', and 'without',
upon the instant. 'By' heart you love her, because your
40 heart cannot come by her; 'in' heart you love her,
because your heart is in love with her; and 'out' of
heart you love her, being out of heart that you cannot
enjoy her.

ARMADO I am all these three.

MOTE And three times as much more, and yet nothing at
all.

ARMADO Fetch hither the swain. He must carry me a
letter.

MOTE A message well sympathized – a horse to be ambas-
50 sador for an ass.

ARMADO Ha, ha, what sayest thou?

MOTE Marry, sir, you must send the ass upon the horse,
for he is very slow-gaited. But I go.

ARMADO The way is but short. Away!

MOTE As swift as lead, sir.

ARMADO The meaning, pretty ingenious? Is not lead a
metal heavy, dull, and slow?

MOTE
    Minime, honest master; or rather, master, no.

ARMADO
　I say lead is slow.

MOTE　　　　　　You are too swift, sir, to say so.
　Is that lead slow which is fired from a gun?　　　　　60

ARMADO Sweet smoke of rhetoric!
　He reputes me a cannon; and the bullet, that's he.
　I shoot thee at the swain.

MOTE　　　　　　Thump then, and I flee.

Exit

ARMADO
　A most acute juvenal, voluble and free of grace!
　By thy favour, sweet welkin, I must sigh in thy face.
　Most rude melancholy, valour gives thee place.
　My herald is returned.

Enter Mote with Costard

MOTE
　A wonder, master! Here's a costard broken in a shin.

ARMADO
　Some enigma, some riddle. Come, thy l'envoy – begin.

COSTARD No egma, no riddle, no l'envoy, no salve in the　70
　mail, sir! O, sir, plantain, a plain plantain! No l'envoy,
　no l'envoy, no salve, sir, but a plantain!

ARMADO By virtue, thou enforcest laughter; thy silly
　thought, my spleen; the heaving of my lungs provokes
　me to ridiculous smiling! O, pardon me, my stars!
　Doth the inconsiderate take *salve* for l'envoy and the
　word 'l'envoy' for a *salve*?

MOTE Do the wise think them other? Is not l'envoy a
　salve?

ARMADO
　No, page; it is an epilogue or discourse to make plain　80
　Some obscure precedence that hath tofore been sain.
　I will example it:
　　The fox, the ape, and the humble-bee
　　Were still at odds, being but three.

33

There's the moral. Now the l'envoy –

MOTE I will add the l'envoy. Say the moral again.

ARMADO

> The fox, the ape, and the humble-bee
> Were still at odds, being but three.

MOTE

> Until the goose came out of door,
> And stayed the odds by adding four.

Now will I begin your moral, and do you follow with
my l'envoy.

> The fox, the ape, and the humble-bee
> Were still at odds, being but three.

ARMADO

> Until the goose came out of door,
> Staying the odds by adding four.

MOTE A good l'envoy, ending in the goose. Would you
desire more?

COSTARD

> The boy hath sold him a bargain, a goose, that's flat.
> Sir, your pennyworth is good, an your goose be fat.
> To sell a bargain well is as cunning as fast and loose.
> Let me see: a fat l'envoy – ay, that's a fat goose.

ARMADO

Come hither, come hither. How did this argument
begin?

MOTE

> By saying that a costard was broken in a shin.
> Then called you for the l'envoy.

COSTARD True, and I for a plantain – thus came your
argument in; then the boy's fat l'envoy, the goose that
you bought – and he ended the market.

ARMADO But tell me, how was there a costard broken in a
shin?

MOTE I will tell you sensibly.

COSTARD Thou hast no feeling of it, Mote. I will speak
    that l'envoy:
    I, Costard, running out, that was safely within,
    Fell over the threshold and broke my shin.

ARMADO We will talk no more of this matter.

COSTARD Till there be more matter in the shin.

ARMADO Sirrah Costard, I will enfranchise thee.

COSTARD O, marry me to one Frances! I smell some
    l'envoy, some goose in this.   120

ARMADO By my sweet soul, I mean setting thee at liberty,
    enfreedoming thy person. Thou wert immured, re-
    strained, captivated, bound.

COSTARD True, true, and now you will be my purgation
    and let me loose.

ARMADO I give thee thy liberty, set thee from durance,
    and in lieu thereof impose on thee nothing but this:
    (*giving Costard a letter*) bear this significant to the
    country maid Jaquenetta. There is remuneration (*giving*
    him a coin), for the best ward of mine honour is re- 130
    warding my dependants. Mote, follow.

MOTE
    Like the sequel, I. Signor Costard, adieu.

                      Exeunt Armado and Mote

COSTARD
    My sweet ounce of man's flesh, my incony jew! – Now
    will I look to his remuneration. 'Remuneration'! O,
    that's the Latin word for three farthings. Three far-
    things – remuneration. 'What's the price of this inkle?'
    'One penny.' 'No, I'll give you a remuneration.' Why,
    it carries it! 'Remuneration'! Why, it is a fairer name
    than French crown. I will never buy and sell out of
    this word.   140

    Enter Berowne

BEROWNE My good knave Costard, exceedingly well met.

COSTARD Pray you, sir, how much carnation ribbon may
a man buy for a remuneration?

BEROWNE What is a remuneration?

COSTARD Marry, sir, halfpenny farthing.

BEROWNE Why then, three-farthing worth of silk.

COSTARD I thank your worship. God be wi'you.

BEROWNE Stay, slave. I must employ thee.

As thou wilt win my favour, good my knave,

150 Do one thing for me that I shall entreat.

COSTARD When would you have it done, sir?

BEROWNE This afternoon.

COSTARD Well, I will do it, sir. Fare you well.

BEROWNE Thou knowest not what it is.

COSTARD I shall know, sir, when I have done it.

BEROWNE Why, villain, thou must know first.

COSTARD I will come to your worship tomorrow morning.

BEROWNE It must be done this afternoon.

Hark, slave, it is but this:

160 The Princess comes to hunt here in the park,

And in her train there is a gentle lady;

When tongues speak sweetly, then they name her
name,

And Rosaline they call her. Ask for her,

And to her white hand see thou do commend

This sealed-up counsel.

He gives Costard a letter

There's thy guerdon – go.

He gives him money

COSTARD Guerdon, O sweet guerdon! Better than remuneration – elevenpence farthing better. Most sweet
guerdon! I will do it, sir, in print. Guerdon! Remuneration!   *Exit*

BEROWNE

170 And I, forsooth, in love!

36

I, that have been love's whip,
A very beadle to a humorous sigh,
A critic, nay, a night-watch constable,
A domineering pedant o'er the boy,
Than whom no mortal so magnificent!
This wimpled, whining, purblind, wayward boy,
This Signor Junior, giant-dwarf, Dan Cupid,
Regent of love-rhymes, lord of folded arms,
Th'anointed sovereign of sighs and groans,
Liege of all loiterers and malcontents,   180
Dread prince of plackets, king of codpieces,
Sole imperator and great general
Of trotting paritors – O my little heart!
And I to be a corporal of his field,
And wear his colours like a tumbler's hoop!
What? I love? I sue? I seek a wife?
A woman, that is like a German clock,
Still a-repairing, ever out of frame,
And never going aright, being a watch,
But being watched that it may still go right!   190
Nay, to be perjured, which is worst of all;
And among three to love the worst of all –
A whitely wanton with a velvet brow,
With two pitch-balls stuck in her face for eyes;
Ay, and, by heaven, one that will do the deed
Though Argus were her eunuch and her guard!
And I to sigh for her, to watch for her,
To pray for her! Go to, it is a plague
That Cupid will impose for my neglect
Of his almighty dreadful little might.   200
Well, I will love, write, sigh, pray, sue, and groan;
Some men must love my lady, and some Joan. *Exit*

*

Enter the Princess, Rosaline, Maria, Katharine,
        Boyet and two more attendant Lords,
        and a Forester

PRINCESS

> Was that the King that spurred his horse so hard
> Against the steep-up rising of the hill?

FIRST LORD

> I know not, but I think it was not he

PRINCESS

> Whoe'er 'a was, 'a showed a mounting mind.
> Well, lords, today we shall have our dispatch;
> On Saturday we will return to France.
> Then, forester, my friend, where is the bush
> That we must stand and play the murderer in?

FORESTER

> Hereby, upon the edge of yonder coppice;

10   A stand where you may make the fairest shoot.

PRINCESS

> I thank my beauty, I am fair that shoot,
> And thereupon thou speakest 'the fairest shoot'.

FORESTER

> Pardon me, madam, for I meant not so.

PRINCESS

> What, what? First praise me, and again say no?
> O short-lived pride! Not fair? Alack for woe!

FORESTER

> Yes, madam, fair.

PRINCESS   Nay, never paint me now!

> Where fair is not, praise cannot mend the brow.
> Here, good my glass, take this for telling true;
>   (*She gives him money*)
> Fair payment for foul words is more than due.

FORESTER

20   Nothing but fair is that which you inherit.

PRINCESS

   See, see, my beauty will be saved by merit!

   O heresy in fair, fit for these days!

   A giving hand, though foul, shall have fair praise.

   But come, the bow! Now mercy goes to kill,

   And shooting well is then accounted ill.

   Thus will I save my credit in the shoot:

   Not wounding, pity would not let me do't;

   If wounding, then it was to show my skill,

   That more for praise than purpose meant to kill.

   And out of question so it is sometimes;   30

   Glory grows guilty of detested crimes,

   When, for fame's sake, for praise, an outward part,

   We bend to that the working of the heart;

   As I for praise alone now seek to spill

   The poor deer's blood, that my heart means no ill.

BOYET

   Do not curst wives hold that self-sovereignty

   Only for praise' sake, when they strive to be

   Lords o'er their lords?

PRINCESS

   Only for praise, and praise we may afford

   To any lady that subdues a lord.   40

     Enter Costard

BOYET Here comes a member of the commonwealth.

COSTARD God dig-you-den all! Pray you, which is the
head lady?

PRINCESS Thou shalt know her, fellow, by the rest that
have no heads.

COSTARD Which is the greatest lady, the highest?

PRINCESS The thickest and the tallest.

COSTARD The thickest and the tallest! It is so – truth is
truth.

   An your waist, mistress, were as slender as my wit,   50

One o'these maids' girdles for your waist should be fit.
Are not you the chief woman? You are the thickest
here.

PRINCESS What's your will, sir? What's your will?

COSTARD I have a letter from Monsieur Berowne to one
Lady Rosaline.

PRINCESS

O, thy letter, thy letter! He's a good friend of mine.
She takes the letter
Stand aside, good bearer. Boyet, you can carve –
Break up this capon.

BOYET   I am bound to serve.
He reads the
superscript

60 This letter is mistook; it importeth none here.
It is writ to Jaquenetta.

PRINCESS   We will read it, I swear.
Break the neck of the wax, and everyone give ear.

BOYET (*reading*) *By heaven, that thou art fair is most in-*
fallible; true that thou art beauteous; truth itself that
thou art lovely. More fairer than fair, beautiful than
beauteous, truer than truth itself, have commiseration on
thy heroical vassal. The magnanimous and most illustrate
King Cophetua set eye upon the pernicious and most indu-
bitate beggar Zenelophon, and he it was that might rightly
70 *say* Veni, vidi, vici; *which to anatomize in the vulgar – O*
base and obscure vulgar! – videlicet, *he came, see, and*
overcame. He came, one; see, two; overcame, three. Who
came? The king. Why did he come? To see. Why did he
see? To overcome. To whom came he? To the beggar.
What saw he? The beggar. Who overcame he? The beggar.
The conclusion is victory. On whose side? The king's. The
captive is enriched. On whose side? The beggar's. The
catastrophe is a nuptial. On whose side? The king's. No;

on both in one, or one in both. I am the king, for so stands
the comparison, thou the beggar, for so witnesseth thy   80
lowliness. Shall I command thy love? I may. Shall I
enforce thy love? I could. Shall I entreat thy love? I will.
What shalt thou exchange for rags? Robes. For tittles?
Titles. For thyself? Me. Thus, expecting thy reply, I
profane my lips on thy foot, my eyes on thy picture, and
my heart on thy every part.

> Thine in the dearest design of industry,
>
> Don Adriano de Armado

Thus dost thou hear the Nemean lion roar
 'Gainst thee, thou lamb, that standest as his prey.   90
Submissive fall his princely feet before,
 And he from forage will incline to play.
But if thou strive, poor soul, what art thou then?
Food for his rage, repasture for his den.

PRINCESS
 What plume of feathers is he that indited this letter?
 What vane? What weathercock? Did you ever hear
  better?

BOYET
 I am much deceived but I remember the style.

PRINCESS
 Else your memory is bad, going o'er it erewhile.

BOYET
 This Armado is a Spaniard that keeps here in court;
 A phantasime, a Monarcho, and one that makes sport   100
 To the prince and his book-mates.

PRINCESS   Thou, fellow, a word.
 Who gave thee this letter?

COSTARD   I told you; my lord.

PRINCESS
 To whom shouldst thou give it?

COSTARD   From my lord to my lady.

41

PRINCESS

From which lord to which lady?

COSTARD

From my Lord Berowne, a good master of mine,
To a lady of France that he called Rosaline.

PRINCESS

Thou hast mistaken his letter. Come, lords, away.
(*To Rosaline*)
Here, sweet, put up this; 'twill be thine another day.

Exeunt all except Boyet, Rosaline, Maria, and Costard

BOYET

Who is the suitor? Who is the suitor?

ROSALINE   Shall I teach you to know?

BOYET

Ay, my continent of beauty.

110 ROSALINE   Why, she that bears the bow.
Finely put off!

BOYET

My lady goes to kill horns, but, if thou marry,
Hang me by the neck if horns that year miscarry.
Finely put on!

ROSALINE

Well then, I am the shooter.

BOYET   And who is your deer?

ROSALINE

If we choose by the horns, yourself. Come not near.
Finely put on indeed!

MARIA

You still wrangle with her, Boyet, and she strikes at
the brow.

BOYET

But she herself is hit lower. Have I hit her now?

120 ROSALINE Shall I come upon thee with an old saying that
was a man when King Pepin of France was a little boy,

42

as touching the hit it?

BOYET So I may answer thee with one as old, that was a
    woman when Queen Guinevere of Britain was a little
    wench, as touching the hit it.

ROSALINE
    Thou canst not hit it, hit it, hit it,
        Thou canst not hit it, my good man.

BOYET
    An I cannot, cannot, cannot,
        An I cannot, another can.

Exit Rosaline

COSTARD
    By my troth, most pleasant! How both did fit it!   130

MARIA
    A mark marvellous well shot, for they both did hit it.

BOYET
    A mark! O, mark but that mark! 'A mark', says my
        lady!
    Let the mark have a prick in't, so mete at if it may
        be.

MARIA
    Wide o'the bow hand! I'faith, your hand is out.

COSTARD
    Indeed, 'a must shoot nearer, or he'll ne'er hit the
        clout.

BOYET
    An if my hand be out, then belike your hand is in.

COSTARD
    Then will she get the upshoot by cleaving the pin.

MARIA
    Come, come, you talk greasily; your lips grow foul.

COSTARD
    She's too hard for you at pricks, sir. Challenge her
        to bowl.

BOYET

140   I fear too much rubbing. Good night, my good owl.

                                   Exeunt Boyet and Maria

COSTARD

  By my soul, a swain, a most simple clown!

  Lord, Lord, how the ladies and I have put him down!

  O'my troth, most sweet jests, most incony vulgar wit;

  When it comes so smoothly off, so obscenely as it
      were, so fit.

  Armado to th'one side – O, a most dainty man!

  To see him walk before a lady, and to bear her fan!

  To see him kiss his hand, and how most sweetly 'a
      will swear!

  And his page o't'other side, that handful of wit!

  Ah, heavens, it is a most pathetical nit!

    Shout within

150   Sola, sola!   *Exit*

IV.2   *Enter Holofernes, Nathaniel, and Dull*

NATHANIEL Very reverend sport, truly, and done in the
  testimony of a good conscience.

HOLOFERNES The deer was, as you know, in *sanguis*,
  blood; ripe as the pomewater, who now hangeth like a
  jewel in the ear of *caelum*, the sky, the welkin, the
  heaven, and anon falleth like a crab on the face of
  terra, the soil, the land, the earth.

NATHANIEL Truly, Master Holofernes, the epithets are
  sweetly varied, like a scholar at the least; but, sir, I
10   assure ye it was a buck of the first head.

HOLOFERNES Sir Nathaniel, *haud credo*.

DULL 'Twas not an awd grey doe, 'twas a pricket.

HOLOFERNES Most barbarous intimation! Yet a kind of
  insinuation, as it were, *in via*, in way, of explication;

facere, as it were, replication, or, rather, *ostentare*, to show, as it were, his inclination – after his undressed, unpolished, uneducated, unpruned, untrained, or, rather, unlettered, or, ratherest, unconfirmed fashion – to insert again my *haud credo* for a deer.

DULL I said the deer was not an awd grey doe, 'twas a 20 pricket.

HOLOFERNES Twice-sod simplicity! *Bis coctus!*

O thou monster Ignorance, how deformed dost thou look!

NATHANIEL
Sir, he hath never fed of the dainties that are bred in a book.
He hath not eat paper, as it were; he hath not drunk ink. His intellect is not replenished. He is only an animal, only sensible in the duller parts.
And such barren plants are set before us that we thankful should be –
Which we of taste and feeling are – for those parts that do fructify in us more than he.
For as it would ill become me to be vain, indiscreet, or a fool, 30
So were there a patch set on learning, to see him in a school.
But *omne bene*, say I, being of an old father's mind;
Many can brook the weather that love not the wind.

DULL
You two are book-men – can you tell me by your wit
What was a month old at Cain's birth that's not five weeks old as yet?

HOLOFERNES Dictynna, goodman Dull. Dictynna, goodman Dull.

DULL What is Dictima?

NATHANIEL A title to Phoebe, to Luna, to the moon.

45

HOLOFERNES

40 The moon was a month old when Adam was no more,
And raught not to five weeks when he came to
five-score.
Th'allusion holds in the exchange.

DULL 'Tis true, indeed; the collusion holds in the exchange.

HOLOFERNES God comfort thy capacity! I say th'allusion
holds in the exchange.

DULL And I say the pollution holds in the exchange, for
the moon is never but a month old; and I say beside
that 'twas a pricket that the Princess killed.

50 HOLOFERNES Sir Nathaniel, will you hear an extemporal
epitaph on the death of the deer? And, to humour the
ignorant, call I the deer the Princess killed a pricket.

NATHANIEL *Perge*, good Master Holofernes, *perge*, so it
shall please you to abrogate scurrility.

HOLOFERNES I will something affect the letter, for it
argues facility.
The preyful Princess pierced and pricked a pretty
pleasing pricket;
Some say a sore, but not a sore till now made sore
with shooting.
The dogs did yell; put 'L' to sore, then sorel jumps
from thicket;
Or pricket, sore, or else sorel, the people fall
60 a-hooting.
If sore be sore, then 'L' to sore makes fifty sores
o'sorel:
Of one sore I an hundred make, by adding but
one more 'L'.

NATHANIEL A rare talent!

DULL If a talent be a claw, look how he claws him with a
talent.

HOLOFERNES This is a gift that I have; simple, simple; a
foolish extravagant spirit, full of forms, figures,
shapes, objects, ideas, apprehensions, motions, revolu-
tions. These are begot in the ventricle of memory,
nourished in the womb of *pia mater*, and delivered 70
upon the mellowing of occasion. But the gift is good
in those in whom it is acute, and I am thankful for it.

NATHANIEL Sir, I praise the Lord for you, and so may
my parishioners, for their sons are well tutored by you,
and their daughters profit very greatly under you. You
are a good member of the commonwealth.

HOLOFERNES *Mehercle!* If their sons be ingenious, they
shall want no instruction; if their daughters be capable,
I will put it to them. But *vir sapit qui pauca loquitur*. A
soul feminine saluteth us. 80

Enter Jaquenetta with a letter, and Costard

JAQUENETTA God give you good morrow, Master Parson.

HOLOFERNES Master Parson – *quasi* pierce-one? An if
one should be pierced, which is the one?

COSTARD Marry, Master Schoolmaster, he that is likest to
a hogshead.

HOLOFERNES Piercing a hogshead! A good lustre of conceit in a turf of earth, fire enough for a flint, pearl
enough for a swine. 'Tis pretty; it is well.

JAQUENETTA Good Master Parson, be so good as read me
this letter. It was given me by Costard, and sent me 90
from Don Armado. I beseech you, read it.

HOLOFERNES

Fauste precor gelida quando pecus omne sub umbra
Ruminat –
and so forth. Ah, good old Mantuan, I may speak of thee
as the traveller doth of Venice:
Venetia, Venetia,
Chi non ti vede, non ti pretia.

47

Old Mantuan, old Mantuan! Who understandeth thee
not, loves thee not. (*He sings*) Ut, re, sol, la, mi, fa. —
100 Under pardon, sir, what are the contents? Or, rather,
as Horace says in his — What, my soul, verses?

NATHANIEL Ay, sir, and very learned.

HOLOFERNES Let me hear a staff, a stanze, a verse. *Lege,
domine*.

NATHANIEL (*reading*)
If love make me forsworn, how shall I swear to love?
   Ah, never faith could hold if not to beauty vowed!
Though to myself forsworn, to thee I'll faithful prove;
   *Those thoughts to me were oaks, to thee like osiers
   bowed.*
Study his bias leaves and makes his book thine eyes,
110   *Where all those pleasures live that art would
   comprehend.*
If knowledge be the mark, to know thee shall suffice:
   *Well learnèd is that tongue that well can thee
   commend,*
All ignorant that soul that sees thee without wonder;
   Which is to me some praise, that I thy parts admire.
*Thy eye Jove's lightning bears, thy voice his dreadful
   thunder,*
   Which, not to anger bent, is music and sweet fire.
Celestial as thou art, O, pardon love this wrong,
That sings heaven's praise with such an earthly tongue!

HOLOFERNES You find not the apostrophus, and so miss
120 the accent. Let me supervise the canzonet.

   He takes the letter

Here are only numbers ratified; but, for the elegancy,
facility, and golden cadence of poesy, *caret*. Ovidius
Naso was the man; and why indeed 'Naso' but for
smelling out the odoriferous flowers of fancy, the jerks
of invention? *Imitari* is nothing. So doth the hound his

master, the ape his keeper, the tired horse his rider.
But, damosella virgin, was this directed to you?

JAQUENETTA Ay, sir, from one Monsieur Berowne, one
of the strange Queen's lords.

HOLOFERNES I will overglance the superscript: (*reading*) 130
*To the snow-white hand of the most beauteous Lady Rosa-
line.* I will look again on the intellect of the letter, for
the nomination of the party writing to the person written unto: *Your ladyship's, in all desired employment,
Berowne.* Sir Nathaniel, this Berowne is one of the
votaries with the King; and here he hath framed a
letter to a sequent of the stranger Queen's, which accidentally, or by the way of progression, hath miscarried.
Trip and go, my sweet; deliver this paper into the royal
hand of the King; it may concern much. Stay not thy 140
compliment; I forgive thy duty. Adieu.

JAQUENETTA Good Costard, go with me. Sir, God save
your life.

COSTARD Have with thee, my girl.

*Exeunt Costard and
Jaquenetta*

NATHANIEL Sir, you have done this in the fear of God,
very religiously; and as a certain father saith –

HOLOFERNES Sir, tell not me of the father, I do fear
colourable colours. But to return to the verses: did
they please you, Sir Nathaniel?

NATHANIEL Marvellous well for the pen. 150

HOLOFERNES I do dine today at the father's of a certain
pupil of mine, where, if before repast it shall please
you to gratify the table with a grace, I will, on my
privilege I have with the parents of the foresaid child
or pupil, undertake your *ben venuto*; where I will prove
those verses to be very unlearned, neither savouring of
poetry, wit, nor invention. I beseech your society.

49

NATHANIEL And thank you too, for society – saith the
text – is the happiness of life.

160 HOLOFERNES And, certes, the text most infallibly concludes it. (*To Dull*) Sir, I do invite you too; you shall
not say me nay. *Pauca verba*. Away! The gentles are at
their game, and we will to our recreation.

Exeunt

IV.3   *Enter Berowne with a paper in his hand,*
alone

BEROWNE (*reading*)
    The King he is hunting the deer;
        I am coursing myself –
They have pitched a toil; I am toiling in a pitch – pitch
that defiles. 'Defile' – a foul word! Well, set thee
down, sorrow, for so they say the fool said, and so say
I – and I the fool. Well proved, wit! By the Lord, this
love is as mad as Ajax: it kills sheep, it kills me – I a
sheep. Well proved again o'my side! I will not love; if
I do, hang me! I'faith, I will not. O, but her eye! By
10   this light, but for her eye I would not love her – yes,
for her two eyes. Well, I do nothing in the world but
lie, and lie in my throat. By heaven, I do love, and it
hath taught me to rhyme, and to be melancholy; and
here is part of my rhyme, and here my melancholy.
Well, she hath one o'my sonnets already. The clown
bore it, the fool sent it, and the lady hath it – sweet
clown, sweeter fool, sweetest lady! By the world, I
would not care a pin if the other three were in. Here
comes one with a paper. God give him grace to groan!

    He stands aside
    Enter the King with a paper

20 KING Ay me!

BEROWNE Shot, by heaven! Proceed, sweet Cupid. Thou
hast thumped him with thy bird-bolt under the left
pap. In faith, secrets!

KING (*reading*)
> *So sweet a kiss the golden sun gives not*
> > *To those fresh morning drops upon the rose,*
> *As thy eye-beams when their fresh rays have smote*
> > *The night of dew that on my cheeks down flows.*
> *Nor shines the silver moon one half so bright*
> > *Through the transparent bosom of the deep*
> *As doth thy face, through tears of mine, give light.*   30
> > *Thou shinest in every tear that I do weep;*
> *No drop but as a coach doth carry thee.*
> > *So ridest thou triumphing in my woe.*
> *Do but behold the tears that swell in me,*
> > *And they thy glory through my grief will show.*
> *But do not love thyself; then thou will keep*
> *My tears for glasses and still make me weep.*
> *O queen of queens, how far dost thou excel,*
> *No thought can think, nor tongue of mortal tell!*

How shall she know my griefs? I'll drop the paper.   40
Sweet leaves, shade folly. Who is he comes here?

He stands aside
Enter Longaville with several papers

What, Longaville, and reading! Listen, ear!

BEROWNE
Now, in thy likeness, one more fool appear!

LONGAVILLE Ay me, I am forsworn!

BEROWNE Why, he comes in like a perjure, wearing
papers.

KING
In love, I hope – sweet fellowship in shame!

BEROWNE
One drunkard loves another of the name.

LONGAVILLE

Am I the first that have been perjured so?

BEROWNE

50   I could put thee in comfort – not by two that I know.
Thou makest the triumviry, the corner-cap of society,
The shape of Love's Tyburn, that hangs up simplicity.

LONGAVILLE

I fear these stubborn lines lack power to move.
(*Reading*) *O sweet Maria, empress of my love!* –
These numbers will I tear, and write in prose.

He tears the paper

BEROWNE

O, rhymes are guards on wanton Cupid's hose;
Disfigure not his shop.

LONGAVILLE (*taking another paper*)

This same shall go:
(*Reading*)
Did not the heavenly rhetoric of thine eye,
'Gainst whom the world cannot hold argument,
60   *Persuade my heart to this false perjury?*
Vows for thee broke deserve not punishment.
A woman I forswore, but I will prove –
Thou being a goddess – I forswore not thee.
My vow was earthly, thou a heavenly love;
Thy grace, being gained, cures all disgrace in me.
Vows are but breath, and breath a vapour is;
Then thou, fair sun, which on my earth dost shine,
Exhalest this vapour-vow; in thee it is.
If broken, then, it is no fault of mine;
70   *If by me broke, what fool is not so wise*
To lose an oath to win a paradise?

BEROWNE

This is the liver vein, which makes flesh a deity,
A green goose a goddess. Pure, pure idolatry.

God amend us, God amend! We are much out
o'th'way.

Enter Dumaine with a paper

LONGAVILLE

By whom shall I send this? – Company? Stay.

He stands aside

BEROWNE

All hid, all hid – an old infant play.
Like a demi-god here sit I in the sky,
And wretched fools' secrets heedfully o'er-eye.
More sacks to the mill! O heavens, I have my wish!
Dumaine transformed! Four woodcocks in a dish!   80

DUMAINE O most divine Kate!

BEROWNE O most profane coxcomb!

DUMAINE

By heaven, the wonder in a mortal eye!

BEROWNE

By earth, she is not, corporal. There you lie!

DUMAINE

Her amber hairs for foul hath amber quoted.

BEROWNE

An amber-coloured raven was well noted.

DUMAINE

As upright as the cedar.

BEROWNE   Stoop, I say!
Her shoulder is with child.

DUMAINE   As fair as day.

BEROWNE

Ay, as some days; but then no sun must shine.

DUMAINE

O that I had my wish!

LONGAVILLE   And I had mine!   90

KING

And I mine too, good Lord!

53

BEROWNE

Amen, so I had mine! Is not that a good word?

DUMAINE

I would forget her, but a fever she

Reigns in my blood, and will remembered be.

BEROWNE

A fever in your blood? Why, then incision

Would let her out in saucers. Sweet misprision!

DUMAINE

Once more I'll read the ode that I have writ.

BEROWNE

Once more I'll mark how love can vary wit.

DUMAINE (*reading*)

> *On a day – alack the day! –*
> *Love, whose month is ever May,*
> *Spied a blossom passing fair*
> *Playing in the wanton air.*
> *Through the velvet leaves the wind,*
> *All unseen, can passage find;*
> *That the lover, sick to death,*
> *Wished himself the heaven's breath.*
> *Air, quoth he, thy cheeks may blow;*
> *Air, would I might triumph so!*
> *But, alack, my hand is sworn*
> *Ne'er to pluck thee from thy thorn.*
> *Vow, alack, for youth unmeet,*
> *Youth so apt to pluck a sweet!*
> *Do not call it sin in me,*
> *That I am forsworn for thee;*
> *Thou for whom Jove would swear*
> *Juno but an Ethiop were,*
> *And deny himself for Jove,*
> *Turning mortal for thy love.*

100

110

This will I send, and something else more plain,
That shall express my true love's fasting pain.   120
O, would the King, Berowne, and Longaville
Were lovers too! Ill, to example ill,
Would from my forehead wipe a perjured note,
For none offend where all alike do dote.

LONGAVILLE (*advancing*)

Dumaine, thy love is far from charity,
That in love's grief desirest society.
You may look pale, but I should blush, I know,
To be o'erheard and taken napping so.

KING (*advancing*)

Come, sir, you blush! As his your case is such;
You chide at him, offending twice as much.   130
You do not love Maria! Longaville
Did never sonnet for her sake compile,
Nor never lay his wreathèd arms athwart
His loving bosom to keep down his heart.
I have been closely shrouded in this bush
And marked you both, and for you both did blush.
I heard your guilty rhymes, observed your fashion,
Saw sighs reek from you, noted well your passion.
'Ay me!' says one; 'O Jove!' the other cries.
One, her hairs were gold; crystal the other's eyes.   140
(*To Longaville*)
You would for paradise break faith and troth;
(*To Dumaine*)
And Jove, for your love, would infringe an oath.
What will Berowne say when that he shall hear
Faith infringèd, which such zeal did swear?
How will he scorn, how will he spend his wit!
How will he triumph, leap, and laugh at it!
For all the wealth that ever I did see,

I would not have him know so much by me.

BEROWNE *(advancing)*

Now step I forth to whip hypocrisy.

150 Ah, good my liege, I pray thee pardon me.
Good heart, what grace hast thou, thus to reprove
These worms for loving, that art most in love?
Your eyes do make no coaches; in your tears
There is no certain princess that appears;
You'll not be perjured, 'tis a hateful thing;
Tush, none but minstrels like of sonneting!
But are you not ashamed? Nay, are you not,
All three of you, to be thus much o'ershot?
You found his mote, the King your mote did see;

160 But I a beam do find in each of three.
O, what a scene of foolery have I seen,
Of sighs, of groans, of sorrow, and of teen!
O me, with what strict patience have I sat,
To see a king transformèd to a gnat!
To see great Hercules whipping a gig,
And profound Solomon to tune a jig,
And Nestor play at push-pin with the boys,
And critic Timon laugh at idle toys!
Where lies thy grief? O, tell me, good Dumaine.

170 And, gentle Longaville, where lies thy pain?
And where my liege's? All about the breast.
A caudle, ho!

KING   Too bitter is thy jest.
Are we betrayed thus to thy over-view?

BEROWNE

Not you to me, but I betrayed by you;
I that am honest, I that hold it sin
To break the vow I am engagèd in,
I am betrayed by keeping company
With men like you, men of inconstancy.

When shall you see me write a thing in rhyme?
Or groan for Joan? Or spend a minute's time   180
In pruning me? When shall you hear that I
Will praise a hand, a foot, a face, an eye,
A gait, a state, a brow, a breast, a waist,
A leg, a limb –
KING   Soft! Whither away so fast?
A true man or a thief that gallops so?
BEROWNE
I post from love. Good lover, let me go.
          Enter Jaquenetta with a letter,
          and Costard
JAQUENETTA
God bless the King!
KING   What present hast thou there?
COSTARD
Some certain treason.
KING   What makes treason here?
COSTARD
Nay, it makes nothing, sir.
KING   If it mar nothing neither,
The treason and you go in peace away together.   190
JAQUENETTA
I beseech your grace let this letter be read.
Our parson misdoubts it; 'twas treason, he said.
KING Berowne, read it over.
          Berowne reads the letter
Where hadst thou it?
JAQUENETTA Of Costard.
KING Where hadst thou it?
COSTARD Of Dun Adramadio, Dun Adramadio.
          Berowne tears the letter
KING
How now, what is in you? Why dost thou tear it?

BEROWNE

  A toy, my liege, a toy. Your grace needs not fear it.

LONGAVILLE

200 It did move him to passion, and therefore let's hear it.

DUMAINE (*gathering up the pieces*)

  It is Berowne's writing, and here is his name.

BEROWNE (*to Costard*)

  Ah, you whoreson loggerhead, you were born to do
    me shame!

  Guilty, my lord, guilty! I confess, I confess!

KING

  What?

BEROWNE

  That you three fools lacked me fool to make up the mess.

  He, he, and you – and you, my liege! – and I,

  Are pick-purses in love, and we deserve to die.

  O, dismiss this audience, and I shall tell you more.

DUMAINE

  Now the number is even.

BEROWNE   True, true, we are four.

  Will these turtles be gone?

210 **KING**   Hence, sirs, away!

COSTARD

  Walk aside the true folk, and let the traitors stay.

                    Exeunt Costard and Jaquenetta

BEROWNE

  Sweet lords, sweet lovers, O, let us embrace!

    As true we are as flesh and blood can be.

  The sea will ebb and flow, heaven show his face;

    Young blood doth not obey an old decree.

  We cannot cross the cause why we were born;

  Therefore of all hands must we be forsworn.

KING

  What, did these rent lines show some love of thine?

BEROWNE

    'Did they?' quoth you! Who sees the heavenly Rosa-
        line

    That, like a rude and savage man of Inde   220

      At the first opening of the gorgeous east,

    Bows not his vassal head and, strucken blind,

      Kisses the base ground with obedient breast?

    What peremptory eagle-sighted eye

      Dares look upon the heaven of her brow

    That is not blinded by her majesty?

KING

    What zeal, what fury hath inspired thee now?

    My love, her mistress, is a gracious moon;

      She, an attending star, scarce seen a light.

BEROWNE

    My eyes are then no eyes, nor I Berowne.   230

      O, but for my love, day would turn to night!

    Of all complexions the culled sovereignty

      Do meet as at a fair in her fair cheek,

    Where several worthies make one dignity,

      Where nothing wants that want itself doth seek.

    Lend me the flourish of all gentle tongues –

      Fie, painted rhetoric! O, she needs it not!

    To things of sale a seller's praise belongs:

      She passes praise; then praise too short doth blot.

    A withered hermit, five-score winters worn,   240

      Might shake off fifty, looking in her eye.

    Beauty doth varnish age, as if new-born,

      And gives the crutch the cradle's infancy.

    O, 'tis the sun that makes all things shine!

KING

    By heaven, thy love is black as ebony!

BEROWNE

    Is ebony like her? O wood divine!

A wife of such wood were felicity.
O, who can give an oath? Where is a book?
That I may swear beauty doth beauty lack
250 If that she learn not of her eye to look.
No face is fair that is not full so black.

KING

O paradox! Black is the badge of hell,
The hue of dungeons, and the school of night;
And beauty's crest becomes the heavens well.

BEROWNE

Devils soonest tempt, resembling spirits of light.
O, if in black my lady's brows be decked,
It mourns that painting and usurping hair
Should ravish doters with a false aspect;
And therefore is she born to make black fair.
260 Her favour turns the fashion of the days,
For native blood is counted painting now;
And therefore red, that would avoid dispraise,
Paints itself black, to imitate her brow.

DUMAINE

To look like her are chimney-sweepers black.

LONGAVILLE

And since her time are colliers counted bright.

KING

And Ethiops of their sweet complexion crack.

DUMAINE

Dark needs no candles now, for dark is light.

BEROWNE

Your mistresses dare never come in rain,
For fear their colours should be washed away.

KING

270 'Twere good yours did; for, sir, to tell you plain,
I'll find a fairer face not washed today.

BEROWNE

I'll prove her fair, or talk till doomsday here.

KING

   No devil will fright thee then so much as she.

DUMAINE

   I never knew man hold vile stuff so dear.

LONGAVILLE

   Look, here's thy love (*showing his shoe*); my foot and
      her face see.

BEROWNE

   O, if the streets were pavèd with thine eyes,
   Her feet were much too dainty for such tread.

DUMAINE

   O, vile! Then, as she goes, what upward lies
   The street should see as she walked overhead.

KING

   But what of this? Are we not all in love?   280

BEROWNE

   O, nothing so sure, and thereby all forsworn.

KING

   Then leave this chat, and, good Berowne, now prove
   Our loving lawful and our faith not torn.

DUMAINE

   Ay, marry, there; some flattery for this evil!

LONGAVILLE

   O, some authority how to proceed!
   Some tricks, some quillets, how to cheat the devil!

DUMAINE

   Some salve for perjury.

BEROWNE

                 'Tis more than need.
   Have at you then, affection's men-at-arms!
   Consider what you first did swear unto:
   To fast, to study, and to see no woman –   290
   Flat treason 'gainst the kingly state of youth.
   Say, can you fast? Your stomachs are too young,
   And abstinence engenders maladies.
   O, we have made a vow to study, lords,

And in that vow we have forsworn our books;
For when would you, my liege, or you, or you,
In leaden contemplation have found out
Such fiery numbers as the prompting eyes
Of beauty's tutors have enriched you with?
300 Other slow arts entirely keep the brain,
And therefore, finding barren practisers,
Scarce show a harvest of their heavy toil;
But love, first learnèd in a lady's eyes,
Lives not alone immurèd in the brain,
But with the motion of all elements
Courses as swift as thought in every power,
And gives to every power a double power,
Above their functions and their offices.
It adds a precious seeing to the eye:
310 A lover's eyes will gaze an eagle blind.
A lover's ear will hear the lowest sound
When the suspicious head of theft is stopped.
Love's feeling is more soft and sensible
Than are the tender horns of cockled snails.
Love's tongue proves dainty Bacchus gross in taste.
For valour, is not Love a Hercules,
Still climbing trees in the Hesperides?
Subtle as Sphinx; as sweet and musical
As bright Apollo's lute, strung with his hair.
320 And when Love speaks, the voice of all the gods
Make heaven drowsy with the harmony.
Never durst poet touch a pen to write
Until his ink were tempered with Love's sighs.
O, then his lines would ravish savage ears
And plant in tyrants mild humility.
From women's eyes this doctrine I derive:
They sparkle still the right Promethean fire;
They are the books, the arts, the academes,
That show, contain, and nourish all the world;

Else none at all in aught proves excellent.   330
Then fools you were these women to forswear,
Or, keeping what is sworn, you will prove fools.
For wisdom's sake, a word that all men love,
Or for love's sake, a word that loves all men,
Or for men's sake, the authors of these women,
Or women's sake, by whom we men are men –
Let us once lose our oaths to find ourselves,
Or else we lose ourselves to keep our oaths.
It is religion to be thus forsworn,
For charity itself fulfils the law,   340
And who can sever love from charity?

KING
Saint Cupid, then! And, soldiers, to the field!

BEROWNE
Advance your standards, and upon them, lords!
Pell-mell, down with them! But be first advised
In conflict that you get the sun of them.

LONGAVILLE
Now to plain-dealing. Lay these glosses by.
Shall we resolve to woo these girls of France?

KING
And win them too! Therefore let us devise
Some entertainment for them in their tents.

BEROWNE
First from the park let us conduct them thither;   350
Then homeward every man attach the hand
Of his fair mistress. In the afternoon
We will with some strange pastime solace them,
Such as the shortness of the time can shape;
For revels, dances, masques, and merry hours
Forerun fair Love, strewing her way with flowers.

KING
Away, away! No time shall be omitted
That will betime and may by us be fitted

BEROWNE
Allons! Allons!

Exeunt King, Longaville, and Dumaine
Sowed cockle reaped no corn,
360   And justice always whirls in equal measure.
Light wenches may prove plagues to men forsworn;
If so, our copper buys no better treasure.   *Exit*

❋

V.1   *Enter Holofernes, Nathaniel, and Dull*
HOLOFERNES *Satis quod sufficit.*
NATHANIEL I praise God for you, sir. Your reasons at
dinner have been sharp and sententious, pleasant
without scurrility, witty without affection, audacious
without impudency, learned without opinion, and
strange without heresy. I did converse this *quondam*
day with a companion of the King's, who is entitled,
nominated, or called Don Adriano de Armado.
HOLOFERNES *Novi hominem tanquam te.* His humour is
10   lofty, his discourse peremptory, his tongue filed, his
eye ambitious, his gait majestical, and his general
behaviour vain, ridiculous, and thrasonical. He is too
picked, too spruce, too affected, too odd, as it were,
too peregrinate, as I may call it.
NATHANIEL A most singular and choice epithet.
He draws out his table-book
HOLOFERNES He draweth out the thread of his verbosity
finer than the staple of his argument. I abhor such
fanatical phantasimes, such insociable and point-
device companions, such rackers of orthography, as to
20   speak 'dout' *sine* 'b', when he should say 'doubt', 'det'
when he should pronounce 'debt' – d, e, b, t, not d, e,
t. He clepeth a calf 'cauf', half 'hauf'; neighbour

vocatur 'nebour', neigh abbreviated 'ne'. This is abhominable, which he would call 'abominable'. It insinuateth me of insanie. *Ne intelligis, domine?* To make frantic, lunatic.

NATHANIEL *Laus Deo, bone intelligo.*

HOLOFERNES *Bone?* 'Bone' for 'bene'! Priscian a little scratched; 'twill serve.

 Enter Armado, Mote, and Costard

NATHANIEL *Videsne quis venit?*   30

HOLOFERNES *Video et gaudeo.*

ARMADO Chirrah!

HOLOFERNES *Quare* 'chirrah', not 'sirrah'?

ARMADO Men of peace, well encountered.

HOLOFERNES Most military sir, salutation.

MOTE (*to Costard*) They have been at a great feast of languages and stolen the scraps.

COSTARD (*to Mote*) O, they have lived long on the alms-basket of words! I marvel thy master hath not eaten thee for a word, for thou art not so long by the head as 40 *honorificabilitudinitatibus.* Thou art easier swallowed than a flap-dragon.

MOTE Peace! The peal begins.

ARMADO (*to Holofernes*) Monsieur, are you not lettered?

MOTE Yes, yes! He teaches boys the horn-book. What is a, b, spelt backward with the horn on his head?

HOLOFERNES Ba, *pueritia*, with a horn added.

MOTE Ba, most silly sheep with a horn. You hear his learning.

HOLOFERNES *Quis, quis,* thou consonant?   50

MOTE The last of the five vowels, if you repeat them; or the fifth, if I.

HOLOFERNES I will repeat them: a, e, i –

MOTE The sheep. The other two concludes it – o, u.

ARMADO Now, by the salt wave of the Mediterraneum, a

sweet touch, a quick venue of wit! Snip, snap, quick
and home! It rejoiceth my intellect. True wit!

MOTE Offered by a child to an old man — which is wit-
old.

60 HOLOFERNES What is the figure? What is the figure?
MOTE Horns.

HOLOFERNES Thou disputes like an infant. Go whip thy
gig.

MOTE Lend me your horn to make one, and I will whip
about your infamy *manu cita*. A gig of a cuckold's horn!

COSTARD An I had but one penny in the world, thou
shouldst have it to buy gingerbread. Hold, there is the
very remuneration I had of thy master, thou halfpenny
purse of wit, thou pigeon-egg of discretion. O, an the
70 heavens were so pleased that thou wert but my bastard,
what a joyful father wouldst thou make me! Go to,
thou hast it *ad dunghill*, at the fingers' ends, as they
say.

HOLOFERNES O, I smell false Latin! 'Dunghill' for
'*unguem*'.

ARMADO Arts-man, preambulate. We will be singuled
from the barbarous. Do you not educate youth at the
charge-house on the top of the mountain?

HOLOFERNES Or *mons*, the hill.

80 ARMADO At your sweet pleasure, for the mountain.
HOLOFERNES I do, *sans question*.

ARMADO Sir, it is the King's most sweet pleasure and
affection to congratulate the Princess at her pavilion in
the posteriors of this day, which the rude multitude
call the afternoon.

HOLOFERNES The posterior of the day, most generous
sir, is liable, congruent, and measurable for the
afternoon. The word is well culled, choice, sweet, and
apt, I do assure you, sir, I do assure.

66

ARMADO Sir, the King is a noble gentleman, and my 90
familiar, I do assure ye, very good friend. For what is
inward between us, let it pass – I do beseech thee,
remember thy courtesy; I beseech thee, apparel thy
head. And among other importunate and most serious
designs, and of great import indeed, too – but let that
pass; for I must tell thee, it will please his grace, by the
world, sometime to lean upon my poor shoulder, and
with his royal finger thus dally with my excrement,
with my mustachio – but, sweet heart, let that pass. By
the world, I recount no fable! Some certain special 100
honours it pleaseth his greatness to impart to Armado,
a soldier, a man of travel, that hath seen the world –
but let that pass. The very all of all is – but, sweet
heart, I do implore secrecy – that the King would have
me present the Princess – sweet chuck – with some
delightful ostentation, or show, or pageant, or antic, or
firework. Now, understanding that the curate and your
sweet self are good at such eruptions and sudden
breaking out of mirth, as it were, I have acquainted
you withal, to the end to crave your assistance. 110

HOLOFERNES Sir, you shall present before her the Nine
Worthies. Sir Nathaniel, as concerning some entertainment of time, some show in the posterior of this day,
to be rendered by our assistance, the King's command,
and this most gallant, illustrate, and learned gentleman,
before the Princess – I say, none so fit as to present the
Nine Worthies.

NATHANIEL Where will you find men worthy enough to
present them?

HOLOFERNES Joshua, yourself; this gallant gentleman, 120
Judas Maccabaeus; this swain, because of his great
limb or joint, shall pass Pompey the Great; the page,
Hercules –

ARMADO Pardon, sir – error! He is not quantity enough
for that Worthy's thumb; he is not so big as the end of
his club.

HOLOFERNES Shall I have audience? He shall present
Hercules in minority. His enter and exit shall be stran-
gling a snake; and I will have an apology for that
130 purpose.

MOTE An excellent device! So if any of the audience hiss,
you may cry 'Well done, Hercules! Now thou crushest
the snake!' That is the way to make an offence gracious,
though few have the grace to do it.

ARMADO For the rest of the Worthies?

HOLOFERNES I will play three myself.

MOTE Thrice-worthy gentleman!

ARMADO Shall I tell you a thing?

HOLOFERNES We attend.

140 ARMADO We will have, if this fadge not, an antic. I
beseech you, follow.

HOLOFERNES *Via*, goodman Dull! Thou hast spoken no
word all this while.

DULL Nor understood none neither, sir.

HOLOFERNES *Allons!* We will employ thee.

DULL I'll make one in a dance, or so; or I will play on
the tabor to the Worthies, and let them dance the
hay.

HOLOFERNES Most dull, honest Dull! To our sport,
150 away!   *Exeunt*

V.2   *Enter the Princess, Rosaline, Maria, and Katharine*

PRINCESS
   Sweet hearts, we shall be rich ere we depart
   If fairings come thus plentifully in.
   A lady walled about with diamonds!

68

Look you what I have from the loving King.

ROSALINE

Madam, came nothing else along with that?

PRINCESS

Nothing but this? Yes, as much love in rhyme
As would be crammed up in a sheet of paper,
Writ o' both sides the leaf, margin and all,
That he was fain to seal on Cupid's name.

ROSALINE

That was the way to make his godhead wax,   10
For he hath been five thousand year a boy.

KATHARINE

Ay, and a shrewd unhappy gallows too.

ROSALINE

You'll ne'er be friends with him; 'a killed your sister.

KATHARINE

He made her melancholy, sad, and heavy;
And so she died. Had she been light, like you,
Of such a merry, nimble, stirring spirit,
She might ha' been a grandam ere she died.
And so may you, for a light heart lives long.

ROSALINE

What's your dark meaning, mouse, of this light word?

KATHARINE

A light condition in a beauty dark.   20

ROSALINE

We need more light to find your meaning out.

KATHARINE

You'll mar the light by taking it in snuff;
Therefore, I'll darkly end the argument.

ROSALINE

Look what you do, you do it still i'th'dark.

KATHARINE

So do not you, for you are a light wench.

69

ROSALINE
Indeed I weigh not you, and therefore light.

KATHARINE
You weigh me not? O, that's you care not for me!

ROSALINE
Great reason, for past cure is still past care.

PRINCESS
Well bandied both! A set of wit well played.

30 But, Rosaline, you have a favour too –
Who sent it? And what is it?

ROSALINE   I would you knew.
An if my face were but as fair as yours,
My favour were as great. Be witness this –
Nay, I have verses too, I thank Berowne;
The numbers true, and, were the numbering too,
I were the fairest goddess on the ground.
I am compared to twenty thousand fairs.
O, he hath drawn my picture in his letter!

PRINCESS
Anything like?

ROSALINE
40 Much in the letters, nothing in the praise.

PRINCESS
Beauteous as ink – a good conclusion.

KATHARINE
Fair as a text B in a copy-book.

ROSALINE
'Ware pencils, ho! Let me not die your debtor,
My red dominical, my golden letter.
O that your face were not so full of O's!

PRINCESS
A pox of that jest, and I beshrew all shrews.
But, Katharine, what was sent to you from fair Du-
maine?

KATHARINE

Madam, this glove.

PRINCESS   Did he not send you twain?

KATHARINE

Yes, madam; and, moreover,
Some thousand verses of a faithful lover;   50
A huge translation of hypocrisy,
Vilely compiled, profound simplicity.

MARIA

This, and these pearls, to me sent Longaville.
The letter is too long by half a mile.

PRINCESS

I think no less. Dost thou not wish in heart
The chain were longer and the letter short?

MARIA

Ay, or I would these hands might never part.

PRINCESS

We are wise girls to mock our lovers so.

ROSALINE

They are worse fools to purchase mocking so.
That same Berowne I'll torture ere I go.   60
O that I knew he were but in by th'week!
How I would make him fawn, and beg, and seek,
And wait the season, and observe the times,
And spend his prodigal wits in bootless rhymes,
And shape his service wholly to my hests,
And make him proud to make me proud that jests!
So pair-taunt-like would I o'ersway his state
That he should be my fool, and I his fate.

PRINCESS

None are so surely caught, when they are catched,
As wit turned fool. Folly, in wisdom hatched,   70
Hath wisdom's warrant and the help of school
And wit's own grace to grace a learnèd fool.

ROSALINE

The blood of youth burns not with such excess
As gravity's revolt to wantonness.

MARIA

Folly in fools bears not so strong a note
As foolery in the wise when wit doth dote,
Since all the power thereof it doth apply
To prove, by wit, worth in simplicity.

Enter Boyet

PRINCESS

Here comes Boyet, and mirth is in his face.

BOYET

80   O, I am stabbed with laughter! Where's her grace?

PRINCESS

Thy news, Boyet?

BOYET   Prepare, madam, prepare!
Arm, wenches, arm! Encounters mounted are
Against your peace. Love doth approach disguised,
Armèd in arguments. You'll be surprised.
Muster your wits, stand in your own defence,
Or hide your heads like cowards and fly hence.

PRINCESS

Saint Denis to Saint Cupid! What are they
That charge their breath against us? Say, scout, say.

BOYET

Under the cool shade of a sycamore
90   I thought to close mine eyes some half an hour,
When, lo, to interrupt my purposed rest,
Toward that shade I might behold addressed
The King and his companions! Warily
I stole into a neighbour thicket by,
And overheard what you shall overhear —
That, by and by, disguised they will be here.
Their herald is a pretty knavish page

72

That well by heart hath conned his embassage.
Action and accent did they teach him there:
'Thus must thou speak' and 'thus thy body bear'. 100
And ever and anon they made a doubt
Presence majestical would put him out;
'For', quoth the King, 'an angel shalt thou see;
Yet fear not thou, but speak audaciously.'
The boy replied 'An angel is not evil;
I should have feared her had she been a devil.'
With that all laughed and clapped him on the shoulder,
Making the bold wag by their praises bolder.
One rubbed his elbow thus, and fleered, and swore
A better speech was never spoke before. 110
Another, with his finger and his thumb,
Cried 'Via, we will do't, come what will come!'
The third he capered and cried 'All goes well!'
The fourth turned on the toe, and down he fell.
With that they all did tumble on the ground,
With such a zealous laughter, so profound,
That in this spleen ridiculous appears,
To check their folly, passion's solemn tears.

PRINCESS

But what, but what? Come they to visit us?

BOYET

They do, they do, and are apparelled thus, 120
Like Muscovites or Russians, as I guess.
Their purpose is to parley, court, and dance,
And every one his love-suit will advance
Unto his several mistress, which they'll know
By favours several which they did bestow.

PRINCESS

And will they so? The gallants shall be tasked;
For, ladies, we will every one be masked,
And not a man of them shall have the grace,

73

Despite of suit, to see a lady's face.
130 Hold, Rosaline, this favour thou shalt wear,
And then the King will court thee for his dear.
Hold, take thou this, my sweet, and give me thine;
So shall Berowne take me for Rosaline.
And change you favours too; so shall your loves
Woo contrary, deceived by these removes.

ROSALINE
Come on, then, wear the favours most in sight.

KATHARINE
But in this changing what is your intent?

PRINCESS
The effect of my intent is to cross theirs.
They do it but in mockery merriment,
140 And mock for mock is only my intent.
Their several counsels they unbosom shall
To loves mistook, and so be mocked withal
Upon the next occasion that we meet,
With visages displayed, to talk and greet.

ROSALINE
But shall we dance if they desire us to't?

PRINCESS
No, to the death we will not move a foot;
Nor to their penned speech render we no grace,
But while 'tis spoke each turn away her face.

BOYET
Why, that contempt will kill the speaker's heart,
150 And quite divorce his memory from his part.

PRINCESS
Therefore I do it, and I make no doubt
The rest will ne'er come in, if he be out.
There's no such sport as sport by sport o'erthrown,
To make theirs ours, and ours none but our own.
So shall we stay, mocking intended game,

And they, well mocked, depart away with shame.
          A trumpet sounds

BOYET

The trumpet sounds. Be masked – the masquers come.
          Enter blackamoors with music, Mote with a speech,
          and the King and the rest of the lords disguised like
          Russians and visored

MOTE

All hail, the richest beauties on the earth!

BOYET

Beauties no richer than rich taffeta.

MOTE

A holy parcel of the fairest dames   160
          (*The ladies turn their backs*
          to him)
That ever turned their – backs – to mortal views!

BEROWNE

'Their eyes', villain, 'their eyes'!

MOTE

That ever turned their eyes to mortal views!
Out –

BOYET

True! 'Out' indeed!

MOTE

Out of your favours, heavenly spirits, vouchsafe
Not to behold –

BEROWNE

'Once to behold', rogue!

MOTE

Once to behold with your sun-beamèd eyes –
With your sun-beamèd eyes –   170

BOYET

They will not answer to that epithet.
You were best call it 'daughter-beamèd eyes'.

MOTE

    They do not mark me, and that brings me out.

BEROWNE

    Is this your perfectness? Be gone, you rogue!

                                  Exit Mote

ROSALINE

    What would these strangers? Know their minds,
        Boyet.

    If they do speak our language, 'tis our will

    That some plain man recount their purposes.

    Know what they would.

BOYET   What would you with the Princess?

BEROWNE

    Nothing but peace and gentle visitation.

ROSALINE

180   What would they, say they?

BOYET

    Nothing but peace and gentle visitation.

ROSALINE

    Why, that they have, and bid them so be gone.

BOYET

    She says you have it and you may be gone.

KING

    Say to her, we have measured many miles

    To tread a measure with her on this grass.

BOYET

    They say that they have measured many a mile

    To tread a measure with you on this grass.

ROSALINE

    It is not so. Ask them how many inches

    Is in one mile. If they have measured many,

190   The measure then of one is easily told.

BOYET

    If to come hither you have measured miles,

And many miles, the Princess bids you tell
How many inches doth fill up one mile.

BEROWNE
Tell her we measure them by weary steps.

BOYET
She hears herself.

ROSALINE   How many weary steps,
Of many weary miles you have o'ergone,
Are numbered in the travel of one mile?

BEROWNE
We number nothing that we spend for you.
Our duty is so rich, so infinite,
That we may do it still without account.   200
Vouchsafe to show the sunshine of your face,
That we like savages may worship it.

ROSALINE
My face is but a moon, and clouded too.

KING
Blessèd are clouds, to do as such clouds do.
Vouchsafe, bright moon, and these thy stars, to shine –
Those clouds removed – upon our watery eyne.

ROSALINE
O vain petitioner, beg a greater matter!
Thou now requests but moonshine in the water.

KING
Then in our measure vouchsafe but one change.
Thou biddest me beg; this begging is not strange.   210

ROSALINE
Play music then! Nay, you must do it soon.
Not yet? No dance! Thus change I like the moon.

KING
Will you not dance? How come you thus estranged?

ROSALINE
You took the moon at full, but now she's changed.

77

Instruments strike up

KING

Yet still she is the moon, and I the man.
The music plays; vouchsafe some motion to it.

ROSALINE

Our ears vouchsafe it.

KING   But your legs should do it.

ROSALINE

Since you are strangers and come here by chance,
We'll not be nice. Take hands. We will not dance.

KING

Why take we hands then?

220 **ROSALINE**   Only to part friends.
Curtsy, sweet hearts. And so the measure ends.

KING

More measure of this measure! Be not nice.

ROSALINE

We can afford no more at such a price.

KING

Price you yourselves. What buys your company?

ROSALINE

Your absence only.

KING   That can never be.

ROSALINE

Then cannot we be bought; and so adieu –
Twice to your visor, and half once to you!

KING

If you deny to dance, let's hold more chat.

ROSALINE

In private then.

KING   I am best pleased with that.

They converse apart

BEROWNE

230   White-handed mistress, one sweet word with thee.

78

PRINCESS
Honey, and milk, and sugar – there is three.
BEROWNE
Nay then, two treys, an if you grow so nice,
Metheglin, wort, and malmsey. Well run, dice!
There's half a dozen sweets.
PRINCESS   Seventh sweet, adieu.
Since you can cog, I'll play no more with you.
BEROWNE
One word in secret.
PRINCESS   Let it not be sweet.
BEROWNE
Thou grievest my gall.
PRINCESS   Gall? Bitter.
BEROWNE   Therefore meet.
        They converse apart
DUMAINE
Will you vouchsafe with me to change a word?
MARIA
Name it.
DUMAINE Fair lady –
MARIA   Say you so? Fair lord!
Take that for your 'fair lady'.
DUMAINE   Please it you,   240
As much in private, and I'll bid adieu.
        They converse apart
KATHARINE
What, was your visor made without a tongue?
LONGAVILLE
I know the reason, lady, why you ask.
KATHARINE
O for your reason! Quickly, sir; I long.
LONGAVILLE
You have a double tongue within your mask,

And would afford my speechless visor half.

KATHARINE

'Veal', quoth the Dutchman. Is not 'veal' a calf?

LONGAVILLE

A calf, fair lady!

KATHARINE   No, a fair lord calf.

LONGAVILLE

Let's part the word.

KATHARINE   No, I'll not be your half.

250   Take all and wean it; it may prove an ox.

LONGAVILLE

Look how you butt yourself in these sharp mocks.
Will you give horns, chaste lady? Do not so.

KATHARINE

Then die a calf before your horns do grow.

LONGAVILLE

One word in private with you ere I die.

KATHARINE

Bleat softly then. The butcher hears you cry.

They converse apart

BOYET

The tongues of mocking wenches are as keen
    As is the razor's edge invisible,
Cutting a smaller hair than may be seen;
    Above the sense of sense, so sensible
260 Seemeth their conference. Their conceits have wings
Fleeter than arrows, bullets, wind, thought, swifter
            things.

ROSALINE

Not one word more, my maids; break off, break off!

BEROWNE

By heaven, all dry-beaten with pure scoff!

KING

Farewell, mad wenches. You have simple wits.

Exeunt the King, lords,
and blackamoors

PRINCESS

Twenty adieus, my frozen Muscovits.
Are these the breed of wits so wondered at?

BOYET

Tapers they are, with your sweet breaths puffed out.

ROSALINE

Well-liking wits they have; gross, gross; fat, fat.

PRINCESS

O poverty in wit, kingly-poor flout!
Will they not, think you, hang themselves tonight?   270
Or ever but in visors show their faces?
This pert Berowne was out of countenance quite.

ROSALINE

They were all in lamentable cases.
The King was weeping-ripe for a good word.

PRINCESS

Berowne did swear himself out of all suit.

MARIA

Dumaine was at my service, and his sword.
'*Non point*', quoth I; my servant straight was mute.

KATHARINE

Lord Longaville said I came o'er his heart;
And trow you what he called me?

PRINCESS   Qualm, perhaps.

KATHARINE

Yes, in good faith.

PRINCESS   Go, sickness as thou art!   280

ROSALINE

Well, better wits have worn plain statute-caps.
But will you hear? The King is my love sworn.

PRINCESS

And quick Berowne hath plighted faith to me.

KATHARINE

And Longaville was for my service born.

MARIA

Dumaine is mine as sure as bark on tree.

BOYET

Madam, and pretty mistresses, give ear:
Immediately they will again be here
In their own shapes, for it can never be
They will digest this harsh indignity.

PRINCESS

Will they return?

290 **BOYET** They will, they will, God knows;
And leap for joy though they are lame with blows.
Therefore change favours, and, when they repair,
Blow like sweet roses in this summer air.

PRINCESS

How 'blow'? How 'blow'? Speak to be understood.

BOYET

Fair ladies masked are roses in their bud;
Dismasked, their damask sweet commixture shown,
Are angels vailing clouds, or roses blown.

PRINCESS

Avaunt, perplexity! What shall we do
If they return in their own shapes to woo?

ROSALINE

300 Good madam, if by me you'll be advised,
Let's mock them still, as well known as disguised.
Let us complain to them what fools were here,
Disguised like Muscovites in shapeless gear;
And wonder what they were, and to what end
Their shallow shows and prologue vilely penned,
And their rough carriage so ridiculous,
Should be presented at our tent to us.

BOYET

Ladies, withdraw. The gallants are at hand.

PRINCESS

Whip to our tents, as roes runs o'er the land.

Exeunt the Princess and ladies
Enter the King, Berowne, Longaville, and Dumaine,
having shed their disguises

KING

Fair sir, God save you. Where's the Princess?   310

BOYET

Gone to her tent. Please it your majesty
Command me any service to her thither?

KING

That she vouchsafe me audience for one word.

BOYET

I will; and so will she, I know, my lord.   *Exit*

BEROWNE

This fellow pecks up wit, as pigeons peas,
And utters it again when God doth please.
He is wit's pedlar, and retails his wares
At wakes and wassails, meetings, markets, fairs;
And we that sell by gross, the Lord doth know,
Have not the grace to grace it with such show.   320
This gallant pins the wenches on his sleeve.
Had he been Adam, he had tempted Eve.
'A can carve too, and lisp. Why, this is he
That kissed his hand away in courtesy.
This is the ape of form, Monsieur the Nice,
That, when he plays at tables, chides the dice
In honourable terms. Nay, he can sing
A mean most meanly; and in ushering
Mend him who can. The ladies call him sweet.
The stairs, as he treads on them, kiss his feet.   330
This is the flower that smiles on everyone,

83

To show his teeth as white as whale's bone;
And consciences that will not die in debt
Pay him the due of 'honey-tongued Boyet'.

KING

A blister on his sweet tongue, with my heart,
That put Armado's page out of his part!

*Enter the Princess, Rosaline, Maria, and Katharine,
having unmasked and exchanged favours, with
Boyet*

BEROWNE

See where it comes! Behaviour, what wert thou
Till this man showed thee, and what art thou now?

KING

All hail, sweet madam, and fair time of day.

PRINCESS

340   'Fair' in 'all hail' is foul, as I conceive.

KING

Construe my speeches better, if you may.

PRINCESS

Then wish me better; I will give you leave.

KING

We came to visit you, and purpose now
To lead you to our court. Vouchsafe it then.

PRINCESS

This field shall hold me, and so hold your vow.
Nor God nor I delights in perjured men.

KING

Rebuke me not for that which you provoke.
The virtue of your eye must break my oath.

PRINCESS

You nickname virtue – 'vice' you should have spoke;
350   For virtue's office never breaks men's troth.
Now, by my maiden honour, yet as pure
As the unsullied lily, I protest,

A world of torments though I should endure,
   I would not yield to be your house's guest,
So much I hate a breaking cause to be
Of heavenly oaths, vowed with integrity.

KING
O, you have lived in desolation here,
   Unseen, unvisited, much to our shame.

PRINCESS
Not so, my lord. It is not so, I swear.
   We have had pastimes here and pleasant game: 360
A mess of Russians left us but of late.

KING
How, madam? Russians?

PRINCESS   Ay, in truth, my lord;
Trim gallants, full of courtship and of state.

ROSALINE
Madam, speak true! It is not so, my lord.
My lady, to the manner of the days,
In courtesy gives undeserving praise.
We four indeed confronted were with four
In Russian habit. Here they stayed an hour
And talked apace; and in that hour, my lord,
They did not bless us with one happy word.   370
I dare not call them fools, but this I think,
When they are thirsty, fools would fain have drink.

BEROWNE
This jest is dry to me. My gentle sweet,
Your wit makes wise things foolish. When we greet,
With eyes' best seeing, heaven's fiery eye,
By light we lose light. Your capacity
Is of that nature that to your huge store
Wise things seem foolish and rich things but poor.

ROSALINE
This proves you wise and rich, for in my eye –

BEROWNE

380   I am a fool, and full of poverty.

ROSALINE

  But that you take what doth to you belong,
  It were a fault to snatch words from my tongue.

BEROWNE

  O, I am yours, and all that I possess.

ROSALINE

  All the fool mine?

BEROWNE   I cannot give you less.

ROSALINE

  Which of the visors was it that you wore?

BEROWNE

  Where, when, what visor? Why demand you this?

ROSALINE

  There, then, that visor: that superfluous case
  That hid the worse and showed the better face.

KING

  We were descried. They'll mock us now downright.

DUMAINE

390   Let us confess, and turn it to a jest.

PRINCESS

  Amazed, my lord? Why looks your highness sad?

ROSALINE

  Help! Hold his brows! He'll swoon. Why look you
      pale?
  Sea-sick, I think, coming from Muscovy!

BEROWNE

  Thus pour the stars down plagues for perjury.
    Can any face of brass hold longer out?
  Here stand I, lady; dart thy skill at me.
    Bruise me with scorn, confound me with a flout,
  Thrust thy sharp wit quite through my ignorance,
    Cut me to pieces with thy keen conceit,

And I will wish thee never more to dance, 400
  Nor never more in Russian habit wait.
O, never will I trust to speeches penned,
  Nor to the motion of a schoolboy's tongue,
Nor never come in visor to my friend,
  Nor woo in rhyme, like a blind harper's song.
Taffeta phrases, silken terms precise,
  Three-piled hyperboles, spruce affection,
Figures pedantical – these summer flies
  Have blown me full of maggot ostentation.
I do forswear them; and I here protest 410
  By this white glove – how white the hand, God
      knows! –
Henceforth my wooing mind shall be expressed
  In russet yeas and honest kersey noes.
And, to begin: wench – so God help me, law! –
My love to thee is sound, *sans* crack or flaw.

ROSALINE
  Sans 'sans', I pray you.

BEROWNE   Yet I have a trick
Of the old rage. Bear with me, I am sick;
I'll leave it by degrees. Soft, let us see:
Write 'Lord have mercy on us' on those three.
They are infected; in their hearts it lies; 420
They have the plague, and caught it of your eyes.
These lords are visited; you are not free,
For the Lord's tokens on you do I see.

PRINCESS
  No, they are free that gave these tokens to us.

BEROWNE
  Our states are forfeit. Seek not to undo us.

ROSALINE
  It is not so; for how can this be true,
  That you stand forfeit, being those that sue?

BEROWNE

Peace! for I will not have to do with you.

ROSALINE

Nor shall not if I do as I intend.

BEROWNE

430 Speak for yourselves. My wit is at an end.

KING

Teach us, sweet madam, for our rude transgression
Some fair excuse.

PRINCESS   The fairest is confession.
Were not you here but even now disguised?

KING

Madam, I was.

PRINCESS   And were you well advised?

KING

I was, fair madam.

PRINCESS   When you then were here,
What did you whisper in your lady's ear?

KING

That more than all the world I did respect her.

PRINCESS

When she shall challenge this, you will reject her.

KING

Upon mine honour, no.

PRINCESS   Peace, peace, forbear!

440 Your oath once broke, you force not to forswear.

KING

Despise me when I break this oath of mine.

PRINCESS

I will; and therefore keep it. Rosaline,
What did the Russian whisper in your ear?

ROSALINE

Madam, he swore that he did hold me dear
As precious eyesight, and did value me
Above this world; adding thereto, moreover,

That he would wed me or else die my lover.

PRINCESS

God give thee joy of him. The noble lord
Most honourably doth uphold his word.

KING

What mean you, madam? By my life, my troth,   450
I never swore this lady such an oath.

ROSALINE

By heaven you did! And, to confirm it plain,
You gave me this; but take it, sir, again.

KING

My faith and this the Princess I did give.
I knew her by this jewel on her sleeve.

PRINCESS

Pardon me, sir, this jewel did she wear,
And Lord Berowne, I thank him, is my dear.
What! Will you have me, or your pearl again?

BEROWNE

Neither of either; I remit both twain.
I see the trick on't. Here was a consent,   460
Knowing aforehand of our merriment,
To dash it like a Christmas comedy.
Some carry-tale, some please-man, some slight zany,
Some mumble-news, some trencher-knight, some Dick,
That smiles his cheek in years, and knows the trick
To make my lady laugh when she's disposed,
Told our intents before; which once disclosed,
The ladies did change favours, and then we,
Following the signs, wooed but the sign of she.
Now, to our perjury to add more terror,   470
We are again forsworn, in will and error.
Much upon this 'tis. (*To Boyet*) And might not you
Forestall our sport, to make us thus untrue?
Do not you know my lady's foot by the square,
   And laugh upon the apple of her eye?

And stand between her back, sir, and the fire,
  Holding a trencher, jesting merrily?
You put our page out – go, you are allowed;
Die when you will, a smock shall be your shroud.
480 You leer upon me, do you? There's an eye
Wounds like a leaden sword.

BOYET   Full merrily
Hath this brave manage, this career, been run.

BEROWNE

Lo, he is tilting straight. Peace! I have done.

  Enter Costard

Welcome, pure wit! Thou partest a fair fray.

COSTARD

O Lord, sir, they would know
Whether the three Worthies shall come in or no.

BEROWNE

What, are there but three?

COSTARD   No, sir; but it is vara fine,
For every one pursents three.

BEROWNE   And three times thrice is nine.

COSTARD

Not so, sir – under correction, sir – I hope it is not so.
You cannot beg us, sir, I can assure you, sir; we
490   know what we know.
I hope, sir, three times thrice, sir –

BEROWNE   Is not nine?

COSTARD Under correction, sir, we know whereuntil it
  doth amount.

BEROWNE

By Jove, I always took three threes for nine.

COSTARD O Lord, sir, it were pity you should get your
  living by reck'ning, sir.

BEROWNE How much is it?

COSTARD O Lord, sir, the parties themselves, the actors,

sir, will show whereuntil it doth amount. For mine
own part, I am, as they say, but to parfect one man in 500
one poor man – Pompion the Great, sir.

BEROWNE Art thou one of the Worthies?

COSTARD It pleased them to think me worthy of Pompey
the Great. For mine own part, I know not the degree
of the Worthy, but I am to stand for him.

BEROWNE Go bid them prepare.

COSTARD We will turn it finely off, sir; we will take some
care.   *Exit*

KING
Berowne, they will shame us. Let them not approach.

BEROWNE
We are shame-proof, my lord; and 'tis some policy 510
To have one show worse than the King's and his com-
            pany.

KING
I say they shall not come.

PRINCESS
Nay, my good lord, let me o'errule you now.
That sport best pleases that doth least know how –
Where zeal strives to content, and the contents
Dies in the zeal of that which it presents;
Their form confounded makes most form in mirth,
When great things labouring perish in their birth.

BEROWNE
A right description of our sport, my lord.
            Enter Armado

ARMADO Anointed, I implore so much expense of thy 520
royal sweet breath as will utter a brace of words.
            Armado and the King
            converse apart

PRINCESS Doth this man serve God?

BEROWNE Why ask you?

91

PRINCESS 'A speaks not like a man of God his making.

ARMADO That is all one, my fair sweet honey monarch;
for, I protest, the schoolmaster is exceeding fantastical;
too, too vain; too, too vain; but we will put it, as they
say, to *fortuna de la guerra.*
He gives the King a paper
I wish you the peace of mind, most royal couplement.
Exit

530 KING Here is like to be a good presence of Worthies. (*Con-
sulting the paper*) He presents Hector of Troy; the swain,
Pompey the Great; the parish curate, Alexander; Ar-
mado's page, Hercules; the pedant, Judas Maccabaeus.
(*Reading*)
And if these four Worthies in their first show thrive,
These four will change habits and present the other five.

BEROWNE
There is five in the first show.

KING
You are deceivèd. 'Tis not so.

BEROWNE The pedant, the braggart, the hedge-priest, the
fool, and the boy.

540 Abate throw at novum, and the whole world again
Cannot pick out five such, take each one in his vein.

KING
The ship is under sail, and here she comes amain.
Enter Costard as Pompey

COSTARD *as Pompey*
I Pompey am —

BEROWNE   You lie! You are not he.

COSTARD *as Pompey*
I Pompey am —

BOYET   With leopard's head on knee.

BEROWNE
Well said, old mocker. I must needs be friends with
thee.

92

COSTARD *as Pompey*
  I Pompey am, Pompey surnamed the Big –
DUMAINE
  The 'Great'.
COSTARD *as Pompey*
  It is 'Great', sir – Pompey surnamed the Great,
  That oft in field, with targe and shield, did make my foe to
      sweat;
  And travelling along this coast, I here am come by chance,   550
  And lay my arms before the legs of this sweet lass of France.
  If your ladyship would say 'Thanks, Pompey', I had
      done.
PRINCESS Great thanks, great Pompey.
COSTARD 'Tis not so much worth, but I hope I was
  perfect. I made a little fault in 'Great'.
BEROWNE My hat to a halfpenny, Pompey proves the
  best Worthy.
        Enter Nathaniel as Alexander
NATHANIEL *as Alexander*
  When in the world I lived, I was the world's commander;
  By east, west, north, and south, I spread my conquering
      might;   560
  My scutcheon plain declares that I am Alisander.
BOYET
  Your nose says no, you are not; for it stands too right.
BEROWNE
  Your nose smells 'no' in this, most tender-smelling
      knight.
PRINCESS
  The conqueror is dismayed. Proceed, good Alexander.
NATHANIEL *as Alexander*
  When in the world I lived, I was the world's commander –
BOYET
  Most true, 'tis right – you were so, Alisander.
BEROWNE Pompey the Great –

COSTARD Your servant, and Costard.

BEROWNE Take away the conqueror; take away
570 Alisander.

COSTARD (*to Nathaniel*) O, sir, you have overthrown
Alisander the conqueror. You will be scraped out of
the painted cloth for this. Your lion, that holds his
pole-axe sitting on a close-stool, will be given to Ajax.
He will be the ninth Worthy. A conqueror, and afeard
to speak? Run away for shame, Alisander.

Nathaniel retires

There, an't shall please you, a foolish mild man; an
honest man, look you, and soon dashed. He is a marvellous good neighbour, faith, and a very good bowler;
580 but for Alisander, alas, you see how 'tis – a little
o'erparted. But there are Worthies a-coming will speak
their mind in some other sort.

PRINCESS Stand aside, good Pompey.

Enter Holofernes as Judas and Mote as Hercules

HOLOFERNES *as presenter*

Great Hercules is presented by this imp,
    Whose club killed Cerberus, that three-headed *canus*,
And when he was a babe, a child, a shrimp,
    Thus did he strangle serpents in his *manus*.
Quoniam he seemeth in minority,
Ergo I come with this apology.
590 Keep some state in thy exit, and retire.

Mote retires

Holofernes speaks as Judas

Judas I am –

DUMAINE A Judas!

HOLOFERNES Not Iscariot, sir.

(*as Judas*)
Judas I am, yclept Maccabaeus.

DUMAINE Judas Maccabaeus clipped is plain Judas.

BEROWNE A kissing traitor. How, art thou proved
  Judas?

HOLOFERNES *as Judas*
  Judas I am —

DUMAINE The more shame for you, Judas.

HOLOFERNES What mean you, sir? 600

BOYET To make Judas hang himself.

HOLOFERNES Begin, sir; you are my elder.

BEROWNE Well followed: Judas was hanged on an elder.

HOLOFERNES I will not be put out of countenance.

BEROWNE Because thou hast no face.

HOLOFERNES What is this?

BOYET A cittern-head.

DUMAINE The head of a bodkin.

BEROWNE A death's face in a ring.

LONGAVILLE The face of an old Roman coin, scarce 610
  seen.

BOYET The pommel of Caesar's falchion.

DUMAINE The carved bone face on a flask.

BEROWNE Saint George's half-cheek in a brooch.

DUMAINE Ay, in a brooch of lead.

BEROWNE Ay, and worn in the cap of a toothdrawer. And
  now forward, for we have put thee in countenance.

HOLOFERNES You have put me out of countenance.

BEROWNE False! We have given thee faces.

HOLOFERNES But you have outfaced them all. 620

BEROWNE
  An thou wert a lion, we would do so.

BOYET
  Therefore, as he is an ass, let him go.
  And so adieu, sweet Jude. Nay, why dost thou stay?

DUMAINE For the latter end of his name.

95

BEROWNE

For the ass to the Jude? Give it him. Jude-as, away!

HOLOFERNES

This is not generous, not gentle, not humble.

BOYET

A light for Monsieur Judas! It grows dark; he may
stumble.

Holofernes retires

PRINCESS Alas, poor Maccabaeus, how hath he been
baited!

Enter Armado as Hector

630 **BEROWNE** Hide thy head, Achilles! Here comes Hector in
arms.

DUMAINE Though my mocks come home by me, I will
now be merry.

KING Hector was but a Trojan in respect of this.

BOYET But is this Hector?

KING I think Hector was not so clean-timbered.

LONGAVILLE His leg is too big for Hector's.

DUMAINE More calf, certain.

BOYET No; he is best indued in the small.

640 **BEROWNE** This cannot be Hector.

DUMAINE He's a god or a painter; for he makes faces.

ARMADO *as Hector*

The armipotent Mars, of lances the almighty,
Gave Hector a gift –

DUMAINE A gilt nutmeg.

BEROWNE A lemon.

LONGAVILLE Stuck with cloves.

DUMAINE No, cloven.

ARMADO Peace!

(as Hector)

The armipotent Mars, of lances the almighty,

650 Gave Hector a gift, the heir of Ilion;

96

A man so breathed that certain he would fight, yea,
From morn till night, out of his pavilion.
I am that flower –

DUMAINE   That mint!

LONGAVILLE   That columbine!

ARMADO Sweet Lord Longaville, rein thy tongue.

LONGAVILLE I must rather give it the rein, for it runs
against Hector.

DUMAINE Ay, and Hector's a greyhound.

ARMADO The sweet war-man is dead and rotten. Sweet
chucks, beat not the bones of the buried. When he
breathed, he was a man. But I will forward with my   660
device. Sweet royalty, bestow on me the sense of
hearing.

Berowne steps forth and whispers to Costard

PRINCESS Speak, brave Hector; we are much delighted.

ARMADO I do adore thy sweet grace's slipper.

BOYET Loves her by the foot.

DUMAINE He may not by the yard.

ARMADO *as Hector*
This Hector far surmounted Hannibal;
The party is gone –

COSTARD Fellow Hector, she is gone! She is two months
on her way.   670

ARMADO What meanest thou?

COSTARD Faith, unless you play the honest Trojan, the
poor wench is cast away. She's quick; the child brags
in her belly already. 'Tis yours.

ARMADO Dost thou infamonize me among potentates?
Thou shalt die!

COSTARD Then shall Hector be whipped for Jaquenetta
that is quick by him, and hanged for Pompey that is
dead by him.

DUMAINE Most rare Pompey!   680

97

BOYET Renowned Pompey!

BEROWNE Greater than 'Great'! Great, great, great Pompey! Pompey the Huge!

DUMAINE Hector trembles.

BEROWNE Pompey is moved. More Ates, more Ates! Stir them on, stir them on!

DUMAINE Hector will challenge him.

BEROWNE Ay, if 'a have no more man's blood in his belly than will sup a flea.

690 **ARMADO** By the north pole, I do challenge thee.

COSTARD I will not fight with a pole like a northern man. I'll slash; I'll do it by the sword. I bepray you, let me borrow my arms again.

DUMAINE Room for the incensed Worthies.

COSTARD I'll do it in my shirt.

DUMAINE Most resolute Pompey!

MOTE Master, let me take you a buttonhole lower. Do you not see, Pompey is uncasing for the combat. What mean you? You will lose your reputation.

700 **ARMADO** Gentlemen and soldiers, pardon me. I will not combat in my shirt.

DUMAINE You may not deny it. Pompey hath made the challenge.

ARMADO Sweet bloods, I both may and will.

BEROWNE What reason have you for't?

ARMADO The naked truth of it is, I have no shirt. I go woolward for penance.

MOTE True, and it was enjoined him in Rome for want of linen. Since when, I'll be sworn, he wore none but a
710 dishclout of Jaquenetta's, and that 'a wears next his heart for a favour.

Enter a messenger, Monsieur Marcade

MARCADE
God save you, madam.

98

PRINCESS   Welcome, Marcade,
But that thou interruptest our merriment.

MARCADE
I am sorry, madam, for the news I bring
Is heavy in my tongue. The King your father –

PRINCESS
Dead, for my life!

MARCADE   Even so; my tale is told.

BEROWNE
Worthies, away! The scene begins to cloud.

ARMADO For mine own part, I breathe free breath. I have
seen the day of wrong through the little hole of discretion, and I will right myself like a soldier.   720

Exeunt Worthies

KING How fares your majesty?

PRINCESS
Boyet, prepare. I will away tonight.

KING
Madam, not so. I do beseech you, stay.

PRINCESS
Prepare, I say. I thank you, gracious lords,
For all your fair endeavours, and entreat,
Out of a new-sad soul, that you vouchsafe
In your rich wisdom to excuse or hide
The liberal opposition of our spirits,
If over-boldly we have borne ourselves
In the converse of breath. Your gentleness   730
Was guilty of it. Farewell, worthy lord!
A heavy heart bears not a humble tongue.
Excuse me so, coming too short of thanks
For my great suit so easily obtained.

KING
The extreme parts of time extremely forms
All causes to the purpose of his speed,

And often at his very loose decides
That which long process could not arbitrate.
And though the mourning brow of progeny
740 Forbid the smiling courtesy of love
The holy suit which fain it would convince,
Yet, since love's argument was first on foot,
Let not the cloud of sorrow jostle it
From what it purposed; since to wail friends lost
Is not by much so wholesome-profitable
As to rejoice at friends but newly found.

PRINCESS
I understand you not. My griefs are double.

BEROWNE
Honest plain words best pierce the ear of grief;
And by these badges understand the King.
750 For your fair sakes have we neglected time,
Played foul play with our oaths. Your beauty, ladies,
Hath much deformed us, fashioning our humours
Even to the opposèd end of our intents;
And what in us hath seemed ridiculous –
As love is full of unbefitting strains,
All wanton as a child, skipping and vain,
Formed by the eye and therefore, like the eye,
Full of straying shapes, of habits, and of forms,
Varying in subjects as the eye doth roll
760 To every varied object in his glance;
Which parti-coated presence of loose love
Put on by us, if, in your heavenly eyes,
Have misbecomed our oaths and gravities,
Those heavenly eyes, that look into these faults,
Suggested us to make. Therefore, ladies,
Our love being yours, the error that love makes
Is likewise yours. We to ourselves prove false
By being once false for ever to be true

To those that make us both – fair ladies, you.
And even that falsehood, in itself a sin, 770
Thus purifies itself and turns to grace.

PRINCESS

We have received your letters, full of love;
Your favours, the ambassadors of love;
And in our maiden counsel rated them
At courtship, pleasant jest, and courtesy,
As bombast and as lining to the time.
But more devout than this in our respects
Have we not been; and therefore met your loves
In their own fashion, like a merriment.

DUMAINE

Our letters, madam, showed much more than jest. 780

LONGAVILLE

So did our looks.

ROSALINE   We did not quote them so.

KING

Now, at the latest minute of the hour,
Grant us your loves.

PRINCESS   A time, methinks, too short
To make a world-without-end bargain in.
No, no, my lord, your grace is perjured much,
Full of dear guiltiness; and therefore this:
If for my love – as there is no such cause –
You will do aught, this shall you do for me:
Your oath I will not trust; but go with speed
To some forlorn and naked hermitage, 790
Remote from all the pleasures of the world;
There stay until the twelve celestial signs
Have brought about the annual reckoning.
If this austere insociable life
Change not your offer made in heat of blood;
If frosts and fasts, hard lodging and thin weeds,

>Nip not the gaudy blossoms of your love,
>But that it bear this trial, and last love;
>Then, at the expiration of the year,
800 Come challenge me, challenge by these deserts,
>And, by this virgin palm now kissing thine,
>I will be thine; and, till that instance, shut
>My woeful self up in a mourning house,
>Raining the tears of lamentation
>For the remembrance of my father's death.
>If this thou do deny, let our hands part,
>Neither entitled in the other's heart.

KING

>If this, or more than this, I would deny,
>To flatter up these powers of mine with rest,
810 The sudden hand of death close up mine eye!
>Hence hermit then – my heart is in thy breast.

The King and the Princess converse apart

DUMAINE

>But what to me, my love? But what to me?
>A wife?

KATHARINE A beard, fair health, and honesty;
>With threefold love I wish you all these three.

DUMAINE

>O, shall I say 'I thank you, gentle wife'?

KATHARINE

>Not so, my lord. A twelvemonth and a day
>I'll mark no words that smooth-faced wooers say.
>Come when the King doth to my lady come;
>Then, if I have much love, I'll give you some.

DUMAINE

820 I'll serve thee true and faithfully till then.

KATHARINE

>Yet swear not, lest ye be forsworn again.

They converse apart

LONGAVILLE

What says Maria?

MARIA   At the twelvemonth's end
I'll change my black gown for a faithful friend.

LONGAVILLE

I'll stay with patience, but the time is long.

MARIA

The liker you; few taller are so young.
    They converse apart

BEROWNE

Studies my lady? Mistress, look on me.
Behold the window of my heart, mine eye,
What humble suit attends thy answer there.
Impose some service on me for thy love.

ROSALINE

Oft have I heard of you, my Lord Berowne,   830
Before I saw you, and the world's large tongue
Proclaims you for a man replete with mocks,
Full of comparisons and wounding flouts,
Which you on all estates will execute
That lie within the mercy of your wit.
To weed this wormwood from your fruitful brain,
And therewithal to win me, if you please,
Without the which I am not to be won,
You shall this twelvemonth term from day to day
Visit the speechless sick, and still converse   840
With groaning wretches; and your task shall be
With all the fierce endeavour of your wit
To enforce the painèd impotent to smile.

BEROWNE

To move wild laughter in the throat of death?
It cannot be; it is impossible;
Mirth cannot move a soul in agony.

ROSALINE

Why, that's the way to choke a gibing spirit,
Whose influence is begot of that loose grace
Which shallow laughing hearers give to fools.

850 A jest's prosperity lies in the ear
Of him that hears it, never in the tongue
Of him that makes it. Then, if sickly ears,
Deafed with the clamours of their own dear groans,
Will hear your idle scorns, continue then,
And I will have you and that fault withal;
But if they will not, throw away that spirit,
And I shall find you empty of that fault,
Right joyful of your reformation.

BEROWNE

A twelvemonth? Well, befall what will befall,
860 I'll jest a twelvemonth in an hospital.

PRINCESS (*to the King*)

Ay, sweet my lord, and so I take my leave.

KING

No, madam, we will bring you on your way.

BEROWNE

Our wooing doth not end like an old play;
Jack hath not Jill. These ladies' courtesy
Might well have made our sport a comedy.

KING

Come, sir, it wants a twelvemonth and a day,
And then 'twill end.

BEROWNE   That's too long for a play.

Enter Armado

ARMADO Sweet majesty, vouchsafe me –

PRINCESS Was not that Hector?

870 **DUMAINE** The worthy knight of Troy.

ARMADO I will kiss thy royal finger, and take leave. I am
a votary; I have vowed to Jaquenetta to hold the plough

for her sweet love three year. But, most esteemed
greatness, will you hear the dialogue that the two
learned men have compiled in praise of the owl and the
cuckoo? It should have followed in the end of our
show.

KING Call them forth quickly; we will do so.

ARMADO Holla! Approach!

Enter all

This side is Hiems, winter; this Ver, the spring; the 880
one maintained by the owl, th'other by the cuckoo.
Ver, begin.

THE SONG

VER When daisies pied and violets blue
          And lady-smocks all silver-white
     And cuckoo-buds of yellow hue
          Do paint the meadows with delight,
     The cuckoo then, on every tree,
     Mocks married men; for thus sings he:
               'Cuckoo!
     Cuckoo, cuckoo!' O, word of fear,   890
     Unpleasing to a married ear!

     When shepherds pipe on oaten straws,
          And merry larks are ploughmen's clocks,
     When turtles tread, and rooks, and daws,
          And maidens bleach their summer smocks,
     The cuckoo then, on every tree,
     Mocks married men; for thus sings he:
               'Cuckoo!
     Cuckoo, cuckoo!' O, word of fear,
     Unpleasing to a married ear!   900

HIEMS When icicles hang by the wall,
          And Dick the shepherd blows his nail,

And Tom bears logs into the hall,
  And milk comes frozen home in pail,
When blood is nipped, and ways be foul,
  Then nightly sings the staring owl:
        'Tu-whit
Tu-who!' – a merry note,
While greasy Joan doth keel the pot.

910 When all aloud the wind doth blow,
  And coughing drowns the parson's saw,
And birds sit brooding in the snow,
  And Marian's nose looks red and raw,
When roasted crabs hiss in the bowl,
  Then nightly sings the staring owl:
        'Tu-whit
Tu-who!' – a merry note,
While greasy Joan doth keel the pot.

ARMADO The words of Mercury are harsh after the songs
920 of Apollo. You that way; we this way.   *Exeunt*

COMMENTARY

The abbreviations 'Q' and 'F' refer to the Quarto (1598) and first Folio (1623) editions of the play. In notes dealing with textual problems, a general knowledge of the relationship between Q and F (outlined in the Account of the Text) is assumed. In quotations from Q and F, 'long s' (ʃ) is printed as 's'. Biblical quotations are modernized from the Bishops' Bible (1568 etc.), the one most likely to have been read by Shakespeare.

The title

Although the traditional title is *Love's Labour's Lost* ('the labour of love is lost'), a case can be made for *Love's Labours Lost* ('the lost labours of love'). Q's title-page reads, ambiguously, 'Loues labors lost'. The running title at the top of each page of text is, more helpfully, '*Loues Labor's lost*'. This latter form is found throughout F, except in the table of contents, where '*Loues Labour lost*' is used. Thus far, the evidence is strongly in favour of *Love's Labour's Lost*. However, the form in the F table of contents recurs in Robert Tofte's *Alba* (1598): 'Loues Labour Lost, I once did see a Play'. And the title given by Francis Meres in his famous 1598 catalogue – '*Loue labors lost*' – although different again, is nevertheless closer to *Love's Labours Lost* than to *Love's Labour's Lost*. This edition retains the traditional title because those readings which support it are less likely to have been memorially corrupted than those which tell against it.

I.1   (stage direction) *Ferdinand, King of Navarre*. The name *Ferdinand* never appears in the spoken text. In Q and F it occurs only in certain stage directions and speech prefixes in I.1 and II.1. A few prefixes in II.1 have the form '*Nauar.*' and '*Nau.*'. Elsewhere, *Ferdinand* is simply 'King', unnamed like his counterpart, the Princess of France. It has been suggested that Shakespeare added the name *Ferdinand* at a late stage (after the spoken text had been established), to discourage the identification of his King with the contemporary ruler of Navarre, Henry; but it is more likely that he began composing with the name in mind and then, finding no real need for it, quietly dropped it from directions and prefixes alike.

Navarre included parts of present-day northern Spain and southern France until Spanish Navarre was annexed by Ferdinand the Catholic in 1516. French Navarre survived as an independent kingdom until, in 1589, it was united with France by Henry.

Berowne, Longaville, and Dumaine. The name *Berowne* is now usually pronounced 'be' as in 'bet' plus 'roan'; but the Elizabethan pronunciation was more like 'beroon' (hence the rhyme with *moon* at IV.3.228 and 230). Evidently the pronunciation of *Longaville* was variable: it rhymes with *ill* at IV.3.121 and ten lines later with *compile*; yet its last syllable must have been close enough to both 'veal' and 'well' to allow the wordplay of V.2.247. In modern productions 'Longavill' is usual. On the sixteenth-century noblemen whose names have been inherited by *Berowne, Longaville,* and *Dumaine,* see the Introduction, page 10.

1–7   *Let fame, that all hunt after ... eternity.* The most striking parallels with Shakespeare's *Sonnets* are noted in the Introduction, pages 14–15.

2   *brazen tombs* (alluding to Horace's famous assertion that his verse would survive the ravages of Time: *Exegi monumentum aere perennius,* 'I have built a monument more lasting than brass', *Odes* III.xxx.1)

3   *the disgrace of death* (1) the loss of living gracefulness in death; (2) the shaming of death (when the courtiers

win immortality through *fame*)

4   *spite of* despite

cormorant devouring Time. 'Time which devours as greedily as a cormorant' (Shakespeare uses this bird several times as an emblem of ravenous appetite); but there is also a subliminal sense: 'Time which devours even the cormorant which devours'.

5   *breath* (here, as often in the play, including the metonymical sense 'speech')

6   *bate* blunt

8   *brave conquerors*. By using the word *conquerors*, Navarre rashly declares the *war* of line 9 won before it is begun. Military imagery is common in the play, especially when love is under discussion (the love-war trope is an Elizabethan commonplace). It gestures towards the world of public responsibilities which the King and his lords (in contrast with their equivalents in real-life France, involved in the civil war and its political aftermath) have abandoned in favour of private study.

9   *affections* passions

11   *late* recent

13   *academe* (pronounced 'akadeem') academy. Shakespeare has been influenced in this part of the play by Pierre de la Primaudaye's *L'Académie française* (1577; translated by Thomas Bowes in 1586 as *The French Academy*), a book in which four fictional young noblemen of Anjou form an academy and discuss ethics.

14   *Still* calm, constant

living art (1) the art of living a good life (translating the Stoic *ars vivendi*); (2) learning infused with vitality (continuing the idea of disgracing death by study)

20   *hand* (with a quibbling reference to the sense 'handwriting')

21   *branch* clause

22   *armed* prepared (continuing the military imagery of lines 8–10)

28   *mortified* dead to earthly pleasures (a death designed to disgrace death – Dumaine having the King's opening lines in mind)

32   *With all these living in philosophy*. Dr Johnson commented 'I know not certainly to what "all these" is to be referred; I suppose he means that he finds "love, pomp, *and* wealth *in* philosophy."' Most editors have agreed. An alternative interpretation of *all these* is 'my three companions'.

33   *I can but say their protestation over*. Alternatively, 'I can but say – their protestation over –'.

37   *not to see a woman*. Modelled on Plato's school in Athens, renaissance academies inherited the philosopher's anti-feminism. In *The Royal Exchange* (1590), Robert Greene notes: 'Plato admitted no auditor in his academy but such as while they were his scholars would abstain from women; for he was wont to say that the greatest enemy to memory was venery.'

43   *wink* sleep, nod off
       of all the at any point during

44   *think no harm all night* think it no harm to sleep all night. Berowne's ellipsis allows a witty allusion to the proverb 'He that sleeps well thinks no harm.'

50   *an if* if

54   *By yea and nay*. A common oath, especially among puritans, deriving from Matthew 5.37, 'let your communication be Yea, yea; Nay, nay'. Berowne uses the phrase equivocally: he swore and he did not.

55–8   *What is the end ... god-like recompense*. Echoes of Marlowe's *Doctor Faustus*, I.8, 10, 18, and 61–2, suggest that when Shakespeare created the comically misguided schedule signed by the men he had in mind the bond which Faustus signs with the devil.

57   *common sense* ordinary understanding

59   *Com'on*. The Q spelling (F has 'come on') is preserved here to draw attention to Berowne's quibble on the word *common* (line 57).

65   *hard-a-keeping oath* an oath too hard to keep

70   *stops* obstacles

71   *train* lure

76   *falsely.* The word acts two ways at once: truth 'treacherously' makes the looker see 'wrongly'.

       his (the looker's)

77   *Light seeking light.* It was commonly believed that the eye created the beams by which it saw (hence Milton's 'When I consider how my light is spent'). This is why Berowne can refer to the eye seeking *the light of truth* (line 75) as a *Light*. On the ingenuity of the speech, see the Introduction, pages 15–16.

       beguile deprive deceivingly

80   *Study me how* let me study how

82–3   *Who dazzling so ... blinded by.* Dr Johnson's gloss has not been surpassed: 'when he "dazzles," that is, has his eye made weak, "by fixing his eye upon a fairer eye, that *fairer* eye shall be his heed," his "direction" or "lodestar ... and give him light that was blinded by it."'

88   *earthly godfathers of heaven's lights* astronomers (who give names to newly discovered stars much as god-parents give names to children at baptism). Berowne's view of naming here and in the following lines is an old one. It is also very persistent; compare Wittgenstein's *Philosophical Investigations* (1953): 'Naming appears as a *queer* connexion of a word with an object ... And *here* we may indeed fancy naming to be some remarkable act of the mind, as it were a baptism of an object' (§ 38). The mysterious nature of the link between words and things (between, in sixteenth-century terms, the *res* and *verba*) is an important preoccupation of the comedy.

90   *shining* (because starlit)

91   *wot* know

95   *proceeding* (perhaps with a quibbling reference to the sense 'taking a degree at university')

96   *weeds the corn, and still lets grow the weeding* pulls up the wheat and leaves the weeds to flourish

97   *The spring is near when green geese are a-breeding. Green geese* (*Green* because they live not on corn but by grazing) lay their eggs (fall *a-breeding*) when they have grown strong on young grass. In a good year this happens in late February or early March. So Berowne is right to say that the laying of goose eggs anticipates spring (he may be echoing a country saw). But there is more to the line than that: Berowne implies that his fellows are inexperienced ('green' is still used in this sense) and foolish (the goose is even today proverbially silly), attempting something by their oath which is beyond their powers. Interestingly, the line anticipates the *l'envoy* to Armado's *moral*, another four-line setpiece brought to nothing by a *goose* (III.1.82–90).

98   *Fit in* appropriate to

99   *In reason nothing . . . Something then in rhyme* (alluding to the phrase 'neither rhyme nor reason')

100   *sneaping frost* nipping frost. The King takes Berowne's *rhyme* as 'rime'.

101   *infants of the spring* young spring buds and flowers

102–3   *Why should proud summer . . . to sing?* The question seems to have two ingredients. Looking back to lines 97–8: 'is it right to brag about a full achievement before you (*the birds*, the other three scholars) have achieved?' Less strongly, anticipating lines 104–9: 'why should one be glad to reach the *summer* of life (sober studious middle age) without enjoying life's spring (the season which gives *birds* a *cause to sing*)?'

104   *an.* Some editors retain the Q and F 'any', but it seems preferable to assume that the eye of the Q typesetter was caught by 'any cause' in the preceding line of Shakespeare's manuscript and that the error passed unaltered into F.

105–6   *At Christmas . . . new-fangled shows.* Berowne strikingly anticipates the songs of Ver and Hiems (spring and winter) which conclude the play.

106   *shows*. The alternate rhyme scheme is broken by this word, and various 'improvements' have been suggested on the grounds that the printer, not Shakespeare, is responsible. But there are so many inconsistencies of this kind, where the sense is right but not the sound (as with *sworn* at line 114), that it is virtually certain that the irregularity is Shakespearian.

107   *like of* enjoy

109   *Climb o'er the house to unlock the little gate*. In one of its most significant divergences from Q, F reads 'That were to clymbe ore the house to vnlocke the gate.' Presumably the man who checked the copy of Q from which F was printed made some correction here which was added to and mixed up with the line he wanted changed. What makes the F reading so puzzling is that Q seems to be in no need of emendation.

110   *sit you out*. The King imagines Berowne sitting apart at a feast (like Apemantus in *Timon of Athens*, I.2.29–31), unless *sit* is a compositorial misreading of 'set', which would be in keeping with *Go home* and *Adieu* in the second half of the line.

112   *for* on the side of

      barbarism lack of culture (as at V.1.76–7, *We will be singuled from the barbarous*)

115   *each three years' day* each day of the three years

124   *Marry* (a weakened form of 'by the Virgin Mary')

127   *gentility* good manners

132   *in embassy* as an ambassador

134   *complete* (accented on the first syllable)

135   *Aquitaine* (an area of south-west France)

140   *is overshot* misses by shooting over the target

144   *won as towns with fire* (that is, destroyed in the taking)

145   *of force* perforce, necessarily

146   *lie* lodge

      mere absolute, downright

149   *affects* passions
150   *special grace* extraordinary divine assistance
153   *at large* in general
155   *in attainder of* condemned to
156   *Suggestions are to other as to me* I am as open to temptation as the next man
158   *I am the last that will last keep his oath* (1) although I am the last to swear, I will be the last to break my oath; (2) of us four swearers, I am the least likely to keep my oath the longest. Berowne is equivocating again.
159   *quick* lively
160–61 *haunted | With* frequented by
164   *who* whom
166   *compliments* formal manners. The Q reading is 'complements', which could also mean 'accomplishments', and this may be the sense intended here.
167   *mutiny* discord
168   *child of fancy* fantastic creature
       hight is named
169   *For interim to* to break up, to provide intervals in
170   *high-born* noble, lofty. Most editors modernize Q's 'high borne' in this way, but 'high-borne' is sometimes given. Although *high-born* is probably the less interesting reading of the two, it is such a common compound that the theatre audience would hear it even if the actor tried to communicate 'high-borne'.
171   *tawny* (because baked brown by the sun)
       debate strife
172   *How you delight* what delights you
174   *for my minstrelsy* as my court singer
175   *wight* person
176   *fire-new* freshly coined (as in *Twelfth Night*, III.2.20–21: 'some excellent jests fire-new from the mint'). 'Fire-new' was itself *fire-new* in 1595; it has not been recorded before *Richard III* and the present play (which is in general very rich in neologisms).

fashion (not in its restricted modern sense: Armado admires whatever is in vogue, not just clothes)

178   (stage direction) *Dull ... Costard.* Shakespeare often uses names to give clues about character, but he does not (as Ben Jonson does, with Volpone, Subtle, Quarlous, and the rest) use them to define character precisely and limitingly. The constable is 'dull' in that he is not intellectual or articulate, but he is lively enough to *dance* and *play on the tabor* (V.1.146–8). A 'costard' is a variety of apple; the name associates the swain with his agricultural tasks.

179   *the Duke's own person.* It is difficult to be sure whether Shakespeare intends to display Dull's dullness by making him refer to the King here and at I.2.121 as *Duke*, whether he imagines Dull using the monarch's local rather than national title (for kings can be dukes, and at I.2.36 and II.1.38 Armado and the Princess, who might be expected to know about Ferdinand's rank, call him *Duke*), or whether he has simply grown careless about Navarre's status. There are similar inconsistencies in Q and F over the Princess. On two occasions, low characters call her *Queen* (IV.2.129 and 137). Perhaps they do so out of ignorance. However, in a large number of speech prefixes Shakespeare – perhaps having at the back of his creative mind the death of her father, the King of France – calls her *Queen* rather than the strictly correct 'Princess'. (In this edition, prefixes have been standardized, spoken text left intact.)

181   *reprehend.* Dull means 'represent'. Dogberry, the constable in *Much Ado About Nothing*, makes similar verbal blunders.

182   *farborough.* This is Dull's version of 'thirdborough', the lowest rank of constable. F's 'Tharborough' is probably to be explained as the typesetter's baffled attempt to reproduce an ill-written 'correction' of 'Farborough' in his Q copy.

185   *Signeour*. Most editions read 'Signior' (properly 'Signor'). The Q spelling is preserved here because it suggests a mispronunciation which is consistent with Dull's difficulties over 'Armado'. It is perfectly possible – especially in view of the fact that elsewhere in Q the less laboured forms 'signeor' and 'signior' are used – that *Signeour* was the spelling employed by Shakespeare at this point in the manuscript from which Q was printed.

    commends you sends you his greetings

187   *contempts*. Costard means to say 'contents', but his word is not inappropriate, given the lofty denouncement of the swain in Armado's letter. The same confusion is used in *The Merry Wives of Windsor*, I.1.232, when Slender, just persuaded to marry Anne Page, says 'I hope upon familiarity will grow more content'.

188   *magnificent Armado* grandiose Armado. There is an anti-Spanish jibe here, 'magnificent' being a stock adjective for the Armada of 1588 and 'Armado' being an alternative form of 'Armada'. Shakespeare gives his braggart a name which encourages the audience to scorn him, only to reveal, in the closing stages of the play, new and engaging depths to his character.

191   *A high hope for a low heaven*. In a theological context, 'hope' commonly meant 'expectation of heaven'. Thus, when Touchstone declares that Corin will be 'damned' for never having been at court, the shepherd simply replies 'Nay, I hope' (*As You Like It*, III.2.33–4). It is in this sense that Longaville interprets Berowne's *hope in God* (line 189), and he insists that *high words* are a *low* sort of *heaven* to *hope* highly for.

193   *To hear, or forbear hearing?* The theological tone is maintained by an allusion to Ezekiel 2.5: 'And whether they will hear or refuse (for they are a rebellious house), yet they may know that there hath been a Prophet among them.'

196   *style*. Berowne plays on 'stile' (hence *to climb in the merriness*).

198   *is to* relates to

199–200   *taken with the manner* caught in the act. The Anglo-French law-term 'mainoure' (meaning 'work done by the hand') popularly acquired the concrete sense 'things stolen' and was at the same time corrupted into *manner*.

202   *In manner and form following*. A common legal formula in the period. Costard's distinctions anticipate the more spectacular ones in Armado's letter.

204   *form* bench

210   *correction* punishment

210–11   *and God defend the right!* The formal prayer offered before a trial by combat, as in *Richard II*, I.3.101, and *2 Henry VI*, II.3.55. The suggestion that Costard would fight Armado to prove his innocence interestingly anticipates V.2.690, where Armado challenges Costard. Here the clown is fairly accused of paying unlawful attentions to Jaquenetta; Armado is in the same position in the last act.

214   *sinplicity*. It is possible that Q's reading, 'sinplicitie', is a misprint; F emends to 'simplicitie'. On *sinplicity* see the Introduction, page 24.

214–15   *hearken after the flesh* be sexually attracted. On the ambiguity of *hearken*, see the Introduction, page 24.

216   *the welkin's vicegerent* the heavens' deputy

217   *dominator* ruler, lord

222   *but so* not worth much. The equivalent of our 'only so so'.

226   *secrets* private affairs (with bawdy overtones. Compare Hamlet's jest (II.2.231–5): 'Then you live about her waist, or in the middle of her favours? ... In the secret parts of Fortune? O, most true! She is a strumpet.')

228   *humour* mood. On the physiological connotations of the word, see the note to I.2.76–81.

229   *physic* medicine

230–39   *The time when? . . . the ground which . . . the place where.* The form of Armado's letter reflects that of Elizabethan legal indictments.

234   *yclept* called

236   *obscene* disgusting (rather than 'sexually shocking')

237   *snow-white pen.* Armado writes with a white quill. (The associations of *white* as the colour of innocence are probably at work.)

        ebon-coloured black (like ebony)

240   *curious-knotted garden* garden with intricately patterned flower-beds. 'Knot' is still used in the sense 'flower-bed with a fanciful design'.

241   *low-spirited* ignoble (rather than 'gloomy, depressed')

241–2   *minnow of thy mirth* object so insignificant as to be laughable (a *minnow* being a small fresh-water fish)

244   *unlettered* illiterate

246   *vassal* slavish fellow

250   *Sorted* associated

251   *continent canon* law enforcing restraint

252   *passion* grieve

257   *meed* reward (delicately paradoxical with the *punishment* which follows)

259   *estimation* reputation

260   *an't* if it

261   *weaker vessel* woman (a description deriving from scripture: 1 Peter 3.7)

263   *vessel.* This is the reading of Q and F and it makes good sense. However, Theobald's emendation 'vassal' is not unattractive in the wake of *weaker vessel* (line 261), since variation rather than repetition is the hallmark of Armado's style (and since the Q compositor might have set *vessel* from a manuscript 'vassal' because line 261 was still in his head, the reading persisting into F because of the erratic nature of the correction between Q and F).

263–4 *at the least of thy sweet notice* on your instructions at very short notice

264 *bring her to trial.* A bawdy innuendo is likely.

269 *the best for the worst* the best example of something bad, the worst of all

271–84 *wench ... damsel ... virgin ... maid.* Costard tries to evade the law by employing synonymia, the rhetorical scheme just used in Armado's letter: *a child of our grandmother Eve, a female ... a woman ... the weaker vessel* (lines 254, 255, and 261). For the wider implications of his quibbling, see the Introduction, pages 24–5.

278 *damsel.* Q's 'Demsel' may be a reflection of Costard's rustic pronunciation rather than a misprint. However, since nothing is made of it by the King (in contrast to Jaquenetta's rustic pronunciation of *Parson*, remarked by Holofernes at IV.2.82), since it makes no underhand comment on the dramatic situation (as *contempts* and *sinplicity* do at lines 187 and 214), and since the correct word is not at all esoteric (as it could be argued 'third-borough' is, at least for Dull, at line 182), this is unlikely. Moreover, in lines 279 and 280 Q spells the same word 'Damsel'. The F emendation 'Damosell', both here and in lines 279 and 280, is very interesting. Would the annotator of Q for F – not notably conscientious in his work – have deleted three words and written three replacements if he could have got by with the alteration of one letter? It seems likely that he had good grounds for preferring the more elaborate form 'Damosell' to *damsel*. Against this must be set the fact that Q, based on Shakespeare's manuscript, has the same reading two and nearly three times: such authority must outweigh the likely good grounds for F's emendation.

282 KING. Q has the speech prefix '*Ber.*', which F emends to '*Fer.*'. Q may be right, but the exchange between Costard and the King is so well-established by this

stage of the scene that an interruption by Berowne seems out of place. Presumably the Q compositor read an indistinct manuscript '*Fer.*' as '*Ber.*'.

285 *This 'maid' will not serve your turn* using the word 'maid' will not get you out of difficulties

286 *will serve my turn.* Costard exploits the bawdy sense of *turn*. Compare *Antony and Cleopatra*, II.5.58–9, where the Messenger tells Cleopatra that Antony is 'bound unto Octavia'; 'For what good turn?' she asks, and he replies 'For the best turn i'th'bed.'

289–90 *mutton and porridge* mutton broth (probably with a glance at the slang sense of *mutton*, 'whore')

295 *lay* wager
goodman yeoman. Dull is addressed as *goodman* at IV.2.36 and V.1.142.

298 *I suffer for the truth.* Costard is thus a comic equivalent of the four scholars, who undertake a painful course of study in their academy to find *the light of truth* (line 75).

300–301 *prosperity! Affliction.* Like Dull at I.2.123, Costard says the opposite of what he intends.

301–2 *sit thee down, sorrow!* (probably proverbial; connotations uncertain; see *set thee down, sorrow* at IV.3.4–5 and the note)

I.2 (stage direction) *Armado and Mote.* On Armado's name and nature, see the note to I.1.188. The argument for modernizing the Q and F 'Moth' (which other editors have preserved) to *Mote* goes as follows. As a result of changes in pronunciation, that form of the word 'moth' which derived from the Old English *mohðe* developed a hard final 't' and became indistinguishable in Elizabethan and Jacobean English from the word 'mote', derived from Old English *mot*. This led to the spellings 'moth' and 'mote' where we would have 'mote' and 'moth'. Setting aside references to Armado's page and

Titania's fairy (with whom similar difficulties arise), of the sixteen appearances of 'mo(a)th(e)(s)' in the Quartos and F, five mean 'insect(s)' and eleven (including four at IV.3.159 of Q and F *Love's Labour's Lost*) 'particle(s)'. 'Moats' occurs once, in the Shakespearian part of *Pericles* (1609 Q). In view of the ambiguity of 'moth' in these texts (including several set from Shakespeare's manuscripts and therefore likely to reflect his own spelling), the modernizing editor must decide which sense is dominant in the case of Armado's page. Since there are no references to his being insect-like but several to his being tiny (as at V.1.40–42 and 124–6) and like a word (V.1.39–40) – a joke which relies on a pun with the French word for 'word', *mot*, which had a sounded final 't' in the sixteenth century – the primary sense is undoubtedly 'particle'. So, despite the spelling of Q and F, *Mote* must be the page's name in a modern-spelling text. Modern actors should pronounce the name as they would 'mote', although Shakespeare's players probably said something like 'mott'.

There is general agreement that the relationship between the braggart and his boy owes something to that between Sir Tophas and his page Epiton in John Lyly's *Endymion* (1588).

5   *imp* child (literally 'young shoot' or 'sapling')

7   *part* distinguish between

8   *juvenal* youth. Armado probably uses this affected word to pun on the name of the Roman satirist Juvenal, thus complimenting Mote on his sharpness.

9   *working* operation (of these emotions)

10   *signor* (a pun on 'senior'; compare III.1.177)

13–14   *congruent epitheton appertaining to* suitable description of. *Epitheton*, an early form of the word 'epithet', is taken from Q's 'apethaton' (F has 'apathaton'). Note, however, the plausible suggestion that editors should read 'appellation', Q's 'apethaton' deriving from 'appellaton' written indistinctly in Shakespeare's manuscript.

15 *nominate* name

16 *appertinent* appropriate

18 *Pretty and apt* (the standard Elizabethan way of saying 'pretty apt', 'quite smart'. Mote playfully interprets the praise as two adjectives in parallel.)

21 *pretty, because little*. Armado parries his page's witty thrust by invoking the proverb 'Little things are pretty'.

25 *condign* well-deserved

28 *quick* full of life

29-30 *Thou heatest my blood* (by making him angry)

33 *speaks the mere contrary* has got it quite the wrong way round. Here, as always in Elizabethan English, 'mere' has the strong sense 'absolute', 'sheer', 'downright'.

33-4 *crosses love not him* coins (some of which carried the image of a cross) rarely come his way

39 *told* counted

40 *I am ill at reckoning*. This is the first of a number of references in the play to mathematical incompetence. The root of the joke seems to be that for all their studying the academicians are baffled by the simplest sums.

41 *tapster* barman. There is a similar slighting reference to 'tapster's arithmetic' in *Troilus and Cressida*, I.2.108.

42 *gamester* gambler

43 *varnish* finish, gloss

43-4 *a complete man* a man possessed of all the civilized accomplishments (such a man as emerges as the ideal in a conduct book like Henry Peacham's *The Complete Gentleman*, 1622)

46 *deuce-ace* a two and a one (in dice)

48 *vulgar* common people

53 *the dancing horse*. Probably Morocco, a performing horse brought to London in 1591. Morocco could beat

out numbers with its hoof and gained considerable renown as an arithmetician.

54   *figure* turn of rhetoric or logic

55   *cipher* zero. Mote takes Armado's *figure* in the sense 'numeral'.

58-9   *drawing my sword against ... affection.* Compare the King's proposed combat at I.1.8-10.

58   *humour* disposition

59   *affection.* See I.1.9 and note.

61   *new-devised curtsy* new-fangled kind of bow

61-2   *think scorn* disdain

62   *outswear* swear to do without

67   *carriage* demeanour. Mote immediately introduces the sense 'carrying power'.

69-70   *he carried the town-gates on his back* (according to Judges 16.3)

71   *well-knit* well-constructed

72   *my rapier.* Armado is as fashionable in weaponry as in words; the rapier was replacing the old-fashioned long-sword in the 1590s.

76-81   *Of what complexion? ... one of the four complexions?* The four *complexions* or humours (phlegm, blood, choler, and melancholy) were thought to be body fluids which, singly or in combination (hence lines 77-8), formed a person's character. They also determined the colours of his or her skin (hence the modern sense of the word *complexion*). Armado's question, *Is that one of the four complexions?*, shows that character is in his mind, but Mote is more interested in skin. By *sea-water green* the page means that Delilah's *complexion* was, like the sea, moist, briny, and ill-coloured. However, he is also implying that *Samson's love* had the 'green-sickness', an anaemic condition, chlorosis, commonly affecting young women and giving their skin a greenish tint.

83   *Green indeed is the colour of lovers. Green* is frequently associated with love in renaissance iconography;

Andrew Marvell draws on this tradition in 'The Garden': 'No white nor red was ever seen | So am'rous as this lovely green' (lines 17–18).

85   *affected her for her wit* loved her for her mental powers. The modern sense of *wit* is post-Shakespearian.

86   *she had a green wit.* It has been suggested that Mote is making quibbling reference to the seven green withes which Delilah used to bind Samson (Judges 16.7); but it is far from certain that such a pun could register in Elizabethan pronunciation. Mote's joke is more likely to be this: if Samson *affected* his mistress's *wit*, then he must have admired it and, as a lover, found it lovable and therefore, in view of what has been said about *green, green*; but a *green wit* is a childish one (drawing on a sense of *green* also used by Berowne at I.1.97) and hardly to be admired after all. Such a jest, anatomized, is a dead thing; on stage, spoken with energy, it is lively enough.

88   *maculate* impure

90.   *Define* explain yourself

93   *pathetical* touching

96   *blushing.* Q and F's odd spelling, 'blush-in' (which might be authorial), draws attention to a secondary sense in the line: (1) 'blushing cheeks are bred by faults'; (2) 'a blush is bred in the cheeks by faults'.

101   *native she doth owe* she owns naturally. The conclusion of Mote's song only makes sense if he is beginning to imply that Jaquenetta's *white and red* (lines 94 and 102–3) are not so much *native* as taken out of cosmetic jars. If a woman's face is plastered with ceruse and rouge, blushing and pallor cannot be seen. This is the first of a number of disparaging references to cosmetics in the play.

102–3 *dangerous rhyme . . . against the reason of white and red* poem warning of the dangers involved in trusting *white and red*. Like Berowne at I.1.99, Mote is alluding to the phrase 'neither rhyme nor reason'

104–5   *ballad ... of the King and the Beggar*. The closest
approximation we have to this old popular song is the
literary reworking of it published in 1612 and collected
in Percy's *Reliques* (1765) under the title 'King Cophetua and the Beggarmaid'. Armado gives the essentials
of the couple's relationship at IV.1.67–84.

108–9   *it would neither serve for the writing nor the tune* both
the text and the tune would be found unacceptable by
contemporary standards

111   *digression* lapse from propriety

113   *rational hind* intelligent yokel

114–15   *To be whipped – and yet a better love than my master.*
Jaquenetta is no better than a whore (prostitutes were
punished by whipping in the sixteenth century); but
even so she deserves a better lover than Armado.

117   *light* (1) the opposite of *heavy* (line 116); (2) wanton.
Katharine exploits the same ambiguity at V.2.14–15.

122   *suffer him to.* From Q; F's 'let him' is distinctly inferior, but differs enough from Q to suggest that it is
not the work of the F compositor.

123   *penance.* Either Dull is trying to say 'pleasance' or he,
like Costard with *prosperity* (I.1.300), is innocently
using a word which means the opposite of what he
thinks it means.
  'a he (a common Elizabethan form of the pronoun)

124–5   *allowed for the dey-woman* approved to serve as dairymaid

129   *lodge.* Presumably a hunting-lodge; but possibly a
gate-house at the entrance to the park – a nicely
ambiguous trysting-place in that, by using it, Armado
would just about keep his promise to stay in Navarre's
rural academy and would also just about escape the
jurisdiction of the academic *schedule*, with its strict
rules against seeing women (he has, after all, no reason
to believe that they have been relaxed), in a kind of
geographical equivocation.

130   *hereby* near here

134 *With that face?* A slang sarcasm roughly equivalent to 'You don't say so!'

139 DULL. Q and F both have '*Clo.*' It has been suggested that *Come, Jaquenetta, away!* is, in fact, Costard's line, and that *Come* is an interruption of her exchange with Armado. This view finds further support in the '*Exit.*' marked for Dull at line 125 in F. However, since both Q and F have '*Exeunt.*' at line 139 and since neither Armado, Costard, nor Mote can accompany Jaquenetta off stage here (because they all speak within the next dozen lines), the suggestion is not entirely persuasive. The most likely explanation for the confusion is as follows: the Q compositor misread a manuscript '*Co.*' at line 139 as '*Clo.*' (capital 'C' sometimes resembles 'Cl' and the compositor had a series of '*Clo.*' prefixes coming up which would encourage him to misread) and therefore deprived the constable of his line; then the annotator, coming upon what looked like an exit because of the dialogue (*Fare you well* at line 125) and finding no more lines for Dull because of the Q compositor's mistake, added the '*Exit.*' which appears in F. If this explanation is correct, F can be ignored and the Q attribution of line 139 changed from Costard to Dull. This produces a neater sequence of exits than can be derived from F. It also makes Dull's *Fare you well* more than a routine parting comment: knowing the rules about scholars and women (he has just taken Costard to the King), the constable draws Jaquenetta away, but Armado prevents him and begins to woo; only at line 139, when the braggart has finished, can Dull take her off stage, which he does with *Come, Jaquenetta, away!*

140 *Villain* (1) peasant; (2) rascal

142-3 *on a full stomach* (with a quibble on the sense 'courageously')

145 *fellows* servants

151 *fast and loose* not playing fairly

153–4   *desolation* (another malapropism)
158   *words*. Dr Johnson's suggested emendation, 'wards' (in
        the sense 'prison-cells'), draws attention to a pun which
        may or may not be conscious on Costard's part.
161   *affect* love
163   *be forsworn* break my oath
164   *argument* evidence, proof
166   *familiar* attendant evil spirit
168   *Solomon so seduced*. On Solomon's love of 'outlandish
        women', his sensuality, and his huge harem, see 3 (or
        1) Kings 11.1–8, the so-called Song of Solomon, and
        the apocryphal book Sirach.
169   *butt-shaft* unbarbed arrow (often assigned to Cupid,
        probably because, being the kind of arrow used in
        field exercises, it is appropriate to his youth)
171   *The first and second cause*. It was widely held that there
        were two provocations or 'causes' which would incite a
        gentleman to fight a duel. They are summarized in Sir
        William Segar's *The Book of Honour and Arms* (1590):
        'I say then that the causes of all quarrel whereupon it
        behoveth to use the trial of arms may be reduced into
        two: ... whensoever one man doth accuse another of
        such a crime as meriteth death, in that case the combat
        ought to be granted. The second cause of combat is
        honour, because, among persons of reputation, honour
        is preferred above life.' Armado means that Cupid
        will not fight like a gentleman, according to the rules.
172   *passado* a forward thrust with the sword, one foot
        being advanced at the same time
        duello code of duelling
174–5   *Adieu, valour; rust, rapier; be still, drum*. Compare
        Othello's farewell to arms (III.3.344–54), one of sev-
        eral points of contact between the two braggart sol-
        diers.
175   *manager* employer, user
176   *extemporal god of rhyme* god of impromptu poetry
177   *turn sonnet* become a sonnet·writer. Note that in the

127

renaissance any short poem not self-evidently a song
might – especially if its subject was love – be called a
sonnet; the notion that a *sonnet* must have fourteen
lines is a modern one.

178   *folio* (large format)

II.1   (stage direction) *Boyet* (pronounced 'boy-yet')

1   *summon up your dearest spirits* collect yourself (with
playful reference to the idea of conjuring devils)

3   *embassy* message

5   *inheritor* one who has inherited, possessor

6   *owe* own

7   *Navarre* (that is, the King of Navarre)
the plea that which is claimed

9–10   *dear ... dear* precious ... costly (because grown so
scarce)

11   *did starve the general world beside* withheld grace from
all the world apart from you

16   *uttered* (1) spoken; (2) offered for sale (as in *Romeo
and Juliet*, V.1.67–8: 'Such mortal drugs I have. But
Mantua's law | Is death to any he that utters them')
chapmen traders (continuing the double sense of
uttered)

17   *tell* (1) describe; (2) count up

18   *counted* accounted (but with a hint of the second sense
of *tell*)

20   *task the tasker* (1) chastise him who has been setting
tasks (as Boyet did in lines 1–12); (2) set a task for one
who sets tasks. The Princess suggests that she will
now, after a light rebuke (lines 13–19), really castigate
Boyet; but sense 1 then softens into sense 2.

21   *You ... fame.* The redundant '*Prin.*' which heads this
line in F may mark the point at which Act II began in
performance.

23   *painful* (1) careful; (2) full of bodily discomfort

25   *to's* to us

28   *Bold of your worthiness* confident of your worth

29   *best-moving fair solicitor* most elegantly persuasive
      petitioner

32   *Importunes* (accented on the second syllable)

36   *All pride is willing pride, and yours is so.* Boyet offers
      his pride and willingness as a pair of virtues. The
      Princess wittily interprets his *Proud* in terms of the
      vice *pride*, and points out that since no one is forced to
      be *Proud* then it goes without saying that his *pride is
      willing.*

42   *solemnizèd* (with an accent on the second syllable)

44   *sovereign parts* outstanding qualities. The reading is
      F's. The two best explanations of Q's 'soueraigne peere-
      lsse' are these: (1) 'pertes' (that is, *parts*) stood in the
      manuscript but it was misread as 'perles' ('pearls') and
      printed in the drawn-out Q spelling; (2) 'peerelsse' is
      Q's misprint for 'peerelesse' which stood in the manu-
      script as a replacement for 'soueraigne' (deleted be-
      cause it sounded like a challenge to the King) – that is,
      the compositor, confused by the revision, printed both
      adjectives instead of one and left out the noun. If the
      first explanation is correct, F's reading can be accepted
      gladly; if the second, F might as well be followed,
      because it makes as much sense as any editor's guess
      could. For suggested emendations see collations list 3.

45   *arts* intellectual accomplishments

46   *Nothing becomes him ill that he would well* anything he
      wants to do well he does well and looks admirable for it

47   *soil* sullying mark

49–51 *a sharp wit ... within his power.* Longaville's flawed
      will makes him *still* ('constantly') use the cutting *edge*
      of his *wit* ('intelligence') against anyone in range.

57   *Of* by

58–60 *Most power to do most harm ... had no wit.* Dumaine
      has the power to do *harm* unwittingly, being so inno-
      cently good, a dangerous state of affairs when it is
      realized that he is also clever enough to make the *ill*

shape of an evil thing seem like the *good* shape of
a virtuous one (with a play on 'to make good' or
'improve'). Katharine then pays Dumaine a more
direct compliment, pivoting her speech on the word
shape: so goodly is he in *shape* that even if he were
not clever, which we know he is, he would *win grace*
from women or (alluding to the religious issues raised
in lines 58–9) from God to cancel out any *ill* acts
done in his goodness.

62   *much too little* far short

63   *to* compared with

66   *Berowne ... but a merrier man.* Rosaline puns on the
word 'brown' (which could sound, in Elizabethan pronunciation, rather like the 'beroon' of *Berowne*),
a colour associated with melancholy; hence
but.

68   *withal* with

69   *begets occasion* finds opportunities

72   *conceit's expositor* the explicator of an ingeniously witty
idea

74   *play truant at his tales* stray from serious matters to
listen to his stories instead

76   *voluble* fluent

79   *bedecking ornaments of praise.* The Princess is as wary
of the ladies' *praise* as she had been of Boyet's (see
lines 13–19).

80   *admittance* permission to enter

82   *competitors* partners

83   *addressed* made ready

85   *field* (the meadowland of Navarre's park)

88   *unpeopled* lacking servants

91–4   *'Fair' I give ... mine.* The Princess communicates her
displeasure by rebuffing Navarre's verse with prose.

91   *give you back again* return to you

92   *The roof of this court* (that is, the sky)

99   *by my will* (a common mild oath)

100   *will shall break it; will, and nothing else.* The Princess

takes up Navarre's *will* in the sense 'desire'. Her observation is prophetic.

104   *sworn out house-keeping* renounced hospitality

108   *To teach a teacher.* The King has made himself an academic. Compare *to task the tasker* (line 20).

110   *suddenly* immediately

114–28   *Lady, I will commend you . . . I cannot stay thanksgiving.* Q prints these lines after line 179 and has the following exchange after line 113:

> *Berowne.* Did not I dance with you in *Brabant* once?
> *Kather.* Did not I dance with you in *Brabant* once?
> *Ber.* I know you did.
> *Kath.* How needles was it then to aske the question?
> *Ber.* You must not be so quicke.
> *Kath.* Tis long of you that spur me with such questions.
> *Ber.* Your wit's too hot, it speedes too fast, twill tire.
> *Kath.* Not till it leaue the rider in the mire.
> *Ber.* What time a day?
> *Kath.* The houre that fooles should aske.
> *Ber.* Now faire befall your maske.
> *Kath.* Faire fall the face it couers.
> *Ber.* And send you manie louers.
> *Kath.* Amen, so you be none.
> *Ber.* Nay then will I be gon.

F follows Q in printing this after line 113, but it attributes all Katharine's lines to Rosaline. This edition is the first to alter Q and F by reorganization and excision. The adjustment is justified in the Account of the Text, pages 243–4. Berowne's exchange with Rosaline parallels that between Armado and the uncooperative Jaquenetta in the previous scene.

119   *fool* poor thing (rather than the restricted modern sense 'idiot')

121   *let it blood* bleed it. The phrase has two ways of mean-

ing one thing: either 'let its blood out' ('it' being an old form of the possessive, as in *King Lear*, I.4.211–12, 'The hedge-sparrow fed the cuckoo so long | That it's had it head bit off by it young'), or 'make it bleed' ('to blood' being a now rare verb meaning 'to cause blood to flow from'). Bloodletting was a common medical practice in the sixteenth century.

123   *physic* knowledge of medicine

124   *prick't with your eye* use your eye (the *ay* of line 123) to bleed my heart

125   *Non point, with my knife*. Rosaline will 'by no means' (the French sense of *Non point*) use her *eye* to *prick* Berowne's heart, for her *eye* has 'no point'; she will use her *knife* instead. The bilingual pun worked for Shakespeare's audience because French *point*, like English 'point', had a sounded final 't'. The Q and F reading, '*No poynt*', seems to draw attention to the wordplay by using English spelling with the italics appropriate to French; but a tilde (representing a final 'n') may have been lost from '*No*'. Compare V.2.277.

128   *stay thanksgiving* spare the time to thank you

129–49   *Madam, your father here ... gelded as it is*. Navarre says that, of the 200,000 crowns owed to his father by the King of France, 100,000 were never paid – though France now claims that they were – and that *part of Aquitaine* was given to his father in surety for the rest, though not in fact worth 100,000 crowns. Navarre then announces that if the King of France would pay but 100,000 crowns – half the sum outstanding – he would give up his right in *Aquitaine | And hold fair friendship with his majesty*. But France, it seems, is demanding 100,000 crowns from Navarre, rather than offering that sum to him to buy back the lost territory (*have his title live in Aquitaine*). Understandably, Navarre thinks this unreasonable.

129   *intimate* refer to, communicate

131   *entire* (accented on the first syllable)

137   *valued to the money's worth* equal in value to the money
      which it secures

147   *depart withal* give up

149   *gelded* (because part has been cut away)

155   *wrong the reputation of your name*. The comment cuts
      deep because of Navarre's obsession with *fame*.

156   *so unseeming to* thus not appearing to

157   *that which hath so faithfully been paid*. Presumably *that*
      refers to the 100,000 crowns which France claims to
      have paid to Navarre's father (line 130). But if it does,
      and if the Princess is right in saying that it has been
      paid, her father's conduct is still unreasonable, because
      he is demanding 100,000 crowns when he should be
      paying it as the other half of the debt. The only way to
      make France's conduct seem fair is to interpret *that* as
      referring either to a total of 200,000 crowns or to
      100,000 crowns, being the second instalment of the
      total, and take the *hundred thousand crowns* of line 130
      to be this second instalment, which Navarre thinks is a
      first instalment which was not paid in any case. France
      would thus be justly annoyed that Navarre kept part
      of Aquitaine despite a full repayment and would be
      entitled to ask for 100,000 crowns as payment for it
      (that being the value put upon it by Navarre's father),
      and the Princess would be properly angered that
      Navarre blames her father when he is himself to blame
      for not keeping up with his own father's finances. Of
      course, no one could grasp these ramifications in the
      theatre, and it is far from certain that Shakespeare
      worked them out himself; he was simply concerned to
      produce a hopeless diplomatic tangle which required
      the *acquittances* (line 161) to be sent for.

160   *arrest your word* seize upon your promise as security

165   *specialties* sealed contracts

168   *All liberal reason* any civilized argument

171   *Make tender of* offer

174   *As* that

178 *consort* attend

181 *Katharine*. Q's '*Rosalin*' here and the '*Katharin*' (for *Rosaline*) at line 196 have caused scholarly controversy. See the Account of the Text, pages 243–4.

183 *What* who

184 *an* if

185 *light in the light* wanton if properly perceived

189 *God's blessing on your beard!* Jesting references to a man's beard were considered very insulting.

198 *or so* or something of that kind

199 *You are welcome*. From F; Q has 'O you are welcome'. This is the first of a number of lines in Q in which the last letter of a '*Bero.*' speech prefix in Shakespeare's manuscript seems to have been printed in the text and '*Ber.*' given as the attribution.

200 *welcome to you* you are welcome to go

203 *take him at his word* (1) arrest his promise (at line 160); (2) interpret what he said literally (as at lines 91–4)

204 *grapple ... board* (as in a sea-battle when grappling irons, flung from ship to ship, bind opposed vessels together and prepare for hand-to-hand fighting)

205 *Two hot sheeps*. Katharine calls the fighting vessels *sheeps* rather than *ships* (the words sounded alike in Elizabethan English) because a sheep was a type of stupidity. *Hot* draws attention to the bawdy overtones of Boyet's *grapple* and *board*.

207 *pasture ... jest*. The *jest* presumably lies in *pasture* as a quibble on 'pastor' ('shepherd').

208 *gentle beast* (that is, *sheep*)

209 *My lips are no common, though several they be* my lips are not common pasture (or 'plentiful' or 'available to every man'), although they are private enclosed grazing land (or 'multiple' or 'parted'). An alternative punctuation – 'common though, several' – turns *though* out of the sense 'although' into 'however'. A skilful actress might be able to communicate both meanings at once, adding yet another quibble to the line.

211   *jangling* wrangling
      gentles gentlefolk

213   *book-men* scholars
      abused misapplied

215   *still rhetoric* silent oratory

218   *affected* overwhelmed by the affections (the forces supposedly conquered by the scholars)

220-21 *all his behaviours . . . his eye.* Navarre could do nothing except gaze at the Princess.

221   *thorough* through

222   *agate with your print impressed* agate engraved with an image of you. Such stones were often set in lovers' rings.

223   *his form* (that is, the Princess's *form* (or 'shape'), made a possession of the King's *heart* (and so becoming his, the *heart's*) by virtue of being *impressed* there)

224   *all impatient to speak and not see* frustrated because able only to speak to, not see, the Princess

226   *repair* resort

229   *crystal* crystal-glass. Boyet extends a common image; compare *Henry V*, II.3.51: 'Go, clear thy crystals.'

230   *Who* which
      tendering (two syllables) showing forth, offering

231   *point* direct

232   *His face's own margin did quote such amazes.* In Elizabethan books the margin often carried notes on the text. *Quote* refers to the quotations contained in such commentaries and also has the sense 'indicate' (as in 'quote a price'). The amazement on the King's face is a clear indication of and comment on his feelings about the Princess. The imagery is probably suggested to Boyet by *glassed* (with a pun on 'glossed') and *point you* (as a note in the margin, often equipped with an arrow or pointing finger, directed the Elizabethan reader to something in the text).

236   *disposed* inclined to be merry

240-44 The attribution of these lines is uncertain because Q only numbers the speakers and the naming in F is incomplete and unconvincing. This edition matches '*Lad.*', '*Lad. 2.*', and '*Lad. 3.*' of Q with their (numbered) equivalents at lines 40, 56, and 64 (where what is said declares the identity of the speaker), though it is far from certain that Shakespeare intended such a correlation.

243   *mad* high-spirited

244   *hard* difficult to outwit

III.1   (stage direction) *Enter Armado and Mote*. Q has 'Enter *Braggart* and his *Boy*', F '*Enter Broggart and Boy.* | Song'. Two interpretations of F are possible: either Mote sings, stops, is asked to *Warble, child*, and does so, singing *Concolinel* (an arrangement which interestingly anticipates *As You Like It*, II.5.1–42, where Jaques enjoys a 'stanzo' of Amiens's 'Under the greenwood tree' and then encourages him – 'Come, warble, come' – to sing another), or the Q annotator glossed the strange word *Concolinel* with the marginal comment 'Song', and the F compositor, finding this remark near the top of the scene, took it to be an addition to the Q stage direction. This edition adopts the latter explanation.

1–4   *Warble, child … Sweet air*. Shakespeare associates music with love melancholy on a number of occasions. Compare Orsino at the beginning of *Twelfth Night*, as love-sick for Olivia as is Armado for Jaquenetta: 'If music be the food of love, play on …'; or Cleopatra, when Antony is away in Rome: 'Give me some music – music, moody food | Of us that trade in love' (II.5.1–2).

3   *Concolinel*. Presumably this is the title of Mote's song. The most likely candidate is the Irish lyric '*Can cailin gheal*' (pronounced 'con colleen yal'), meaning 'Sing, maiden fair' (compare the corruption of an Irish song

136

in *Henry V*, IV.4.4). Another attractive suggestion
is that the song begins *'Quand Colinelle'*, for Mote refers shortly afterwards to a *French brawl* (lines 7–8).

5   *enlargement* freedom

      festinately quickly

8   *brawl* (a French dance – the *branle* – or its music)

9   *Brawling* quarrelling noisily

10   *jig off a tune* sing the tune of some jig or some jig-
like tune

11   *canary to it with your feet* dance to it in the style of the
canary (a lively Spanish dance supposed to have origi-
nated among the natives of the Canary Isles)

15–18 *your hat ... rabbit on a spit.* Mote describes the
conventional postures of the Elizabethan melancholic.
Compare John Heminges's description of the dramatist
Ford: 'Deep in a dump Jack Ford alone was got |
With folded arms and melancholy hat' ('Elegy on
Randolph's Finger', lines 81–2).

16   *penthouse-like* like a projecting roof

17   *thin-belly* (with an unpadded lower portion, to emphasize the lover's slender waist)

18   *after* in the style of

19   *the old painting.* It is most unlikely that Mote is thinking of a specific painting. Compare his words with
Borachio's in *Much Ado About Nothing*, III.3.129–33,
describing the effect of fashion on young gallants:
'sometimes fashioning them like Pharaoh's soldiers in
the reechy painting, sometime like god Bel's priests in
the old church-window, sometime like the shaven
Hercules in the smirched worm-eaten tapestry'.

20   *snip* snatch

      compliments gentlemanly manners

20–21 *humours* characterful moods

21   *nice* coy

22   *of note* of distinction

22–3   *do you note me?* Q has 'do you note men' and F reprints
Q. It is possible that Mote turns to the 'men' in the

audience here, like Leontes in *The Winter's Tale*, I.2.192–6.

23   *affected to these* fond of these (*compliments* and *humours*)

25   *penny*. Armado's word *purchased* guides this emendation of the Q and F 'penne' (a reading which, absurdly, has been used to support the identification of Mote with Thomas Nashe, a writer who certainly used a 'pen').

27   *The hobby-horse is forgot*. Mote mockingly takes Armado's sighs as part of a popular adage or song. In *Hamlet*, III.2.144, the Prince gives the complete line: 'For O, for O, the hobby-horse is forgot!'

28–30   *hobby-horse ... colt ... hackney*. All three words had the slang sense 'whore'.

45–6   *And three times as much more, and yet nothing at all*. (1) Armado loves three times as much as Mote has said, but his love is still nothing of note; (2) Mote could say three times as much about Armado's love, but it would still be just rhetorical 'division' and not worth the hearing.

49   *sympathized* matched

49–53   *a horse to be ambassador for an ass ... slow-gaited*. Now obscure: perhaps Costard is *a horse* because he is intelligent, strong, but silent, while the *ass* is stupid and brays; perhaps the jokes are bawdy. Compare the Fool's quip in *King Lear*, I.5.33.

58   *Minime* (Latin) by no means

61   *smoke* (often applied to language by Shakespeare; see, for example, *The Rape of Lucrece*, line 1027: 'This helpless smoke of words')

63   *Thump then, and I flee*. Either 'bang, off I go' or 'say "bang" and I'll go' (leaving Armado to make the appropriate noise).

65   *welkin* sky

66   *gives thee place* gives way to you

68   *Here's a costard broken in a shin*. Costard has indeed cut his shin (see lines 114–15); Mote is amused that

138

Costard should be *broken in a shin* because 'a costard'
was slang for 'a head' (which has no shin); he may also
have in mind Armado's success over Costard in love,
for to be *broken in a shin* was (on the basis of *Romeo
and Juliet*, I.2.52) to be disappointed by a mistress and
left seeking another.

69   *l'envoy* explanation. See Armado's fuller account in
        lines 80–81.

70   *No egma, no riddle, no l'envoy.* Costard takes Armado's
        enigma, *riddle*, and *l'envoy* as suggested remedies for
        the broken shin, which the braggart has apparently not
        yet noticed. Conceivably he confuses *enigma* or *egma*
        with 'enema', and thinks that *l'envoy* has something to
        do with the verb 'to lenify' (that is, 'to purge gently').
        Costard returns to *purgation* at lines 124–5.

70–71   *salve in the mail.* Not only will Costard eschew
        Armado's supposed remedies, he will avoid 'ointment
        in the medicine pouch (*mail*)'.

71   *plantain* (herb used for healing cuts and bruises)

73   *silly* naive

74   *spleen* laughter (which was thought to be produced by
        the spleen)

75   *ridiculous smiling* (1) smiling in ridicule; (2) absurd
        smiling. Armado intends only the first sense.

76   *inconsiderate* unthinking person
        salve for l'envoy. Costard's rustic pronunciation of *salve*
        (line 70) has evidently led Armado to interpret it as
        Latin for 'greetings', just the opposite of *l'envoy* in the
        sense 'parting words'.

81   *precedence* preceding matter
        hath tofore been sain has been said previously

83–5   *The fox, the ape . . . the moral.* A 'moral' is 'a hidden
        sense' or 'words with some concealed meaning'. The
        couplet has been supposed to contain a topical allusion,
        the evidence being that Spenser's political allegory,
        'Mother Hubberd's Tale', includes a fox and an
        ape. But it seems more likely that the two authors are

close here not because of a common satirical purpose but because both draw on the tradition of the beast fable. Mote probably finds the hidden sense of the *moral* when he detects the ambiguity of *at odds* ('an uneven number' as well as 'quarrelling'). See the note to IV.3.209.

84   *still* constantly

90   *stayed* ended

        adding four becoming the fourth

97   *l'envoy, ending in the goose* (because the French for 'goose' is *oie*)

99   *sold him a bargain, a goose.* Costard quibbles on the slang sense of 'selling a goose': 'making a fool of'.

103   *argument* topic for discussion, discussion (rather than 'wrangle')

108   *he ended the market* (alluding to the proverb 'Three women and a goose make a market')

109   *how* in what sense. Armado has still not realized that Costard is Mote's *costard* (line 68), but the clown thinks that he has and takes the question to mean 'How did it happen that Costard cut his leg?'

111   *sensibly* (1) with common sense (rather than with round-about wit); (2) with warmth, with feeling

112   *Thou hast no feeling of it.* Costard denies that the page can explain *sensibly* because only he 'senses' or 'feels' the cut.

117   *matter* pus

118   *enfranchise* release from confinement

119–20   *Frances ... goose.* Costard uses another slang sense of *goose* here, 'whore'. *Frances*, a type name for a prostitute, prompts him.

124–5   *be my purgation and let me loose.* Costard quibbles on Armado's *bound*, meaning both 'in bonds' and 'consti-pated'.

128   *significant* (that which signifies; here Armado's letter)

130   *ward* guard

132   *the sequel* (that which follows; with a last glance at the *l'envoy* joke)

133   *incony* fine (a vogue word in the late sixteenth century, quickly dropped from the language)

           jew (more likely to be a diminutive of 'jewel' or 'juvenal' than 'Jew')

135   *three farthings.* A coin of this value (three quarters of a penny) was issued several times in the sixteenth century.

136   *inkle* linen tape

138   *carries it* wins out, clinches the bargain

139   *French crown* (1) a coin; (2) the bald head caused by syphilis, the French pox

139–40 *out of this word* using any other word

142   *carnation* flesh-coloured

165   *counsel* (something which informs; here Berowne's letter)

           guerdon. It may be significant that in lines 166 and 168 Q and F replace this spelling by 'Gardon'. Both forms are correct, but in different ways: 'guerdon' is true to the word's French origin; 'gardon' indicates its received Elizabethan pronunciation. One can imagine Shakespeare imagining Berowne using the word with educated fastidiousness and Costard trying it out phonetically, the respective spellings finding their way into Q and from Q into F.

168   *in print* most exactly (or 'honestly')

170–75 *And I . . . magnificent.* Q prints this as three very long, irregular lines of 'verse'. The F lineation is closer to that printed in this edition.

172   *beadle* parish officer responsible for whipping offenders

           humorous moody

173   *critic* (the first recorded use of this word as a noun)

174   *pedant* schoolmaster. Holofernes is so called at V.2. 533 and 538.

176   *wimpled* wearing a blindfold

176   *purblind* quite blind. The word could also mean 'part-blind', but that does not fit the renaissance Cupid.

177   *Signor Junior*. Berowne gives Cupid a title which his years hardly merit, drawing attention to a quibbling paradox: 'senior junior'.

       Dan (a variant form of 'Don', the contraction of *dominus*, 'master')

178–80 *lord of folded arms ... malcontents*. See Mote's description of the melancholy lover (lines 15–18).

179   *sovereign* (three syllables)

181   *plackets* slits in petticoats

       codpieces pouches on the front of men's breeches designed to conceal and advertise the genitals

182   *imperator* absolute ruler

183   *paritors* officers who summoned offenders to the ecclesiastical courts

184   *corporal of his field* field officer to Cupid the *general*. *Corporal* was a higher rank in the sixteenth century than it is today.

185   *wear his colours like a tumbler's hoop*. Berowne imagines himself decorated with Cupid's ribbons and silks like an acrobat's hoop.

187   *German clock*. Elaborate in construction and highly ornamental (often including automatic figures of persons or animals), German clocks made attractive objects but unreliable timepieces.

188   *frame* order

191   *perjured* (by breaking the oath sworn in I.1)

193   *A whitely wanton with a velvet brow*. Q and F make perfect sense: Rosaline is pale of complexion with a soft-skinned forehead. But because Berowne declares at IV.3.263 that Rosaline's *brow* is *black*, the emendation 'wightly' ('mannish') has been proposed. It seems better to assume a Shakespearian inconsistency and retain *whitely*.

195   *do the deed* engage in sexual intercourse

196   *Though Argus were her eunuch and her guard!* Juno

jealously put Io, loved by her husband Jove, in the
custody of the hundred-eyed monster Argus.

197   *watch* stay awake at night

201   *and groan.* Neither Q nor F has *and*, but some such
          word seems metrically desirable.

202   *Joan.* In using this type name for a woman of the
          lower classes (compare *greasy Joan doth keel the pot*,
          V.2.909, 918) and contrasting it with *my lady* (not
          Rosaline but any noblewoman), Berowne recalls the
          saying 'Joan's as good as my lady.'

IV.1.1–2   *Was that the King ... hill.* She cannot get him out
          of her mind.

2   *steep-up rising.* F alters Q's 'steepe vp rising' to 'steepe
          vprising'; but compare 'steep-up heavenly hill' (Sonnet
          7), 'steep-up hill' ('Fair was the morn' in *The Passionate
          Pilgrim*, 1599), 'steep-down gulfs of liquid fire'
          (*Othello*, V.2.278).

3   FIRST LORD. Q has '*Forr.*'; F '*Boy.*'. See the Account
          of the Text, pages 245–6.

4   *mounting* (1) rising (up the *hill*); (2) aspiring. There is
          probably a quibble on 'mountain', glancing back to
          hill, a jest which anticipates the disputed translation of
          mons at V.1.78–80.

10   *stand* hunter's station (often a specially erected struc-
          ture)
          fairest. The Forester means 'most favourable', but the
          Princess playfully misunderstands him.

16   *never paint me now!* Compare II.1.13–19, where the
          Princess rebukes Boyet for using the *painted flourish*
          of his *praise* to conceal (as though with cosmetic *paint*)
          the flaws in her beauty.

17   *brow* forehead

18   *glass* mirror

20   *inherit* possess

21   *by merit* (1) by its innate worth (which is what the

Forester means at line 20); (2) by giving a reward (as in *Richard II*, I.3.156–8: 'A dearer merit ... Have I deservèd at your highness' hands'); (3) by good works (hence *be saved* and *heresy*, lines 21–2; Elizabethan Protestants held that faith, not good works, won the soul salvation)

22 *in fair* in respect of beauty

these days (of religious dissension)

30 *out of question* undoubtedly

31–5 *Glory grows guilty ... no ill.* See the Introduction, pages 17–18.

31 *Glory* desire for glory

36–8 *Do not curst wives ... their lords?* don't shrewish wives wilfully follow *the working of the heart* precisely *for praise' sake* when they boss their husbands about?

41 *commonwealth* common people

42 *dig-you-den* give you good evening

47 *The thickest and the tallest.* The Princess carries on with Costard's list, but her joke recoils in the clown's next speech.

58–9 *you can carve – | Break up. Carve* means 'make courtly gestures' (as at V.2.323); but *Break up*, a term originally used in deer butchery, draws out the more mundane sense, 'cut up meat'.

59 *capon* (perhaps with a playful reference to the French *poulet*, meaning both 'fowl' and 'love-letter')

60 *is mistook* has been wrongly delivered

62 *Break the neck of the wax* break the seal on the letter (*neck* gives perhaps another hint of the *capon*)

63–4 *infallible* incontrovertible

67 *illustrate* (accented on the second syllable) illustrious

68–9 *King Cophetua ... Zenelophon.* This is Armado's *ballad ... of the King and the Beggar* (I.2.104–5). *indubitate* undoubted

70 *Veni, vidi, vici.* The famous slogan displayed by Julius Caesar in his Pontic triumph (see Suetonius, *Divus*

144

Julius 37.2); Armado translates it at lines 71–2, though substituting *he* for 'I'.

anatomize. Some editors keep the Q and F 'annothanize', suspecting it to be Armado's pseudo-Latin for 'annotate'.

vulgar vernacular

71 *videlicet.* Q and F '*videliset*' reflects Elizabethan pronunciation of Latin.

71,72 *see ... see.* Editors either alter this (the reading of Q and F) to 'saw' or they blame Armado for mistranslating *vidi*. But in Elizabethan English 'see' was perfectly acceptable as a third-person singular past-tense verb.

78 *catastrophe* conclusion

83 *tittles* jots, specks

84 *expecting* awaiting (but with a hint of compulsion, as in 'England expects that every man will do his duty')

87 *dearest design of industry* most precious intent of my laborious gallantry

89 *the Nemean lion.* Hercules killed the ferocious lion of Nemea (in Greece) as the first of his twelve labours.

92 *from forage will incline to play* will turn from preying to playing

94 *repasture* food (that which provides a repast)

95 *indited* wrote

96 *vane* weathervane

98 *going o'er* (1) reading ; (2) climbing over (taking *style* as 'stile')

erewhile recently

99 *keeps* stays

100 *phantasime* one full of fantasies

Monarcho (apparently the nickname of a notably vainglorious hanger-on at Elizabeth's court)

101 *To* for

107 *mistaken* taken to the wrong person

108 *put up* put away

'twill be thine another day (proverbial) your turn will come

145

109   *suitor ... suitor*. The Q and F spelling, 'shooter', draws attention to an ambiguity which allows Rosaline to gloss *suitor* as *she that bears the bow* (line 110).

110   *continent* (something which contains)

111   *put off* evaded

113   *horns ... miscarry* there is a scarcity of horns (an allusion to the fanciful notion that men with unfaithful wives grew horns on the forehead)

115   *deer* (with a pun on 'dear': one of the commonest quibbles in Elizabethan drama)

118   *strikes at the brow* (1) takes good aim (*brow* meaning 'brow-antler', the best mark for an archer shooting at a stag); (2) calls you cuckold

119   *hit lower* (than Boyet as the horned deer. *Hit* has such strong bawdy overtones throughout the exchange that it is clear what is meant by *lower*.)
    hit her understood her correctly

120   *come upon* approach (probably with a bawdy quibble)

121   *King Pepin* (Charlemagne's father, who died in A.D. 768)

122   *the hit it* (the title of a popular song and dance)

124   *Queen Guinevere* (who lived long before Pepin. Boyet names a woman famous for cuckolding her husband, King Arthur, to back up lines 112–13.)

130   *fit it* make words, metre, and subject-matter harmonize (with a bawdy quibble)

131–3   *A mark ... may be*. Maria uses *mark* in the sense 'a shot at a target'. But 'note' (*mark*) the word *mark*, says Boyet, turning it in the following line to the bawdy sense 'pudendum', and elaborating his joke by putting a *prick* (both the 'bull's-eye' of the target and the obvious bawdy meaning) in the *mark* for it *to mete at* (for the prick 'to aim at').

134   *Wide o'the bow hand* shooting too far to the side of the *hand* holding the *bow* (usually the left)
    out (1) out of practice; (2) inaccurate

135   *clout* the *mark* in archery, consisting of a white patch

of cloth in the middle of the target held by the *pin* (see line 137). Costard continues the bawdry.

136 *An if my hand be out, then belike your hand is in* if my hand is *out* (as an archer and in sexual matters), doubtless yours is not. Boyet addresses Maria.

137 *Then will she get the upshoot by cleaving the pin* (1) in that case she will shoot the best shot of the archery competition (with a glance at 'get the better of you, Boyet, in argument') by splitting the *pin* at the centre of the target; (2) in that case she will cause her lover to ejaculate by embracing his *pin* (the *prick* of line 133)

138 *you talk greasily* your badinage is gross

139 *She's too hard for you at pricks ... Challenge her to bowl* (1) since she is better than you at hitting archery targets (again with a hint of 'better than you in argument'), challenge her to a game of bowls instead; (2) since you find her sexually impenetrable, invite masturbation. Costard is unabashed by Maria's rebuke.

140 *rubbing*. In bowls, the 'rub' is an obstacle between the bowler and the jack; hence Hamlet's 'there's the rub' (III.1.65). Boyet means that Maria's wit keeps creating difficulties for him, but he also maintains sense 2 of the previous line.

Good night. Boyet's 'farewell' sets up his joke about the *owl* (a bird associated with *night*).

owl. Maria is an *owl* because she has 'taken offence' ('taken owl' in the proverbial phrase) at the men's bawdry. But she is also an *owl* because the word sounded like ''ole' in the sixteenth century (hence the rhyme with *bowl* in the preceding line) and ''ole' bears here its slang sexual sense.

143 *incony*. See the note to III.1.133.

144 *obscenely*. Whatever Costard means to say here, *obscenely* does very well.

145-8 *Armado ... And his page*. It may be that these characters appeared in an early draft of IV.1 and that Shakespeare forgot to cut Costard's reference to them when

147

composing the manuscript from which Q was set. Alternatively, lines 141–4 can be read as a recapitulation of the stage action and lines 145–9 as a report of behind-the-scenes activity; Armado and Mote do not appear between III.1.132 and V.1.29, and Costard's words usefully remind us of them.

145   *dainty* elegant

149   *pathetical nit* touching little fellow

       (stage direction) *Shout within.* Q has 'Shoot within' and F follows, but this probably reflects Shakespeare's spelling of *Shout*. Bows (which shoot quietly), not guns, have been mentioned as the weaponry of the hunters; and Costard's cry *Sola, sola* (line 150), the proper one for a hunt, seems best interpreted as a response to a cry off stage.

IV.2   (stage direction) *Holofernes.* The pedant's name may derive from that of Gargantua's tutor in Rabelais, but it is more likely to be biblical in inspiration. In the apocryphal Book of Judith, the heroine saves Jerusalem from conquest by decapitating Holofernes, the general of Nebuchadnezzar's army. This Holofernes was a familiar 'tyrant' in medieval Miracle plays.

1   *reverend* worthy of respect

1–2   *in the testimony of a good conscience* with the warrant of a clear conscience. Nathaniel alludes to 2 Corinthians 1.12: 'For our rejoicing is this, the testimony of our conscience, that in simplicity and godly pureness, not with fleshly wisdom, but by the grace of God, we have had our conversation in the world, and most of all to youwards.'

3–4, 5   *in sanguis, blood . . . caelum.* These are emendations of Q and F, which have 'sanguis in blood' and '*Celo*'. The former (as the structure of the speech shows) must be a compositor's failure of memory between manuscript and setting stick, and the latter a misreading of a manuscript '*Celū*' ('e' was acceptable in renaissance Latin for 'ae', and the tilde over the 'u' stood for 'm').

3–4   *in ... blood* in full vigour

4   *pomewater* (a variety of apple)
       who which

4, 6   *now ... anon* at one moment ... at the next

6   *crab* crab-apple

9   *at the least* to make the lowest estimate. Presumably Nathaniel means to imply that Holofernes's verbal gifts, exceeding those of a mere scholar, are those of a veritable poet.

10   *buck of the first head* male deer in its fifth year of life (not, as Holofernes seems to think, a mature beast), having its first full set of antlers

11   *Sir* (the appropriate courtesy title for a priest)
       haud credo I do not believe it

12   *an awd grey doe* (emending Q and F's 'a *haud credo*' to show the primary sense of the words for Dull)
       pricket buck in its second year of life

13   *intimation* intrusion

14   *insinuation* beginning

15   *facere* to make
       replication unfolding, revealing

18   *unconfirmed* inexperienced

19   *insert again* substitute
       my haud credo. If Dull thinks Holofernes's *haud credo* means *awd grey doe*, the misunderstanding also works the other way.

22   *Twice-sod* soaked twice (referring to Dull's double error over *haud credo*)
       Bis coctus (a common tag) cooked twice

27   *sensible* responsive

29   *fructify* bear fruit

31   *a patch set on learning* (1) a blot on the arts (*a patch* on learning's face or garb); (2) a dolt (*patch*) put to his books; (3) a dolt trying to be learned. It is not clear which sense is primary.

32   *omne bene* all's well
     being of an old father's mind agreeing as I do with one
     of the church fathers (such as St Augustine)

33   *Many can brook the weather that love not the wind.* Far
     from being the wise saw of one of the church fathers,
     this is a common proverb meaning 'one can and must
     endure what one doesn't like'. Nathaniel's conclusion
     is trite and inconsequential.

36   *Dictynna . . . Dictynna.* Nathaniel glosses correctly at
     line 39. The term was not much used. The Q reading
     (reprinted in F), '*Dictisima*', presumably derives from
     a misreading of Shakespeare's manuscript – 'y' being
     taken as 'i' plus 'long s', 'nn' as 'im'.

38   *Dictima.* Some editors emend to 'Dictynna', but there
     are no palaeographical grounds for this and it makes
     good theatrical sense for Dull to be baffled by Holo-
     fernes's Latin.

39   *Phoebe* the moon (sister of Phoebus, the sun)

40   *no more* no older

41   *raught* reached

42   *Th'allusion holds in the exchange* the riddle is the same
     with *Adam* as it is with *Cain*

43, 47   *collusion . . . pollution.* Dull's blunders comment on the
     linguistic habits of Holofernes and Nathaniel. A *collu-
     sion* is a 'verbal trick', which can be used, as it is here,
     to create and celebrate *collusion* ('knowing conspiracy').
     As an obscure foreign word used in preference to a
     plain native term, *Dictynna* is an excellent example of
     linguistic *pollution* in action.

45   *comfort* have pity on, console

53   *Perge* (two syllables; hard 'g') proceed

54   *abrogate scurrility* avoid bawdry. Nathaniel is no doubt
     alarmed by the potential of *pricket*.

55   *something affect the letter* employ alliteration to some
     degree

56   *argues* demonstrates

57   *preyful* desirous of prey

150

58   *Some say a sore* some people say that the *pricket* was a
      sore, a buck in its fourth year (perhaps alluding to the
      haud credo controversy)
      but not a sore . . . shooting but it was not a *sore* until the
      Princess's arrows hurt it (*made it sore*)

59   *The dogs did yell; put 'L' to sore, then sorel jumps from
      thicket* the dogs bayed, and when the sore was exposed
      to the alarming noise ('L' being pronounced with a
      prosthetic 'y' by the Elizabethans, so that it sounded
      like *yell*) it jumped from the thicket as a *sorel* (another
      kind of deer, a buck in its third year). Despite Nath-
      aniel's warning at lines 53–4, there may be bawdy
      overtones in the putting of the 'ell' to the 'Sore' (Q
      spelling).

60   *Or pricket, sore, or else sorel, the people fall a-hooting*
      whatever kind of deer the prey actually is, when the
      people see it flushed from cover they cry and shout
      (*Sola, sola!*, presumably). 'Pricket-sore' and 'Sorell'
      (Q punctuation and spelling) may be bawdy.
      Or either

61   *If sore be sore, then 'L' to sore makes fifty sores o'sorel* if
      it's a sore which is hurt, then adding 'L' to the wounded
      deer's name makes *fifty sores* (because 'L' is the Roman
      numeral for 50) as well as *sorel*. Some editors read
      'fifty sores – O, sorel', which is supported by F ('*O
      sorell*') and is compatible with Q's 'o sorell' (for every-
      where else in Q 'a', not 'o', is the abbreviated form of
      'of'); but the next line seems to demand the text as
      printed here.

62   *by adding but one more 'L'*. The joke is clearer in Q and
      F, where *sorel* is spelled with a double 'l'.

64   *If a talent be a claw*. Dull is right: 'talent' is a now
      obsolete form of 'talon'.
      claws him flatters himself, preens

66   HOLOFERNES. The first of a number of misattributions
      involving the curate and pedant in Q and F. (Both
      texts here read '*Nath.*'.) As Gary Taylor has pointed

out to me, the only way to make sense of this confusion, and to explain the shift towards occupational
rather than personal naming for the two characters
which follows it, is to assume that as Shakespeare
composed the second half of his play he became
muddled about the clergyman's and schoolmaster's
names and, to make things easier for himself, used
occupational names instead.

69   *ventricle* section of the brain. The memory was usually
located towards the back of the head, where the spinal
marrow enters the brain.

70   *pia mater* (fine membrane covering the brain)

70–71   *delivered upon the mellowing of occasion* born when the
time is ripe

75   *under you* under your tutelage. The bawdy overtones
of the phrase are brought out in Holofernes's reply
(particularly in *put it to them*, line 79), though both
speakers seem unaware of them.

77   *Mehercle!* by Hercules!

79   *vir sapit qui pauca loquitur* it's a wise man who says
little (a common apophthegm. Holofernes would do
well to mark his own words.)

81   *Parson*. The Q and F 'Person' is just a spelling variant
of *Parson* (which both texts read at line 89). However,
as Holofernes's joke in the next line shows, the spelling
in this instance reflects Jaquenetta's rustic pronunciation, and it may thus be Shakespearian in origin. There
is presumably a parallel between the dairymaid's entry
here *with a letter* and Costard, and the constable's *with
a letter* and Costard at I.1.178. Just as Jaquenetta
immediately greets 'M. Person' (to use the Q and
F form), so Dull asks at once for *the Duke's own
person*.

82   *quasi* as if

pierce-one. This would be much closer to *Parson* in
Elizabethan pronunciation than in our own. Seven-
teenth-century lists of homophones pair 'pierce' with

'parse', and contemporaries record the sounds 'on' and 'un' for 'one'.

84   *likest*. From F; Q's 'liklest' makes 'likeliest' (in the sense 'most like') a possible reading.

85   *hogshead* barrel (with the slang sense 'fat-head')

86   *Piercing a hogshead* broaching a barrel (with the slang sense 'getting drunk'). Q and F have 'Of persing a Hogshead' and give the speech to '*Nath.*'. Perhaps 'Of' is the last syllable of a misread manuscript '*Holof.*'.

86-7 *lustre of conceit* gleam of wit

87-8 *pearl enough for a swine* (twisting the proverb 'to cast pearls before swine')

92-3 *Fauste precor ... Ruminat* I pray thee, O Faustus, when all the cattle ruminate in the cool shade. This, the opening of Mantuan's *Eclogues*, is printed with several mistakes in Q and F. One, '*Facile*' for *Fauste*, is kept by some editors; but it is not a theatrically interesting error, and there are good palaeographical grounds for emending it (an Elizabethan manuscript 'u' could easily be read as 'ci', a short-tailed 'long s' as 'l', and 'te' as a full 'e').

94   *Mantuan*. Baptista Spagnolo Mantuanus (1447–1516), a Carmelite friar whose *Eclogues* became standard reading in Elizabethan grammar schools (hence Holofernes's interest).

96-7 *Venetia, Venetia ... pretia* Venice, Venice, only those who do not see you fail to prize you. The near-gibberish of Q and F (see collations list 4) was probably created by the Q compositor's misreading of a partly phonetic rendering of the Italian in Shakespeare's manuscript. This edition prints the proverb in the form recorded in a number of Elizabethan sources.

99   *Ut, re, sol, la, mi, fa*. Some editors have suggested that Holofernes tries to sing a scale but muddles the order of the names (*Ut* is the old name for 'doh', *sol* is 'soh'). It seems more likely that the order is correct and that

what he sings is a self-satisfied snatch of melody. Compare Edmund's 'Fa, sol, la, mi' (*King Lear*, I.2.136).

103   *a staff, a stanze*. Both mean 'a stanza'.

103–4   *Lege, domine* read, master

105–18   *If love make me . . . tongue*. This sonnet, together with the poems of Longaville and Dumaine (IV.3.58–71 and 99–118), was reprinted with slight verbal changes in *The Passionate Pilgrim* (1599), a miscellany of poems by Shakespeare and other authors.

108   *Those thoughts to me were oaks* those thoughts which seemed to me as firm as oaks
         osiers willows

109   *Study his bias leaves and makes his book thine eyes* the student turns away from his labours (with a hint of 'his eccentric course') and makes your eyes his book. Berowne's argument is similar to that used in the first scene (I.1.80–83); he expands it at IV.3.294–330.

117   *pardon love this wrong* excuse my love this fault

118   *sings heaven's praise*. Although this reading is found in Q, F, and *The Passionate Pilgrim* alike, some editors include a monosyllable such as 'in' or 'the' for metrical reasons.

119   *find not the apostrophus* ignore the marks of elision. It is difficult to see where Nathaniel could go wrong, and it may be that Holofernes is simply finding an impressive-sounding excuse to take the letter from him.

120   *supervise* look over
         canzonet song, poem

121–7   *Here are . . . you?* Q (followed by F) attributes this to 'Nath.'. The lines clearly belong to Holofernes; it may be that in the manuscript this passage began '[Sir] Nathaniel, here are . . .' and the compositor set a piece of text as speech prefix.

121   *numbers ratified* metrically correct verses

122   *caret* it is lacking

123   *Naso*. Ovid's family name happens to mean '(big) nose'.

124-5 *jerks of invention* strokes of imagination

125   *Imitari is nothing* to imitate is nothing (without *invention*)

126   *tired* attired (with saddle, reins, and other trappings)

128-9 *from one Monsieur Berowne, one of the strange Queen's lords*. Puzzling: at lines 90–91 Jaquenetta said that the letter *was given me by Costard, and sent me from Don Armado*, and nothing said between 91 and 128 could have introduced Berowne into her mind. It has been suggested that *Monsieur Berowne* was a printer's replacement for 'Don Armado', made to square the speech with what Holofernes says in lines 130–41; but Armado is no more one of the Princess's lords than Berowne. Perhaps Shakespeare became confused at this point in the draft; perhaps he wanted Jaquenetta to seem simple.

129   *strange* foreign

      Queen. On the Princess's sudden elevation in rank here and at line 137, see the Account of the Text, page 242, and the note to I.1.179.

130   *superscript* address

132   *intellect* purport (thus, contents of the letter)

134   *all desired employment* every service which you ask of me

137   *sequent* follower

138   *by the way of progression* on its way

139   *Trip and go* (from a popular song)

140-41 *Stay not thy compliment; I forgive thy duty* do not linger to make the polite farewell which you owe me

144   *Have with thee* I'll go along with you

147-8 *I do fear colourable colours*. Holofernes quibblingly inverts the stock phrase 'I fear no colours' (see *Twelfth Night*, I.5.5), meaning 'I am not afraid of battle-flags' and thus 'I am not afraid'. He claims to *fear* the *colourable* ('ambiguously plausible, each man applying a

155

convenient interpretation to them') *colours* ('excuses')
to be found in the writings of the church fathers.

150   *for the pen* as far as the penmanship, the calligraphy,
was concerned (or, perhaps, 'considering the author').
See V.2.40 and note.

152   *repast* the meal

153   *to gratify the table with a grace* to please the company
with a prayer (more wordplay: *to gratify* means 'to
grace' as well as 'to please')

155   *undertake your ben venuto* ensure your welcome

159   *the text* (probably Ecclesiastes 4.8–12)

160   *certes* (two syllables) certainly

162   *Pauca verba* few words
       gentles gentlefolk

162–3   *at their game*. In a hunt, the *game* ('sport') is to pursue
game ('game animals'). Holofernes pursues the former
sense into *recreation* (line 163).

IV.3   (stage direction) *Enter Berowne with a paper in his hand,
alone*. This follows Q and F. The last word is, strictly
speaking, superfluous, but it draws attention to the
significant movement in the scene from loneliness in
love to what Nathaniel calls *society* (IV.2.158,
IV.3.126), and to the framing effect whereby it begins
and ends with Berowne, solitary.

1–2   *The King . . . myself*. Most editors treat this as part of
Berowne's prose speech; but it is printed as verse in Q
and F. Reading poetry from his *paper*, Berowne anticipates his companions later in the scene.

2   *coursing* (probably a pun on 'cursing')

3   *pitched a toil* set a snare (in the hunt)
       toiling in a pitch struggling in the foul sticky mess
which is love. It is just possible that Berowne has *her
eye* (line 9) in mind already, and that he means that
he is struggling to disengage himself from the *two
pitch-balls* in Rosaline's face (III.1.194).

3–4   *pitch that defiles.* See Ecclesiasticus 13.1: 'Whoso
        toucheth pitch shall be defiled withal'. Like Falstaff in
        1 Henry IV, II.4.405–6 ('This pitch – as ancient writers
        do report – doth defile, so doth the company thou
        keepest'), Berowne works the text into a parody of
        Euphuism, the highly wrought prose style developed
        by John Lyly. Parody is expressive here because
        it suggests both the tangled nature of Berowne's
        feelings and the contempt he has for that entangle-
        ment.

4–5   *set thee down, sorrow.* Berowne may have in mind
        Costard's words at I.1.301–2; but *so they say the fool
        said* tells against this because Berowne heard the clown
        himself. Probably the phrase was proverbial and pro-
        verbially associated with a fool.

7   *as mad as Ajax: it kills sheep.* Mad with fury at being
        denied the armour of the dead Achilles, Ajax attacked
        a flock of sheep which he believed to be the Greek
        army.

18   *in* (1) in the same predicament as myself; (2) in love

22   *bird-bolt* blunt-headed arrow used for shooting birds

22–3   *under the left pap* (and so 'in the heart'. Compare *A
        Midsummer Night's Dream*, V.1.290–91: 'that left
        pap, | Where heart doth hop.')

27   *The night of dew that on my cheeks down flows* (1) the
        tears, plentiful as dew-drops in the night, which flow
        down my cheeks; (2) the tears which flow on my
        cheeks' (or cheek's) down (hearing an apostrophe)

36   *thou will.* Q is not ungrammatical in sixteenth-century
        terms; and F's 'thou wilt', though more acceptable to
        modern ears, is more likely an annotator's or com-
        positor's sophistication than an authorial correction.

37   *glasses* mirrors. The Princess is reflected in the King's
        tears like the mistress in Donne's 'A Valediction: Of
        Weeping'.

41   *shade* cover up

43   *in thy likeness* looking like you (the King)

45   *perjure* perjurer. Berowne's observation anticipates
      Longaville's own at line 60.

45–6 *wearing papers.* Perjurers were commonly forced to
      wear placards on their heads, setting out their offences.
      Presumably Longaville carries *papers* in his hatband.
      Compare Dumaine at line 123.

51   *triumviry* triumvirate, threesome

      corner-cap (cap with three (or four) corners, worn by
      divines, academics, and judges; hence the imagery of
      the next line)

      society sociability, fellowship

52   *The shape of Love's Tyburn.* Tyburn was a famous place
      of execution; gallows were built of three timbers.

53   *stubborn* harsh, rugged

55   *numbers* verses

56   *guards* trimmings

57   *shop* codpiece (by extension from the slang sense,
      'phallus')

58–71 *Did not the heavenly ... paradise.* See the note to
      IV.2.105–18.

59   *whom* (for 'which')

65   *Thy grace, being gained, cures all disgrace in me.* Longa-
      ville echoes ironically *And then grace us in the disgrace of
      death* (I.1.3).

68   *Exhalest this vapour-vow.* It was thought that the sun
      drew vapours from the earth, causing will-o'-the-
      wisps, meteors, and suchlike.

72   *liver vein* idiom of love. The liver was considered the
      source of amorous desire.

73   *green goose* fresh young strumpet

74   *amend* put to rights, improve

76   *All hid, all hid – an old infant play. All hid* was a cry in
      the children's game Hodman-blind; see Ben Jonson's
      Epicoene, IV.5.341. But Berowne is comparing the
      eavesdropping scene to a medieval Miracle play as well
      as to a game played by infants. In such a play, the
      actor performing God sat aloft, as though in heaven,

and, according to line 77 (*Like a demi-god here sit I in the sky*), that is where Berowne sits. The most likely arrangement of actors on Shakespeare's stage at line 76 is this: Berowne has found his way (at line 19 or later) to the 'lords' room' (a space above and behind the stage used to seat select members of the audience, and, on occasion, for such elevated bits of action as scenes on city walls), while the King and Longaville have concealed themselves down stage, behind the pillars used to support the 'heavens' or 'canopy' which covered part of the playing area. Thus when Dumaine enters from one of the two doors in the back wall of the stage he can be observed and remarked on by his fellows from three angles at once.

79   *More sacks to the mill* (proverbial)

80   *woodcocks* (considered very foolish)

84   *she is not, corporal* (1) she is not, soldier (like Berowne at the end of Act III, Dumaine has become a *corporal* in Cupid's army); (2) she is not heavenly, she is fleshly

85   *Her amber hairs for foul hath amber quoted* her hair is so beautifully amber that it seems to allude to amber (the semi-precious stone) only to make amber look ugly (or, elliptically, 'her amber-coloured hair is so beautiful that it has caused amber itself to be cited as something ugly'). Modernization of Q and F 'coted' has suppressed a pun: 'coted' means 'overtaken, outstripped' as well as 'quoted'.

86   *raven*. Berowne takes Dumaine's line in the sense 'her amber hairs have caused amber to be cited as a fowl'. If this is the case, he observes, then someone must think that the *raven* is amber, because that is the bird which most resembles Katharine's supposedly fairer-than-amber hair.

87   *Stoop, I say* (elliptical: 'unlike the cedar, I say, your mistress has a stoop', perhaps adding 'come down to earth about this')

88   *with child* bulging (as though pregnant)

92   *Is not that a good word?* (1) isn't that kind of me? (2) isn't the word *Amen* known to be good?

95   *incision* bloodletting

96   *in saucers* (1) into the saucers used for catching the blood; (2) by the saucerful

        misprision (1) misinterpretation (of Dumaine's words); (2) release (for Katharine, from her lover's veins)

98   *vary wit* inspire a man to express himself with variety or novelty

99–118   *On a day . . . thy love.* Reprinted in the anthology *England's Helicon* (1600) as well as in *The Passionate Pilgrim*, on both occasions without lines 113–14 (which tie the poem to the dramatic situation). *Wished* and *thorn* (lines 106 and 110) are taken from the anthologies rather than Q or F.

105   *That* so that

116   *Ethiop* blackamoor (used here as an example of ugliness)

117   *deny himself for Jove* shed his deity (the most Jove-like thing about him)

120   *fasting pain* pain caused by abstinence

122   *example* furnish a precedent for

123   *perjured note.* See the note to lines 45–6.

125   *thy love is far from charity.* Dumaine professes erotic rather than Christian love, *amor* rather than *caritas*.

126   *in love's grief desirest society* (with a glance at the proverb 'It is good to have company in trouble')

133   *wreathèd arms* (the folded arms of love melancholy: see III.1.15–18)

138   *reek* exhale

143   *when that* when

148   *by* about

153–4   *Your eyes . . . princess* (recalling the King's sonnet; see lines 31–3)

158   *to be thus much o'ershot* to have missed the target by so much (strictly, by shooting over it). See I.1.140.

159–60   *You found . . . three.* 'Why seest thou the mote that is in thy brother's eye, but perceivest not the beam that is in thine own eye? Or how wilt thou say to thy brother "Suffer me, I will cast out a mote out of thine eye"; and behold, the beam is in thine own eye? Thou hypocrite, first cast out the beam out of thine own eye: and then shalt thou see clearly to cast out the mote that is in thy brother's eye' (Matthew 7.3–5; compare Luke 6.41–2).

162   *teen* affliction, woe

164   *a gnat* (example of insignificance)

165   *gig* spinning-top

166   *tune a jig* play (or sing) a frivolous dance tune (or song)

167   *Nestor* (an aged and wise Greek general at the siege of Troy)

       push-pin (another children's game, in which pins were pushed in order to cross them)

168   *critic Timon* censorious Timon (the hero of Shakespeare's *Timon of Athens*)

       idle toys foolish trifles

172   *A caudle, ho!* Berowne calls for warm thin gruel for the supposedly ailing King.

178   *With men like you, men of inconstancy.* Q, followed by F, reads 'With men like men of inconstancie'. Adding *you* makes sense of the line, corrects the metre, and assumes a simple printer's error. Moreover, *you* fits the structure of the speech: Berowne begins by contrasting the *I betrayed* with the faithless *you* (line 174) and then elaborates this opposition, listing the merits of *I* (175–6) before rounding on *you*. Some editors prefer 'With moon-like men, men of inconstancy'.

180   *Joan* (as at III.1.202)

181   *pruning me* preening myself

182–4   *a hand, a foot . . . a limb.* The catalogue extends as Berowne, seeing Jaquenetta and Costard coming with his letter, tries to sneak away (hence the King's questions).

183   *state* way of carrying oneself, bearing

185   *true man* honest man (perhaps with an ironic echo of
       true girl at I.1.299, *true* carrying the sense 'having
       the proper attributes and appetites')

186   *post* ride quickly (picking up Navarre's *gallops*)

187   *present* (1) gift; (2) written document (more common
       in the form 'presents')

188   *What makes treason* what is treason up to. Costard
       interprets *makes* more straightforwardly.

192   *Our parson misdoubts it; 'twas treason, he said.* A minor
       inconsistency: *treason* was not mentioned in IV.2; and
       Holofernes more obviously *misdoubts* ('is suspicious
       about') the letter than Nathaniel (see IV.2.135–40).

198–201 *Why dost thou tear it? . . . his name.* Compare *The Two
       Gentlemen of Verona*, I.2.100–136, where Julia tears up
       Proteus's letter and then lovingly picks up and reads
       the pieces.

202   *loggerhead* blockhead

204   *mess* group of four at table

205   *you – and you* (both referring to the King)

206   *deserve to die.* Pickpockets caught in the act were
       executed.

209   *the number is even . . . we are four.* As Mote's *l'envoy*
       (III.1.89–90) was anticipated by I.1.97, so it antici-
       pates this section of IV.3, with the three men *at odds*
       (like *The fox, the ape, and the humble-bee*) made *even* by
       a fourth, Berowne (like *the goose*).

210   *turtles* turtledoves (that is, lovers. Berowne does not
       know that Armado has intervened.)
       sirs (in Elizabethan English a polite form of address
       for women as well as men; compare *Antony and Cleo-
       patra*, IV.15.84)

216   *cross* thwart

217   *of all hands* on every side

218   *rent lines* torn verses

220   *rude* ignorant
       Inde India

224   *peremptory* resolute

eagle-sighted. It was believed that of all birds only the eagle could stare at the sun without damaging its sight. Even an eagle, Berowne says, would be *blinded* by the beauty of Rosaline's brow (lines 225–6).

229   *scarce seen a light* a light hardly to be seen

230   *My eyes are then no eyes.* Probably a playful reminiscence of the opening line of the most famous soliloquy in Thomas Kyd's *The Spanish Tragedy* (*c.* 1589): 'O eyes, no eyes, but fountains fraught with tears' (III.2.1.).

232   *the culled sovereignty* those picked out as the best

234   *several worthies make one dignity* several good qualities combine in one excellence

235   *nothing wants that want itself doth seek* nothing that desire desires and looks for is lacking

236   *flourish* (1) eloquence; (2) adornment

237   *painted rhetoric* flowery language added like paint to sense

238   *of sale* offered for sale

239   *praise too short doth blot* praise could only spoil Rosaline's reputation (*blot* it) because what she is surpasses praise

245   *thy love is black as ebony.* A connexion with the dark lady of the *Sonnets* is often made; see the Introduction, pages 30–32.

246   *wood.* The Q and F reading, 'word', is not impossible in this verbally conscious play.

247   *A wife of such wood were felicity.* Perhaps a comic version of Pygmalion's wish to marry an ivory statue (Ovid's *Metamorphoses* X).

248   *who can give an oath? Where is a book?* The *book* is to swear on (a bible) but, taken with *oath*, it inevitably recalls the broken vow of study.

250   *If that she learn not of her eye to look* if she (beauty) does not get her (Rosaline's) beautiful eye to look with

251   *No face is fair that is not full so black.* Like the Duke of Venice describing Othello ('far more fair than

black', I.3.287), Berowne exploits the double sense of 'fair', 'light in colour' and 'beautiful'.

253   *the school of night*. See the Introduction, pages 9–10.

254   *beauty's crest*. That is, the sun, which (as Berowne himself says at line 244) lightens *the heavens* rather than darkening *hell*. *Crest* was presumably suggested by *badge* (line 252).

255   *Devils soonest tempt, resembling spirits of light*. Berowne begins his assault on the traditional association (bolstered by neo-platonism) between light, beauty, and virtue by invoking 2 Corinthians 11.14: 'Satan himself is transformed into an angel of light'. *Resembling* has here the sense 'when they resemble'.

257   *usurping hair* false hair, wigs

258   *aspect* (accented on the second syllable) appearance

260   *favour* face
        turns the fashion of the days sets a new fashion

261–3   *native blood is counted ... her brow* rouge is now so common that the red blood of a healthy complexion is ashamed to declare itself (knowing that it will simply be accounted *painting*), and it therefore makes itself *black*, imitating Rosaline's forehead

266   *Ethiops of their sweet complexion crack* blackamoors boast of having attractive complexions (Rosaline's darkness making them seem light)

267   *dark is light* (in comparison with Rosaline; unless Dumaine means that Berowne has removed all distinction between dark and light by making *black fair*)

268–9   *Your mistresses ... washed away*. A double-edged joke: hyperbolical (the women are so nearly colourless that a shower would leave them blank) and more literal (they are blank already, their *colours* being cosmetics, liable to run in the *rain*).

273   *No devil will fright thee then* (on *doomsday*, collecting souls)

284   *some flattery for this evil* something plausibly pleasing (to cover) this evil

285   *some authority how to proceed!* Compare I.2.65, where Armado asks Mote for *authority* to excuse his love for Jaquenetta.

286   *quillets* subtleties

288   *Have at you* here goes (often associated with attack, and so perhaps suggested by the second half of the line) *affection's men-at-arms*. See I.1.8–10; the men have defected to the enemy.

291   *state* (1) condition; (2) majesty

293   After this line Q (followed by F) prints the following, evidently an early draft of lines 294–330:

> And where that you haue vowd to studie (Lordes)
> In that each of you haue forsworne his Booke.
> Can you still dreame and poare and thereon looke.
> For when would you my Lord, or you, or you,
> Haue found the ground of Studies excellence,
> Without the beautie of a womans face?
> From womens eyes this doctrine I deriue,
> They are the Ground, the Bookes, the Achadems,
> From whence doth spring the true *Promethean* fire
> Why vniuersall plodding poysons vp
> The nimble spirites in the arteries,
> As motion and long during action tyres
> The sinnowy vigour of the trauayler.
> Now for not looking on a womans face,
> You haue in that forsworne the vse of eyes:
> And studie too, the causer of your vow.
> For where is any Authour in the worlde,
> Teaches such beautie as a womas eye:
> Learning is but an adiunct to our selfe,
> And where we are, our Learning likewise is.
> Then when our selues we see in Ladies eyes,
> With our selues,
> Do we not likewise see our learning there?

Shakespeare's declining confidence in the speech presumably explains 'With our selues', a false start for 'Do we not likewise see our learning there'. Dissatisfied, he picked up the threads from line 293 (though writing on in the manuscript) and remodelled the argument in the form which stands in this text.

297   *leaden* heavy, dull, and slow (see III.1.56–7)

298   *fiery numbers* (the poems we have just heard)

300   *keep* stay within

304   *immurèd* walled up

307   *to every power a double power* double strength to every faculty

310   *gaze an eagle blind* (by being more brilliant than the sun. See the second note to line 224.)

312   *the suspicious head of theft is stopped* the wary ears of a thief can hear nothing. The common emendation of *head* to 'heed' seems unnecessary.

313–14 *more soft and sensible | Than are the tender horns of cockled snails.* Compare 'Or as the snail, whose tender horns being hit, | Shrinks backward in his shelly cave with pain' (*Venus and Adonis*, 1033–4).

314   *cockled* having a shell

317   *the Hesperides.* The last of Hercules' twelve labours involved taking golden apples from the garden of the Hesperides, the daughters of Hesperus. Here Shakespeare follows the common practice of calling the garden itself *the Hesperides.*

318   *Subtle as Sphinx* (because the Sphinx told riddles)

321   *Make* (governed by *voice.* An Elizabethan would not find this ungrammatical.)

326   *From women's eyes this doctrine I derive.* The best line of the early draft (see the note to line 293) found its way into the final text.

327   *the right Promethean fire* the very fire which Prometheus stole from heaven to give to mankind

330   *Else none at all in aught proves excellent* without their help, no one achieves excellence in anything

334   *loves all men* is friend to all men

340   *charity itself fulfils the law* (an allusion to Romans 13.8: 'he that loveth another hath fulfilled the law')

341   *who can sever love from charity?* Sophistical: *caritas* can be translated either 'charity' or 'love', but it is hardly the same as *amor*. See Longaville's quip at line 125.

343   *Advance your standards* (with a bawdy as well as a military sense)

344   *be first advised* take care first of all

345   *get the sun of them* attack them with the sun in their eyes (with the quibbling sense 'beget sons on them', maintaining the bawdry of lines 343–4)

346   *glosses* (referring to Berowne's comments on their love)

351   *attach* (a legal term) seize

353   *strange* fresh, novel

358   *betime* be appropriate (with a play on 'be time', which is the reading of Q and F)

       be fitted be employed (with a play on 'be found fitting for our purposes')

359   *Allons! Allons!* let's go! let's go! The Q and F 'Alone alone' is initially attractive, because what Berowne goes on to say is very different from the kind of things he has been saying to his fellows; but a parallel with the end of the next scene, where Holofernes, also planning an entertainment for the visitors, says to Dull 'Alone, we will employ thee' (where the sense must be *Allons!*), tells against it.

       (stage direction) *Exeunt King, Longaville, and Dumaine*. No exits are marked in Q; F's general '*Exeunt*.' after line 362 does not seem compatible with the tone of Berowne's speech. The arrangement in this edition (with Berowne lingering briefly after *Allons! Allons!*) is often used on stage.

       Sowed cockle reaped no corn if darnel is sown, the field will yield no grain. Berowne may have the imagery of Matthew 13.25–6 in mind.

361   *Light* frivolous, wanton

362   *copper* (coin)

V.1.1   *Satis quod sufficit* that is enough which suffices (our
        proverb 'enough is as good as a feast'). Holofernes is
        presumably referring to the dinner.

2   *reasons* discourses, conversation

3   *sententious* pithy

4   *affection* affectation

5   *opinion* dogmatism

6–7   *quondam day* former day (presumably 'yesterday': an
        affected use of the Latin)

9   *Novi hominem tanquam te* I know the man as well as I
        know you. In this as in other places Shakespeare's
        audience would know that the pedant's Latin comes
        straight from the classroom; here the source is the
        Brevissima Institutio, 'Lyly's Grammar'.

10   *peremptory* resolute

        his tongue filed his language smooth and refined (as in
        Ben Jonson's poem in the Folio: 'the race | Of Shake-
        speare's mind and manners brightly shines | In his
        well-turnèd and true-filèd lines')

12   *thrasonical* boastful. Thraso is a braggart soldier in
        Terence's comedy *Eunuchus*.

13   *picked* fastidious

        odd, as it were. Holofernes apologizes for stretching
        the sense of the word; in the sense 'unusual, strange',
        'odd' is not recorded before the 1590s.

14   *peregrinate* affectedly foreign

15   (stage direction) *table-book* notebook

17   *staple* fibre

        argument subject-matter

18   *fanatical phantasimes* extravagant and fantastic fellows

        insociable impossible to associate with

18–19   *point-device* affectedly precise

19   *rackers of orthography* torturers of spelling. Holofernes

believes that pronunciation should follow spelling, a
common view among Elizabethan educators.

20   *'dout' sine 'b'* 'dout' without the letter 'b'. Most editors
follow the Q and F 'dout fine', but it is not clear what
this means; 'sine' in the manuscript could easily have
been read as 'fine' ('f' for 'long s') and the isolated 'b'
overlooked.

22   *clepeth* calls

23   *vocatur* is called

24   *abhominable, which he would call 'abominable'*. The
form with 'h' is so general in English from Wyclif to
the mid-seventeenth century that the joke is probably
restricted to Holofernes's fussy insistence that all
spelled letters must be spoken. But it is possible that
Shakespeare knew that the form without 'h' was based
on a correct etymology and that with 'h' on a false one
(*abominari*, 'to deprecate as an ill omen', rather than *ab
homine*, 'away from man, inhuman'), and that he
thought of Holofernes's pedantry as ill-informed as
well as *insociable and point-device*.

25   *insinuateth me of insanie* introduces frenzy into me,
makes me mad. Evidently the Q compositor (followed
in F) was as baffled by the word as the curate, printing
'infamie'.

    Ne intelligis, domine? do you understand, sir?

27   *Laus Deo, bone intelligo* God be praised, I understand
good (using *bone* in error for *bene* ('well'), as Holofernes
points out)

28–9   *Priscian a little scratched; 'twill serve*. Priscian's gram-
mars, written in the early sixth century, were still standard. Thus, 'your Latin is slightly wrong, but it will
do well enough'.

30   *Videsne quis venit?* do you see who is coming?

31   *Video et gaudeo* I see and I rejoice. For *gaudeo* Q and F
have '*gaudio*' ('with joy'), which is not necessarily
wrong; but the complacently balanced emended
reading seems more in character.

32   *Chirrah!* Probably Armado's attempt at χαῖρε (*chaire*),
        a Greek greeting (Elizabethan pronunciation uncertain)
        familiar to Shakespeare's audience through its inclusion
        in the first part of the Erasmian schoolbook, *Familiaria
        Colloquia*. Most editors make the same mistake as Holo-
        fernes and assume that the braggart means 'Sirrah!'

33   *Quare* why

38-9   *alms-basket* (basket in which scraps of food were col-
        lected for the poor)

39-40   *hath not eaten thee for a word*. Mote's name puns with
        mot, French for 'word'. See the first note to I.2.

40   *long by the head* tall. The idiom survives in 'taller by a
        head'.

41   *honorificabilitudinitatibus*. Considered the longest word
        in existence (a renaissance equivalent of 'antidis-
        establishmentarianism'); it is the dative-ablative plural
        of a medieval Latin word meaning, in the nominative,
        'the state of being honoured'.

42   *flap-dragon* (a flaming raisin or the like floated on ale
        or wine and drunk off)

43   *The peal begins*. Mote compares the conversation of
        Armado and Holofernes to the clanging of bells.

44   *lettered* a man of reading (as in 'man of letters'). Mote
        takes the question literally.

45   *horn-book* (leaf of paper held by a wooden handle and
        protected by a thin sheet of horn, containing the alph-
        abet)

45-65   *What is . . . a cuckold's horn*. Strongly reminiscent of
        The Two Gentlemen of Verona, I.1.70-100, where Pro-
        teus proves Speed a sheep. Katharine does the same
        for Boyet, in a more courtly idiom, at II.1.205-10.

47, 48 *Ba* (close enough to the 'baa' of a sheep to make Mote's
        joke)
        pueritia childishness (hence, 'child')

50   *Quis, quis, thou consonant?* who, who, you nonentity (a
        consonant being the absence of sound between
        vowels)?

170

51-4   *The last of the five vowels . . . o, u.* Some editors emend *last* to 'third', but this spoils the development of Mote's jest. Lines 51-2 tempt Holofernes to repeat the vowels by suggesting that the identity of the *silly sheep* depends on which of them is *u*. When the pedant recites, to make *u* Mote, the boy interrupts to point out the implications of *i* and captures *u* as well.

55   *Mediterraneum* (an affectedly pedantic form of 'Mediterranean'; Latin *Mare mediterraneum* means 'sea surrounded by land' or 'sea in the middle of the earth')

56   *touch* hit (of an opponent in a fencing-match)
        venue sword-thrust

57   *home* to the point aimed at

58-9   *wit-old* (thus 'wittold' or 'wittol', a 'contented cuckold')

60   *figure* (of speech, 'conceit')

61   *Horns.* Mote's wit has transformed the *horn* of the *silly sheep* (line 48) into the even more insulting *Horns* of cuckoldry.

62   *disputes* (a common form of the second person singular; compare V.2.208, *Thou now requests*)

63   *gig* spinning-top

65   *manu cita* with a ready hand

66   *An* if

68-9   *halfpenny purse* small purse ('for holding silver halfpence' rather than 'costing a halfpenny')

69   *pigeon-egg* (example of something small)

72   *ad dunghill.* Costard's error for *ad unguem*, 'to a nicety' (literally 'to the fingernail', borrowed from sculpture).

76   *Arts-man, preambulate* man of learning, walk forth. The Q and F reading, '*Arts-man preambulat*' ('the artsman walks forth'), is distinctly inferior.
        singuled set apart, distinguished. An affected form of 'singled' built on the Latin *singulum* (which also produced widely accepted words like 'singular').

77-8   *the charge-house on the top of the mountain.* More of

171

Erasmus's *Familiaria Colloquia*: Livinus, asked *unde prodis?* ('Where do you come from?'), replies *e collegio Montis acuti* ('From the college of the mountain with the sharp crest'), an allusion, for Erasmus, to the Collège de Mont Aigu in Paris, where he had been educated as a boy.

79   *Or mons, the hill.* The schoolbook lies behind this: Holofernes reminds Armado (as though his pupil) that *mons* (nominative of *montis*) can be translated *hill* as well as *mountain*. The braggart and pedant cannot discuss simple facts without filtering them through a book. See IV.1.4 and the note.

83   *congratulate* give pleasure to

84   *posteriors* hind parts (an affected borrowing from Latin, printed in Q (doubtless following Shakespeare's manuscript), like *preambulate*, in the italics appropriate to a foreign language)

86   *generous* well-born

87   *liable, congruent, and measurable* (synonyms for 'fitting, apt')

90–91   *my familiar, I do assure ye, very good friend.* This is ambiguous, but Armado seems to offer *familiar* not as an adjective but as a noun (meaning *very good friend*).

92   *inward* private
            let it pass never mind about that

93–4   *remember thy courtesy . . . apparel thy head.* Clearly there is some byplay with Holofernes's hat: either Armado asks him to remove it on hearing the King's name (*thy courtesy*) and then invites him to replace it (*apparel thy head*), or he twice asks him to replace what has been removed spontaneously.

98   *excrement* outgrowth (compare *Hamlet*, III.4.122: 'Your bedded hair like life in excrements'). There is also the obvious scatological sense, doubtless not intended by Armado.

103   *all of all* sum of everything

105   *chuck* (a common term of affection) chick

106   *ostentation* display

antic (pageant in which the actors wore grotesque costumes)

116–17   *the Nine Worthies*. This group of notables often appeared in masques and pageants. The nine were usually Hector of Troy, Alexander the Great, and Julius Caesar (three virtuous pagans); Joshua, David, and Judas Maccabaeus (three Old Testament heroes); King Arthur, Charlemagne, and either Godfrey of Boulogne or Guy of Warwick (three Christian warriors). The promotion of Hercules and Pompey (lines 122–3) is unorthodox.

120–23   *Joshua, yourself ... Hercules*. Shakespeare evidently settled the casting of the entertainment very late. In the event, Joshua does not appear and Nathaniel plays Alexander; and Holofernes, not Armado, plays Judas Maccabaeus. The superfluous phrase 'my selfe, and', which appears in Q and F after *Joshua, yourself*, is no doubt inherited from Shakespeare's manuscript and suggests his uncertainty at this point in composition.

122   *pass* (pass muster as; and so 'impersonate tolerably well', '*present* competently enough')

127   *have audience* be heard

128   *in minority* as a child. The first exploit of Hercules was to strangle two serpents sent by Juno to kill him in his cradle.

     enter entrance

129   *apology* formal justification

140   *We will have, if this fadge not, an antic*. Armado is unaware of the ironic truth ('if the pageant is not well received, never mind, it will serve as an antic instead') underlying his intended 'if the pageant works out badly in rehearsal we will put together an antic instead'. The verb *fadge* ('fit', 'be found suitable') was *fire-new* in the 1590s.

142   *Via* come on

146   *make one* join

147   *tabor* (small drum)

148   *hay* (country dance with winding configurations)

V.2.2	*fairings* complimentary gifts (originally the kind bought or given at fairs)
3	*A lady walled about with diamonds*. Navarre has sent a brooch or pendant which includes the picture of a lady in a surround of diamonds. Such jewels were popular in Elizabethan England.
9	*fain* obliged
	to seal on Cupid's name. Navarre's letter was so packed with writing that the seal had to be applied over part of the text, covering the name *Cupid* with wax.
10	*wax* increase (quibbling on the stuff of the seal)
11	*five thousand year* (thought to be the age of the world)
12	*shrewd* curst, evil
	unhappy bringing misfortune ('unhap')
	gallows gallows-bird, knave fit to be hanged
18	*a light heart lives long* (proverbial)
19	*dark meaning* hidden sense
	mouse (a term of endearment)
	light word frivolous utterance
20	*A light condition in a beauty dark* a wanton character in a dark-complexioned beauty
22	*taking it in snuff* taking offence at it. Katharine makes use of the origin of the phrase – disgust at the smell of a candle being snuffed (trimmed or extinguished) – to suggest, playfully, that the *light* shed on lines 15–18 by line 20 is like candle-light.
24	*Look what* whatever (but with a hint of 'look out and make sure that')
	you do it still i'th'dark (*do* developing its bawdy sense)
26	*I weigh not you* I do not outweigh you, you are fatter than I. Katharine picks up an alternative sense of the phrase in line 27.
27	*that's* that means
28	*past cure is still past care* (proverbial)
29	*bandied . . . set* (tennis terms)
30	*favour* love-token. At line 33 Rosaline uses the word in the sense 'personal appearance'.

35   *numbers* metre
       numbering estimate (of her worth)
37   *fairs* beautiful women
40   *Much in the letters, nothing in the praise.* Berowne's
       letter is an accurate *picture* of Rosaline's beauty in that
       its *letters* are well-penned (perhaps an echo of Nath-
       aniel at IV.2.150); but in what it says (*the praise*) it is
       inaccurate.
42   *Fair as a text B in a copy-book.* The letter *B* in the
       formal style of handwriting known as 'text hand' is
       particularly elaborate. Rosaline is as *Fair* ('beauteous')
       as that letter, but since that letter uses much *ink* she is
       not, after all, *Fair* ('light in colour').
43   *'Ware pencils, ho!* be wary of bringing writing imple-
       ments, such as the pencil, into the argument. Line 45
       shows why.
       not die your debtor repay your insult
44   *red dominical* (red letter S used to mark Sundays in
       almanacs. If Rosaline is dark, Katharine is ruddy.)
       golden letter (also used to mark Sundays and holy days.
       Rosaline has in mind the *amber hairs* so praised by
       Dumaine.)
45   *O's* (letters here signifying the scars left by smallpox.
       Rosaline here explores an alternative sense of *pencils*,
       'finely-pointed brushes used in applying make-up to
       blemishes'.)
46   *A pox of that jest* (registering Rosaline's jest but also
       rebuking her for it)
       beshrew all shrews wish mischief on all scolds. Moder-
       nization of Q and F 'Shrowes' blurs the rhyme with
       O's.
51   *translation* communication
52   *profound simplicity* (1) wise silliness; (2) complete folly.
       The latter sense of *profound* was novel in the 1590s.
57   *or I would these hands might never part.* Maria wraps
       the pearls round her hands like a prisoner held by a
       chain.

175

59   *purchase* procure

61   *in by th'week* caught hopelessly. The origin of the phrase is uncertain.

62-3   *make him . . . wait the season, and observe the times* make him wait until I inclined to see him, and have him come and go as I chose

64   *bootless* fruitless

65   *hests*. The Q (and F) reading, 'deuice', is probably a compositor's bad guess at an unclear *hests* in the manuscript; but it may be Shakespearian – either a simple irregularity or the beginning of an abortive movement into alternative rhyme.

66   *make him proud to make me proud that jests*. Berowne would be so thoroughly in Rosaline's power that he would be grateful if she deigned to mock him disdainfully.

67   *pair-taunt-like* like a winning hand of cards in the game Post and Pair (consisting of four cards of the same value, such as four aces). Rosaline will, in modern terms, 'trump' Berowne constantly. Some editors prefer to emend Q and F 'perttaunt like' to 'planet-like', beginning an astrological metaphor which ends in the next line with *fate*.

74   *gravity's revolt to wantonness*. Perhaps Rosaline is being ironic when she attributes *gravity* to the witty Berowne (the lords have, after all, set up as austere scholars). Perhaps *gravity* was forced on her by a dramatist hunting antitheses too earnestly.

75   *note* stigma

76   *foolery* (two syllables)

82   *Encounters mounted are* skirmishes are afoot

84   *surprised* taken off your guard

87   *Saint Denis* (the patron saint of France)

88   *charge their breath*. Boyet uses *charge* in the sense 'attack at a gallop', continuing the speech–military imagery of line 84, *Armèd in arguments*.

92   *addressed* approaching

95	*overhear* hear over
98	*conned his embassage* learned his message
101	*made a doubt* expressed fear that
102	*put him out* make him forget his lines
104	*audaciously* boldly
109	*rubbed his elbow* (a sign of satisfaction, like rubbing hands)
	fleered grinned
111	*with his finger and his thumb* (snapping them)
114	*turned on the toe* pirouetted
117	*spleen ridiculous* ludicrous fit of laughter (unless *ridiculous* governs *passion's solemn tears* in the next line)
121	*Like Muscovites or Russians*. Such costumes were common in pageantry, but Shakespeare may have been directly inspired by an entertainment offered at Gray's Inn (the lawyers' college) on Twelfth Night 1595. As part of the Christmas Revels (which had included a performance of *The Comedy of Errors* on 28 December), an 'ambassador' from 'the mighty Emperor of Russia and Muscovy' came to the Inn 'in attire of Russia, accompanied with two or three of his own country, in like habit'. (Quotations are from a contemporary report first published in a late-seventeenth-century account of the Revels, *Gesta Grayorum*.) Law students constituted an important section of Shakespeare's audience in the public theatre; no doubt he bore them in mind while composing.
123	*love-suit*. Some editors follow the Q and F 'Loue-feat', glossing it as 'exploit inspired by love'; but the strong case for *love-suit* is clinched by line 129, where the Princess quibblingly echoes Boyet with *Despite of suit*.
124	*several* respective
	which they'll know (elliptical; the sense is 'which mistress each will know')
126	*tasked* put to trial
129	*Despite of suit* (1) despite his asking; (2) despite his

love-suit (line 123); (3) for all his elaborate (Russian) costuming

130–31   *Hold, Rosaline ... his dear*. It has been suggested that Shakespeare replaced this couplet by the next and that it was printed in error. But they say quite different things, though dealing with one exchange of favours.

134   *change* exchange

135   *removes* exchanges

136   *most in sight* conspicuously

139   *mockery* (two syllables) mocking (which is indeed the F reading)

141   *unbosom shall* will disclose

146   *to the death* (as in 'fight to the death'. The imagery has become military again.)

147   *penned* composed specially

152   *be out* is made to forget his lines

153   *such sport as* sport to compare with

154   *theirs* their sport

157   (stage direction) *blackamoors*. Not, of course, real *blackamoors* (rarely seen in renaissance Europe), but attendants in negroid disguise. Such characters were not uncommon in masques and pageants.

159   *Beauties no richer than rich taffeta* (because the women are wearing masks made of the glossy silk cloth known as *taffeta*)

160   *parcel* small group

165   *'Out' indeed!* See line 152; the women have succeeded.

172   *daughter-beamèd eyes* (taking *sun* as 'son' and offering a female equivalent)

174   *Is this your perfectness?* do you call this being word-perfect?

177   *plain* plain-spoken

184–5   *measured many miles | To tread a measure* walked many miles to join her in the paces of a stately dance. Rosaline exploits another sense of *measured* in her reply.

203 *but a moon* (because Rosaline borrows light from the Princess)

  clouded. The cloud is Rosaline's mask.

205 *bright moon, and these thy stars*. Compare the King's imagery at IV.3.228–9.

206 *eyne* eyes

208 *moonshine in the water* (proverbial) nothing

209 *change* round (of a dance)

210 *not strange* not odd (though the begging is done by someone *strange*, 'foreign')

215 *she is the moon, and I the man*. They have a natural affinity, like the man in the moon and his home.

216 *motion* movement. Rosaline takes the word in the sense 'response'.

219 *nice* fastidious

222 *More measure* a larger amount. Courtly Elizabethan dances began with holding hands, curtsying, and kissing. Thus *The Tempest*, I.2.375–9:

> Come unto these yellow sands,
> And then take hands.
> Curtsied when you have and kissed
> The wild waves whist,
> Foot it featly here and there. . . .

Rosaline grants the first two courtesies and denies the third.

227 *Twice to your visor, and half once to you!* (obscure)

232 *treys* threes

233 *Metheglin* (a Welsh drink brewed from honey and spices)

  wort (sweet unfermented beer)

  malmsey (strong sweet wine)

235 *cog* cheat

237 *Thou grievest my gall* you cause pain by rubbing my sore. But the Princess takes *gall* in the sense 'bile', the *Bitter* secretion of the liver.

237   *meet* appropriate (perhaps quibbling on the sense 'have
       a meeting')

242–6   *was your visor . . . visor half.* Visors were held in place
       by a projection or *tongue* taken into the mouth. Kath-
       arine alludes to this when she asks Longaville why he
       is so silent. If he is silent, he replies, she is *double*-
       tongued ('saying enough for two', 'quibbling', and
       'deceiving'), one *tongue* being her own and the other
       the mask's. And that is why she inquires about his
       silence: she would like to dispose of *half* her fluency
       by giving him one of her tongues.

247   *'Veal', quoth the Dutchman.* The Dutchman is trying
       to say 'well', which represents Katharine's sarcastic
       judgement on Longaville's *reason*. At the same time,
       Veal puns on 'veil' (often spelled 'veal'), this being
       Katharine's substitution for the *speechless visor* of
       the preceding line. Further, *Veal*, when tacked on
       to Katharine's last spoken word, *long* (line 244),
       makes up her wooer's name. By adopting Longaville's
       half (uttering *half* his name to make up the whole),
       Katharine demonstrates her ability to see through the
       Veal on the suitor's face.
       Is not 'veal' a calf? It is in French, where *le veau*
       means both (compare *capon* at IV.1.59); or perhaps
       Katharine means that *veal* is made from *a calf* (as
       'pork is a pig'). The question draws out an insult latent
       in the first half of the line: Longaville is *a calf* or
       'dunce'.

249   *Let's part the word.* Longaville means 'let's strike a
       compromise over this', but Katharine takes him liter-
       ally, treating *calf* as she had 'Longaville'.
       I'll not be your half (1) I refuse to share with you; (2)
       I'll not be your wife, your 'better half'; (3) I'll not be
       the sound ' 'alf', second *half* of the word *calf* (but
       neither will I be 'ca', the other *half*, and the first
       syllable of 'Katharine')

250   *Take all* (of the calf, that baby *ox*)

wean it bring it up

251 *butt yourself* injure yourself with horns. The jest is
unfolded in the next line: by giving her lover (as Longaville mistakenly thinks himself) an *ox*, Katharine
gives him *horns*; but 'giving horns' means 'cuckolding',
and cuckolding injures the reputation of the horning
woman as well as the horned man.

259–60 *Above the sense of sense, so sensible | Seemeth their con-
ference* their conversation is sharper than sense can
perceive. Unqualified praise is not in Boyet's nature,
and he probably intends the sarcastic implication that
the brilliance is so far beyond sense as to be not
sense.

260 *conceits* witty remarks

263 *dry-beaten* bruised (*dry* because no blood has been
drawn)

268 *Well-liking* sleek, plump

269 *poverty in wit, kingly-poor flout!* The Princess agrees
that the men are poor *in wit* but also directs the charge
of intellectual *poverty* against Rosaline, implying that
the pun *Well-liking* ('well-like-king') is but a *kingly-
poor flout*. She eludes the charge herself by including
within it both a reversed form of *liking* (*kingly*) and a
variation on *poverty* (*poor*).

272 *out of countenance* (1) masked; (2) ashamed

273 *all in lamentable cases* (1) each in a sorry condition; (2)
all wearing horrible masks and costumes

274 *weeping-ripe* almost weeping
good word kind comment (from Rosaline)

275 *out of all suit* (1) beyond all reasonableness; (2) like
himself rather than the Russian which his *suit* ('costume') declared him to be; (3) in the wrong *love-suit*,
wooing the Princess instead of Rosaline

277 *Non point* not at all (with a quibble on the *point* of the
sword). See II.1.125 and note.

279 *trow you* do you know
Qualm sudden feeling of sickness. *Came o'er* still has

	this association; *heart* suggests that the *Qualm* here is produced by 'heartburn'.
281	*statute-caps* (woollen caps worn on Sundays and holy days by persons of low social rank in deference to an Elizabethan law)
288	*In their own shapes* without disguises
289	*digest* accept, stomach
292	*repair* return
293	*Blow* bloom (quibbling on *blows*, line 291; hence the Princess's uncertainty)
296	*damask* white and red (often used of roses; here of the complexion)
	commixture mingling
297	*Are angels vailing clouds* they (the *Fair ladies*) are like angels letting clouds fall. Boyet uses the mask-cloud imagery introduced by Rosaline and the King at lines 203–6.
298	*Avaunt, perplexity!* away with confusion! (also 'away, Perplexity!', treating Boyet as the embodiment of the effect he causes)
301	*as well known as disguised* as thoroughly when they come to be recognized as when they came in disguise
303	*shapeless gear* badly cut clothes
306	*rough carriage* graceless bearing. The men evidently adopted in their masque the unrefined manners associated with Russians by the Elizabethans.
309	*Whip* dash (as though on horseback)
	as roes runs o'er the land. The Princess forces grammar to win (and advertise) a quibble: 'as roe deer speed o'er the land'; 'as the rose sends out runners and spreads over the ground'. The women will go to their tent like the roses Boyet has said they are (lines 293–7).
317	*wit's pedlar, and retails his wares* (exploiting the double sense of *utters it*, 'says it' and 'sells it')
318	*wakes and wassails* festivals and revels
319	*by gross* wholesale

321 *pins the wenches on his sleeve* (wearing them like favours)

322 *had* would have

323 *carve* make courtly gestures

lisp. Compare Hamlet's disapproval of affected lisping (III.1.145).

325 *ape of form* slavish follower of etiquette

Monsieur the Nice Mr Fastidious

326 *tables* backgammon

327 *In honourable terms* politely

327-8 *sing | A mean most meanly* sing a middle part (alto or tenor) well enough

328 *ushering* ordering ceremony (the task of a gentleman usher)

329 *Mend him who can* no one can improve on his performance

332 *white as whale's bone*. So traditional an image that what might be complimentary is rendered sarcastic. *Whale's* has two syllables.

337 *Behaviour* fine manners

338 *this man showed thee* Boyet showed you how very fine manners could be. For *man* Q and F read 'mad man' and 'madman', which might be correct, though metrically irregular; but *madam* in the next line suggests how a mistaken 'mad' could have found its way into the text.

340 *'Fair' in 'all hail' is foul*. The Princess takes the King's greeting, *hail*, in the sense 'hailstorm'; and that kind of *hail* is certainly enough to make a *fair* day *foul*.

346 *Nor* neither

348 *virtue* property, efficacy

349 *nickname* misname

350 *office* operation

361 *mess* group of four

363 *courtship* courtliness (but with more than a hint of 'wooing')

365 *to the manner of the days* as is fashionable nowadays

370   *happy* felicitous, well-chosen

372   *When they are thirsty, fools would fain have drink* (that is, they are fools. In this play even the insults incline to obliquity.)

373   *dry* stale, dull

374–6   *When we greet ∴ . . lose light* when we look the sun in the eye, its light blinds us

387   *case* covering (applied to masks elsewhere; see *Romeo and Juliet*, I.4.29, and *Much Ado About Nothing*, II.1.85)

391   *Amazed* bewildered

394   *Thus pour the stars down plagues.* Certain diseases were thought to be in the power of the planets.

395   *face of brass* brazen-faced impudence

397   *confound* put into confusion, destroy

400   *wish* invite

401   *wait* attend upon you

404   *friend* mistress

405   *blind harper's song.* Blind minstrels, accompanying themselves on fiddle or harp, were a common sight in Elizabethan England.

407   *Three-piled* (like the best-quality velvet)
        spruce affection smart affectation

409   *blown me* laid their eggs in me, made me flyblown

413   *russet* (rough reddish-brown, the colour of peasants' clothes)
        kersey (coarse woollen cloth)

414   *law* (an exclamation usually associated with Shakespeare's low characters)

416   *Sans 'sans'* without 'sans' (because it is affected)

416–17   *Yet I have a trick | Of the old rage* I still have a trace of my old fever

419   *Lord have mercy on us* (written on houses infected by plague)

422   *visited* stricken by disease

423   *the Lord's tokens* (1) plague sores; (2) love-favours given by the men (hearing 'lords' ')

424   *free* (1) not infected by love; (2) generous

425   *Our states are forfeit* (1) we owe you our estates (as *free* wooers who would be husbands); (2) we have lost power over ourselves (being so thoroughly in love)
       undo ruin

426–7   *how can this be true, | That you stand forfeit, being those that sue?* 'How can those be liable to forfeiture that begin the process. The jest lies in the ambiguity of "sue" which signifies to "prosecute by law," or to "offer a petition" ' (Dr Johnson). In Elizabethan English, 'sue' often means 'advance a love-suit'.

434   *well advised* in your right mind

437   *more than all the world I did respect her* I valued her more highly than I did the whole world

438   *challenge* claim

440   *Your oath once broke, you force not to forswear* having once broken your word (by ignoring the regulations of the *academe*), you wouldn't hesitate to break it again

453   *this* (some kind of love-token)

459   *remit* give up

460   *consent* compact

462   *dash* shatter
       Christmas comedy (hinting, perhaps, at a connexion with the embassy of Russians at Gray's Inn; see the note to line 121)

463   *please-man* toady
       slight insignificant
       zany clown (the rustic servant of the *commedia dell'arte* pantaloon)

464   *mumble-news* prattler
       trencher-knight heroic feeder (rather than fighter)
       Dick (a type name) low fellow

465   *smiles his cheek in years* grins his face into wrinkles

469   *she* (each respective mistress)

472   *Much upon this 'tis* that's more or less what happened

474   *square* carpenter's rule. Berowne produces a variant of

the traditional 'have the length of her foot', that is, 'have her measure'.

475 *the apple of her eye* her pupil. Presumably Boyet is in the habit of wittily catching *my lady's* eye.

476 *stand between her back ... and the fire* (to shield her from excessive heat)

477 *Holding a trencher* (to serve her food)

478 *allowed* licensed to jest (like a court fool)

479 *a smock shall be your shroud* you'll die like the woman you are, covered by a smock

481 *Wounds like a leaden sword.* Shakespeare often mentions the leaden or wooden swords used as stage properties.

482 *this brave manage, this career* this splendid gallop, this charge. See the Account of the Text, page 244.

483 *is tilting straight* has immediately returned to his verbal jousting

487 *vara* (a still current dialectal pronunciation of 'very')

490 *beg us* prove us fools. The expression apparently derives from the practice of the sixteenth-century Court of Wards. A petitioner could *beg* this court to adjudge a relative or dependant mentally deficient and to grant him (as guardian) the use of the fool's property. Frequently exploited for private gain, the Court of Wards was suppressed by Charles II.

492 *whereuntil* to what

495–6 *it were pity you should get your living* it would be too bad if you had to earn your living

500 *parfect* The Q spelling reflects Costard's rustic pronunciation of 'perfect', a word here extended beyond its familiar Elizabethan sense, 'execute, complete, accomplish', towards 'perform'.

501 *Pompion* pumpkin

504 *degree* rank

510 *some policy* a good stratagem, a shrewd ploy

512–18 *they shall not ... their birth.* The exchange is similar to that in *A Midsummer Night's Dream*, V.1.81–105,

186

where Hippolyta tries to dissuade Theseus from letting the theatrically unskilled mechanicals perform their play.

515–16 *the contents | Dies in the zeal of that which it presents* the matter of the play is murdered by the earnestness of the performance intended to give it life

517 *Their form confounded makes most form in mirth* the ruin of *great things* (with more than a hint of 'things pretentious') creates more *mirth* than anything else could

519 *our sport* (the Muscovite masque)

520 *Anointed* King. Anointing forms part of the coronation service.

524 *God his* God's

528 *fortuna de la guerra* chance of war

529 *couplement* pair

537 *'Tis not so.* The King is no better at arithmetic than the Worthies (see the note to I.2.40). Perhaps he is here distracted by a guilty recollection that the *first show* of the play, presented by Mote, did indeed include four actors: Berowne, Longaville, Dumaine, and himself.

540–41 *Abate throw at novum ... his vein.* Obscure; but probably: 'set aside a throw of five or nine in the dice-game *novum* and there is nothing in the whole world good enough to be compared with these splendid characters, taken for what they are'. Not enough is known about the rules of *novum*, but five and nine were evidently the highest scores and perhaps regarded as interchangeable (five counting for nine). Certainly Berowne's joke seems to rest on the fact that five actors mean to play nine Worthies.

544 *leopard's head on knee.* Pompey's arms were thought to include a lion or leopard rampant; presumably the beast is blazoned on Costard's shield and he is holding it upside down so that the *head* is resting on his *knee*. Boyet makes a joke of this by alluding to mas-

quine, the representation of beasts' heads (often those of lions and leopards) on the elbows and knees of garments.

549   *targe* (pronounced like 'barge') shield

556   *perfect* word-perfect

561   *scutcheon* coat of arms (probably on Nathaniel's shield). Alexander's arms were thought to include a lion seated on a throne holding a battle-axe; see Costard's comments in lines 573–4.

562   *right* straight. Some authorities (such as Plutarch) say that Alexander had a wry neck.

563   *Your nose smells 'no' in this, most tender-smelling knight.* Boyet has surely detected the imposture by using his own sensitive (*tender-smelling*) nose. Alexander was famed for his sweet-smelling skin.

566   *Most true, 'tis right.* Boyet encourages Nathaniel, but his memory has deserted him.

573   *the painted cloth.* The Nine Worthies were frequently depicted on the painted hangings which covered the walls of Elizabethan chambers.

573–4   *Your lion . . . to Ajax* another hero will deprive you of your *scutcheon* (see the note to line 562). The *close-stool* ('privy') is substituted for Alexander's throne to make it appropriate for *Ajax* ('a jakes', another word for 'privy'). The *pole-axe* which the lion *holds* is an implicitly bawdy substitute for the battle-axe on Alexander's arms.

580–81   *a little o'erparted* not quite equal to the part

584   *imp* child

585   *Cerberus, that three-headed canus* (the dog which guards the gates of Hades). *Canus* should properly be *canis*, but Holofernes needs the rhyme.

587   *manus* hand(s)

588   *Quoniam* since

589   *Ergo* therefore

590   *state* dignity

594   *yclept* called

595   *clipped* (1) cut short (punning on *yclept*); (2) embraced (the sense Berowne draws out in the next line)

602   *Begin . . . you are my elder* hang yourself first, you are senior to me

603   *Judas was hanged on an elder* (an old legend)

606   *this.* Holofernes indicates his face.

607   *cittern-head.* Citterns (guitar-like instruments) often had a grotesque head carved at the neck end of the fingerboard.

608   *bodkin* long pin used for holding the hair in place (with a head which was often lavishly decorated)

609   *death's face in a ring* miniature skull, worn in a ring as a *memento mori*

610–11   *scarce seen* (being so worn away)

612   *pommel of Caesar's falchion* ornamental knob ending the hilt of Caesar's curved sword. Supposed relics of Caesar, including weapons, were in great demand in the sixteenth century.

613   *carved bone face on a flask.* Gunpowder flasks were commonly made of elaborately carved ivory, horn, or bone.

614   *half-cheek* profile

615   *brooch of lead.* A brooch worn in the hat indicated a man's trade. Dentists evidently wore leaden ones.

618   *put me out of countenance* quite disconcerted me. Holofernes begins to retaliate with quibbles of his own.

620   *outfaced them all* mocked them all to shame

621–2   *lion . . . ass.* Holofernes is like the ass in Aesop's fable, who wore the lion's skin until he was detected.

624   *latter end of his name.* Setting up the *Jude-as* joke for Berowne to clinch in the next line, Dumaine gives it an obscene twist (for Jude's *latter end* is his *ass* in the slang sense 'backside').

626   *gentle* courteous, worthy of gentlefolk

630   *Achilles* (Hector's great rival and eventual killer)

632   *Though my mocks come home by me* even if I suffer in

the future by being abused for this abuse. Dumaine recognizes the women's disapproval.

634 *Hector was but a Trojan in respect of this* Hector the man, prince of Troy, was just an agreeable but essentially ordinary fellow (the popular sense of *Trojan*) compared with the Hector presented by Armado

636 *so clean-timbered* such a fine figure of a man

638 *calf* (1) part of the leg; (2) fool

639 *indued* endowed

  small lower part of the leg

641 *makes faces* pulls faces (like the over-acting villain in 'The Murder of Gonzago': see *Hamlet*, III.2.262)

642 *armipotent* mighty in arms

644 *A gilt nutmeg* a nutmeg glazed with egg-yolk, used for spicing wine or ale (a common lover's gift)

645 *A lemon.* Also used for flavouring drinks, especially when *Stuck with cloves* (line 646).

647 *cloven.* Dumaine takes Berowne's *lemon* as 'leman', 'mistress'; the 'leman', being female, is naturally *cloven.*

650 *Ilion* Troy

651 *breathed* well exercised, fit

652 *pavilion* (tent used by the warrior when not fighting)

657 *Hector's a greyhound.* He was famed for his speed in running.

661 *device* dramatic contrivance

662 (stage direction) *Berowne steps forth and whispers to Costard.* The wording of Q and F ('*Berowne steps foorth*') draws attention to a parallel with IV.3.149, where Berowne comes out of hiding to chastise the King: *Now step I forth to whip hypocrisy.* The second stepping forth leads to the public exposure of Armado's love for Jaquenetta much as the first publishes Navarre's love for the Princess. It has been suggested (by T. W. Craik in 'Berowne steppes forth', *Notes and Queries* n.s. 20, 1973, page 133) that Shakespeare wrote 'Clowne' rather than 'Berowne'; but it

seems unlikely that Costard would press himself forward and then wait six lines before challenging Armado.

666 *yard* (with the slang sense 'penis')

668 *party is gone* man is dead

669 *gone* cast away, ruined in reputation

669-70 *two months on her way* two months pregnant. An interesting example of Shakespearian 'double-time': since I.2.135, where Armado declares his love to Jaquenetta, he and the dairymaid have lived for months and the lords and ladies apparently only for days. Some literal-minded readers (the problem never raises itself in the theatre) have tried to resolve the two time schemes by arguing that only a few days pass for the low as well as the high characters, and that Costard got Jaquenetta pregnant several weeks before the start of the play; but Armado is very far from being fool enough to marry another man's whore (see lines 718-20).

672 *Trojan* (as at line 634, making quibbling use of the popular sense of the word)

673 *quick* teeming with life, pregnant

675 *infamonize* defame

677 *whipped* (the punishment for fornication)

685 *Ates* provocations. Ate (pronounced 'ah-té') is the goddess of discord.

691 *with a pole like a northern man*. Staves were particularly associated with men of the north of England and the Scottish borders.

697 *take you a buttonhole lower* (1) unbutton your doublet (so that you can fight in your shirt); (2) take you down a peg or two

698 *uncasing* undressing

704 *bloods* men of spirit

707 *woolward* (with no linen between the woollen outer garments and the skin)

708 MOTE. Some editors give the lines to Boyet (because

the Q and F '*Boy.*' is ambiguous); but Mote is the one likely to know about his master's underclothes.

708-9   *enjoined him in Rome for want of linen.* Lacking linen, Armado has had to go without: there is no question of voluntary *penance*. *In Rome* is a jibe at the Spaniard's Catholicism.

710   *dishclout* dishcloth

711   (stage direction) *Enter a messenger, Monsieur Marcade.* Marcade's name (basically the French surname Marcadé) is intensely suggestive. He comes to 'mar Arcady', reminding those who shelter in Navarre's park (as though he were Death rather than a messenger of death) that *Et in Arcadia ego* is more than a conceit of pastoral. And, because of this connexion with death, Marcade's name also recalls that of Mercury, the god responsible for conducting souls to the underworld; whether consciously or not, when Shakespeare gave his messenger a name with this gloomy resonance (the more striking because of the last speech of the play) he was echoing Robert Wilson's *The Cobbler's Prophecy* (*c.* 1590), a mythological Morality in which the central character, Raph the cobbler, keeps calling the god Mercury 'Markedie'.

716   *Even so* (two syllables)

718-20   *I have seen ... discretion* (based on the proverb 'One may see day at a little hole')

720   *right myself like a soldier* put myself in the *right* ('do the honourable thing'), as befits a soldier

721   *your majesty.* The Princess has become a queen through the death of her father.

727   *hide* put out of sight, disregard

728   *liberal opposition of our spirits* free and easy antagonism in which we souls have indulged

729-30   *over-boldly we have borne ourselves | In the converse of breath* our conversation has been too free and unlady-like. (See the note to I.1.5.)

730   *gentleness* gentility (and the conduct associated with it)

733–4   *coming too short ... easily obtained.* Navarre has settled
the dispute about Aquitaine behind the scenes. In the
opening sequence of *The Comedy of Errors*, the Duke
says that he is powerless to save Egeon from execution
because he 'may not disannul' the laws (I.1.145); but
in the last scene he forgets this and grants him 'life'
(V.1.391). Theseus initially insists that Hermia must
marry Demetrius or suffer the legal consequences
(death or expulsion to a convent), only to 'overbear'
both the laws and Hermia's father near the end of the
play (*A Midsummer Night's Dream*, I.1.38–90,
IV.1.178). The emotional discoveries made during each
action somehow permit the rules and restraints which
precipitated those actions to be transcended. Something similar happens in *Love's Labour's Lost*: the political and legal tangle which brings the lovers together
becomes so insignificant as the action progresses (the
King and Princess coming to an emotional understanding which undercuts the antagonism required of
them by their negotiations) that it can eventually be
disposed of in this perfunctory – satisfying for need-
ing to be no more – pair of lines.

735–6   *The extreme parts ... his speed* as time runs out
time forces decisions to be made on all issues not yet
settled

735   *extreme* (accented on the first syllable)

737   *loose* moment of release (from archery; when the
bowstring is loosed, the arrow is shot and cannot be
recalled)

738   *That which long process could not arbitrate* the kind of
issue which careful consideration and argument could
not settle

739   *mourning brow of progeny* features of a bereaved child,
marked by sorrow

741   *convince* prove

747   *I understand you not. My griefs are double* on top of
my distress at losing my father comes another grief –

that I don't understand you. See the Introduction, pages 32–3.

749 *badges* signs (Berowne's words)

750 *neglected time* frittered our hours away. Conceivably *time* should have a capital letter, because the sense 'ignored the power of that *cormorant devouring* force which we set out to defeat by our original oaths' certainly registers.

753 *Even to the opposèd end of our intents* into the very opposite of what we purposed

754 *what in us* those qualities put in us by *love*

755 *strains* traits, tendencies (with the merest hint of 'tunes, melodies')

756 *vain* foolish

757–60 *Formed by the eye ... glance.* This is close to *A Midsummer Night's Dream*, V.1.12–17, part of Theseus' account of the common 'imagination' of 'The lunatic, the lover, and the poet':

> The poet's eye, in a fine frenzy rolling,
> Doth glance from heaven to earth, from earth to
>   heaven.
> And as imagination bodies forth
> The forms of things unknown, the poet's pen
> Turns them to shapes, and gives to airy nothing
> A local habitation and a name.

758 *straying.* The parallel with *A Midsummer Night's Dream* makes 'strange' an attractive alternative to the Q and F 'straying'. Theseus's speech develops from an assertion that the strange things which the lovers claim to have experienced in the woods are fancied – 'More strange than true'. It is easy to imagine Shakespeare writing 'straing' in his manuscript and the Q compositor, followed in F, misinterpreting.

habits ... forms. Richly general terms (*habits* meaning 'characteristic doings', 'demeanours', and 'modes', *forms* 'shadowy shapes', 'ideal figures', and 'decorous appearances') linked at the prosaic level by two things dear to *love*: 'clothes . . . bodies'.

761–71   *Which parti-coated presence . . . turns to grace.* The sense of these embarrassed and ingenious lines is roughly as follows. 'If we made ourselves look unseemly in your eyes by adopting the habits and conduct (the *presence*) of foolish flirtatious *love*, quite against our oaths and our supposed academic seriousness, it was those very eyes which tempted us into the error in the first place. So, *ladies*, since the love we've given you is now yours, its faults – collected while the love was being handed over – must be yours as well. What's more, though we did break our oaths *once* (abandoning the *academe*), we only did it so that we could be true to you – you who, having made us false, now have the power to make us permanently true – *for ever*. Indeed, love-prompted oath-breaking, in itself so sinful, can redeem itself and become virtuous by turning into a loving and pure oath-keeping.'

761   *parti-coated* in motley (like a fool)

765   *Suggested* tempted

       make. The object of the verb is in the previous line: *these faults.*

774–5   *rated them | At* judged them to be (perhaps with a hint of the critical sense 'chastised them for being merely')

776   *bombast* (1) empty speeches, mere words; (2) woollen padding for clothes (hence *lining to the time*)

777–8   *more devout than this in our respects | Have we not been* we have given your advances no more serious attention than this

781   *quote* interpret

786   *dear* (1) serious (costing Navarre *dear* both morally and in terms of honour); (2) precious (because his *guiltiness* is the product of love for her)

787   *as there is no such cause* (roughly 'although I can't think why *my love* should prompt you to do anything')

790 *naked* unfurnished, austere

792 *twelve celestial signs* (of the Zodiac)

796 *weeds* clothes

798 *last love* remains love

800 *challenge* claim

deserts deservings. A second sense, 'reward' (as in 'just deserts'), though it does not register consciously, prepares for the convinced *I will be thine* of line 802.

802 *I will* (more expressive of desire and purpose than 'I shall')

instance moment. Not much is lost if the F emendation (it is, strictly speaking, more than a modernization), 'instant', is adopted.

807 *entitled in* (1) having a claim to (a legal term); (2) written in (a common conceit in love poetry)

809 *flatter up* pamper

811 *Hence hermit then* off I go, then, as a hermit

thy breast. After this Q (followed by F) prints an exchange between Berowne and Rosaline which must be the first draft of lines 826–60:

> *Berow.* And what to me my Loue? and what to me?
> *Rosal.* You must be purged to, your sinnes are rackt.
>   You are attaint with faultes and periurie:
>   Therefore if you my fauour meane to get,
>   A tweluemonth shall you spende and neuer rest,
>   But seeke the weery beddes of people sicke.

Shakespeare seems to have started by presenting the couples' bargains in order of interest, with Berowne and Rosaline following the King and Princess; then, recognizing that the sequence as it stood or tended was anti-climactic, he extended the exchange of the wittiest couple and put it last. Something similar apparently happened with the dance in *Much Ado About Nothing*, II.1.77–140: Q inconsistencies suggest that Beatrice and Benedick were originally the second couple to parley, not the last.

823   *friend* lover

824   *stay* wait

        long. Maria takes the word in the sense 'tall'. Compare V.1.39–41.

826   *Studies my lady?* Rosaline is deep in thought. Berowne's question involves, perhaps unwittingly, a belated and ironic reminder of the lords' original scheme.

828   *attends* waits for

833   *comparisons* scornful similes

        flouts jeers

834   *all estates* people of all kinds and classes

836   *wormwood* (a bitter-tasting herb)

840   *still* always

843   *the painèd impotent* those left powerless and in pain

848   *loose grace.* Superficially, 'casual charm'; but the phrase has weight and wit because on another level it includes moral senses paradoxically linked. *Loose* means 'sinfully lax', as in 'loose woman', and *grace* is a spiritual gift from God. Rosaline's moral oxymoron aptly expresses her concern that Berowne's merit should be so mingled with error.

853   *dear* heartfelt

862   *bring* accompany

864   *Jack hath not Jill* (inverting the proverb. Contrast *A Midsummer Night's Dream*, III.2.461–3, where, about to use the love-juice to pair the lovers as they should be, Puck remarks 'Jack shall have Jill; | Naught shall go ill. | The man shall have his mare again, and all shall be well.')

        courtesy kind acquiescence

866   *a twelvemonth and a day.* A standard slice of literary time, as in Edward Lear's 'They sailed away for a year and a day'; but the period was also standard in legal agreements, so the lovers become contracted with some formality.

873   *three year*. Armado's vow replaces his earlier promise to *study three years with the Duke* (I.2.35–6).

874   *dialogue*. In Elizabethan usage the word referred to both sung and spoken disputation; but Shakespeare's intention is clear from the title given to the *dialogue* in Q and F, '*The Song*' (line 882).

874–5   *the two learned men* (Holofernes and Nathaniel. No doubt the pair take the parts of the owl and the cuckoo in the *dialogue* which follows.)

881   *maintained* argued for, defended

884   *lady-smocks* cuckoo-flowers. The plant is known to botanists as *cardamine pratensis*.

885   *cuckoo-buds of yellow hue*. It is by no means certain what a *cuckoo-bud* is. The most popular candidate is the buttercup. However, Matts Rydén, who has done a great deal of work on Shakespeare's plant names, argues in 'Shakespeare's Cuckoo-buds' (*Studia Neophilologica* 49, 1977, pages 25–7) that the dramatist invented the flower so that he could cunningly allude to cuckoldry (the associations of *cuckoo* are clear from the lyric, and *buds* could mean 'horns', the ornaments supposedly sported by a man with an unfaithful wife).

888   *Mocks married men* (because the bird's cry suggests 'cuckold')

894   *turtles tread* turtledoves mate
       daws jackdaws

902   *blows his nail* (1) blows on his fingernails (to keep warm); (2) stands idle (as in 'twiddles his thumbs')

905   *ways be foul*. Probably an unconscious echo of Musidorus's speech at the end of Chapter 18 of Book I of Sir Philip Sidney's *The Countess of Pembroke's Arcadia* (published in 1590): 'But O love, it is thou that does it; thou changest name upon name; thou disguisest our bodies, and disfigurest our minds. But indeed thou hast reason, for, though the ways be foul, the journey's end is most fair and honourable'.

906 *staring* (his eyes being wide-open and watchful)

907–8 *Tu-whit | Tu-who!* The owl is sometimes given an
extra 'Tu-whit' or 'Tu-who' to balance the three cries
of the cuckoo, but since Q (followed by F) has 'Tu-
whit to-who' not once but twice the reading given is
likely to be Shakespearian; presumably the owl's cry
was sung as melismata.

909 *keel* cool (to stop *the pot* boiling over)

911 *saw* moral saying

914 *crabs* crab-apples

919–20 *The words of Mercury are harsh after the songs of Apollo.*
In Q this extraordinary line stands alone, after the
play, as a kind of *l'envoy*; some reasons for accepting
the F attribution to Armado are offered in the Account
of the Text, page 245. The line's primary sense
stems from Armado's position as presenter of the
dialogue: he gives it an epilogue (balancing the equally
brief prologue of lines 880–82) which declares that
speech would seem *harsh* after such fine singing. But
because the braggart is effectively providing an
epilogue for the whole play, the line has wider and
subtler implications: (1) the *words* of Marcade (for the
connexion with Mercury, see the note to line 711) had
indeed seemed *harsh* after the songs, sonnets, and lyri-
cal wooing of the lovers (for the link between Apollo,
song, and Love, see IV.3.318–25); (2) the true study
which the scholars must now undertake in the *harsh*
world outside the park (Mercury's association with
scholarship was a commonplace; see, for example,
Marlowe's *Hero and Leander*, Sestiad I, 386–485) is
in contrast to their life within it. The coupling of
Mercury and Apollo is not unusual; a number of
renaissance authors use the gods as a pair (Ben
Jonson, for example, in *Neptune's Triumph*). What is
remarkable is, rather, that in context the coupling
seems at once unpredictable and resonantly con-
clusive.

920   *You that way; we this way.* From F; not in Q. Perhaps
Shakespeare's Armado parted the audience from the
characters; more likely, he directed the lords and ladies
out of one of the doors in the back wall of the stage
and went with the other low characters out of the
second; more likely still (though it overrules the King's
assertion at line 862 that the lords will bring the ladies
on their way), Armado sent the ladies out of one door
(back to France) while he, the other low characters,
and the lords left by the other. Most modern productions adopt or adapt the third arrangement. Compare
Timon of Athens, V.1.104, where the hero invites the
Poet and Painter to leave his cave in different directions: 'You that way, and you this'. And note Kent's
words to the anonymous Gentleman at the end of
III.1 in the Q *King Lear* (a text thought to derive from
Shakespearian manuscript): 'Ile this way, you that'.

Love's Labour's Lost was written about 1595, but the first extant edition is dated 1598. This quarto (small-format) text was printed by William White for the publisher Cuthbert Burby. Its title-page reads: 'A Pleasant Conceited Comedie Called, Loues labors lost. As it was presented before her Highnes this last Christmas. Newly corrected and augmented *By W. Shakespere.*' The significance of those last seven words has been much disputed. It used to be argued that Shakespeare had 'corrected and augmented' another man's play and that White was pointing this out to his customers. But it is now generally thought that White's compositor (typesetter) simply omitted a full-stop before *'By W. Shakespere.'* I share this assumption. However, if Shakespeare is assumed to be the sole author of *Love's Labour's Lost*, what is to be made of 'Newly corrected and augmented'? Many scholars believe that Shakespeare revised a *c.* 1595 version of the comedy for the Christmas 1597 performance 'before her Highnes', and that White included the 1597 revisions in his text. In his influential 'Three Notes on Shakespeare's Plants' (*Review of English Studies* n.s. 3, 1952, pages 117–29) J. W. Lever claims to have actually identified one of these revisions. The song of Ver is indebted, he says, to a passage in John Gerard's *Herbal* – a book not published until 1597 and thus not available to Shakespeare when he composed his *c.* 1595 'Pleasant Conceited Comedie'. I have argued elsewhere not only that Lever's claim to have found a specific revision is unfounded but that there is no sign anywhere in the Quarto ('Q') of a 1597 textual reworking (*'Love's Labour's Lost* and Shakespearean Revision': see page 38 above). In my opinion, 'Newly corrected and augmented' was intended to advertise the superiority of White's Q over a now lost 'bad quarto'. When Cuthbert Burby published a replacement for the 'bad quarto' of *Romeo and Juliet* in 1599, it bore a legend strikingly similar to that which had appeared on his *Love's Labour's Lost* in the previous year: '*newly corrected, augmented, and amended*'. Perhaps a 'bad quarto' of *Love's Labour's Lost* will one day be found.

Meanwhile, editors have to work with the text in hand. What lies behind Q? There seems to be overwhelming evidence in every part of Q that it was set from an authorial manuscript – either directly or (if, as seems unlikely, it is the reprint of a 'good quarto' set from such a manuscript) at one remove. First of all, there are a number of unusual spellings in Q (such as 'annothanize' for 'anatomize', 'Shoot' for 'shout', and 'doon' for 'done') which recur in editions of Shakespeare's plays demonstrably set from his papers. The Q compositors, that is, were influenced by Shakespeare's orthography. Secondly, the names of characters in the speech prefixes and in stage directions are highly inconsistent. Individual and type names are freely interchanged: 'Costard' is sometimes 'Clown', 'Ferdinand' both 'Navarre' and 'King', 'Nathaniel' 'Curate', and 'Holofernes' 'Pedant'. (On Shakespeare's confusion between the curate and pedant see the note to IV.2.66.) Throughout the play – not just after she hears of her father's death and inherits his kingdom – the Princess is apt to be called 'Queen'. And in Act II the ladies have no names at all in two patches of prefixes, being '1. *Lady*.', '2. *Lad*.', '3. *Lad*.', or, still more anonymously, '*Lad*.'. Such inconsistencies and obscurities are characteristic of a text printed from 'foul papers' – that is, from an author's working manuscript. When a play was transferred into a company prompt-book, the names were largely regularized, for convenience both in rehearsal and in performance, so that plays printed from prompt-books tend to be well-ordered in their naming of parts. Thirdly, the Q stage directions are vague ('*Enter the King and the rest*', V.2.309), inaccurate ('*Exit* Boy', when he stays on to speak, V.2.590), misplaced ('*Exit Curat*' at V.2.582, six lines too late), or simply omitted (as at III.1.63). Again, no prompter would allow such chaos in his book, but an author at work might well leave such details to be settled after the completion of the dialogue. Fourthly, at a number of points (see the Commentary to IV.3.293, V.1.120–23, and V.2.811) Q prints material which Shakespeare obviously rejected and which would have been left out of any fair copy or prompt-book of the play. (The presence of these loose ends and duplicates also shows, of course, that Q cannot be based on a report of the comedy in performance.)

None of the above presents serious editorial problems. Speech prefixes are easily standardized, stage directions supplied, and so on. The notorious Katharine–Rosaline tangle of Act II is a different matter. In Q, Berowne first woos Katharine (in the exchange preserved in the note to II.1.114–28), then flirts with Rosaline (in the dialogue printed in this edition at II.1.114–28), only to conclude the confusion by asking Boyet about Katharine (see the note to II.1.181). It is odd both that Berowne should woo two women and that he should give more attention to Katharine than to Rosaline, the woman with whom he is paired in the rest of the play. Various explanations have been offered for this, the most popular being that when the lords and ladies first meet, the ladies are masked, so that Berowne is confused about which woman is the Rosaline he likes. In 'Shakespeare at Work: The Katharine–Rosaline Tangle in *Love's Labour's Lost*' (see page 38 above), I point out the serious weaknesses of the masking theory and suggest the following alternative: when Shakespeare wrote Act II in the foul papers he had only a hazy sense of the women (hence the numbered as opposed to named prefixes), and his tentative linking of Berowne with 'Katharine' (thus the first encounter and the question to Boyet) was later contradicted by a pairing with 'Rosaline'; looking back to Act II at a later stage in composition, Shakespeare noticed this contradiction and, deleting the first encounter, he added, on a loose sheet inserted into the foul papers, a replacement exchange between Berowne and Rosaline (he did not leave the first encounter intact and change its 'Katharine' prefixes because Rosaline had developed into a woman who needed harder-hitting lines than the text provided), forgetting to adjust the exchange with Boyet to compensate for his revision; the compositors who set Act II printed both the first and (where it seemed to stand, not where it should have stood) the second encounters of Berowne and left the exchange with Boyet intact. If this interpretation of the tangle is correct, the editor must dispose of the first Berowne encounter and replace it by the second, and he should make the correction to Berowne's exchange with Boyet which Shakespeare forgot to make for himself. Both these alterations of Q have been made in this edition.

Interestingly, in Act II of the *Love's Labour's Lost* which appears in the folio (large-format) edition of Shakespeare's works (published and printed by Isaac Jaggard in 1623), a redistribution of Q's speech prefixes has produced a structure very similar to that which the bibliographical evidence suggests was in the foul papers. (It gives Rosaline all the lines assigned to Katharine in the exchange printed in the note to II.1.114–28, and it makes over to Boyet most of the Berowne attributions in the exchange originally printed after II.1.179.) Although the text in the Folio ('F') is basically a reprint of Q, it contains a large number of variant readings, not all of which can be discounted as compositorial inventions. Evidently someone had annotated the copy of Q from which Jaggard's compositors worked. Consider V.2.481–2, where this edition has 'Full merrily | Hath this brave manage, this career, been run' (Boyet is mocking Berowne for abusing him): for 'manage' Q reads 'nuage' and F 'manager'. If Q is nonsense (produced by a poor attempt to decipher Shakespeare's handwriting), F declares itself unacceptable by its context. And yet 'manager' is so daring and suggestive (it leads so naturally to the excellent 'manage' – that is, 'gallop') that it can scarcely be the work of a compositor. Would a compositor cunning enough to replace 'nuage' by such a suggestive reading also print such a self-evidently wrong one? What seems to have happened is this: the annotator corrected Q's 'nuage' to 'manage', but Jaggard's compositor misread his emendation and set 'manager'.

At V.2.481–2 only a detail is at stake; but there are a number of F readings which contribute significantly to the text of the play. The most striking of these is certainly to be found at the end. Modern editors have tended to ignore the last words of F ('*Brag.* The words of Mercurie, | Are harsh after the songs of Apollo: | You that way; we this way'), preferring Q's unadorned and unattributed 'The wordes of Mercurie, are harsh after the songes of Apollo'. But both alterations of Q are Shakespearian. Once it is noticed that towards the end of the play Armado emerges from the sub-plot to take up a central position (see the Introduction, pages 25–7), then nothing seems more natural than for him to speak the comedy's epilogue. As for the addition of 'You that way; we this way': this makes the end of the play resemble other Shakespearian endings (involving, as they invariably do, a request for applause, a general dance, or a motivated departure: 'Let your indulgence set me free', 'Strike up, pipers', 'let's away, | To part the glories of this happy day') without sacrificing one jot of the ambiguity which makes the ending of *Love's Labour's Lost* special.

Did the annotator work from manuscript or from his memory of the play in performance? In 'The Copy for the Folio Text of *Love's Labour's Lost*' (see page 38 above) Stanley Wells argues that the annotator used a Shakespearian manuscript in a post-foul-paper state. My own view is that if the annotator used such a manuscript, his access to it was severely limited. The half-solutions (of the Act II tangle, for example) and plain guesses (consider 'euer' instead of 'hermit' for 'herrite' at V.2.811) which litter the F text certainly look like the product of ingenuity working on a fallible memory.

A word, finally, about an editorial paradox. Although one can be generally eclectic about Q–F variants – choosing at will those alternatives which seem most Shakespearian – there is a series of F readings which, although they look authorial, must be rejected. It is clear that Shakespeare originally gave Boyet two companion lords. In Q, they appear in the stage directions which head II.1 and IV.1, they are referred to and indeed addressed by other characters (at II.1.37–8, for example), and two half-lines of dialogue are attributed to them (II.1.39, 79). It is almost certain, moreover, that in the foul papers IV.1.3 was spoken by one or other of the lords – that it was compositorial misreading of a manuscript '*Lor*.' which gave rise to Q's unsatisfactory '*Forr*.' at this point. (Since the Princess invites the Forester to join the dialogue at IV.1.7–8, it is inappropriate for him to speak at line 3.) However, the absence of the lords from the second half of Q strongly suggests that Shakespeare abandoned the characters during the course of composition. Perhaps he saw the dramatic advantages which would accrue if he concentrated his and his audience's attention on Boyet; or perhaps he needed the actors who had been earmarked to play the lords elsewhere. Whatever his motivation, the course of his revision is clear: after finishing the foul papers, he set about removing the lords from the first half of the play – presumably in a fair copy of the text. The annotator reports some, but not all, of Shakespeare's changes. He redistributes II.1.79 (to Maria) and IV.1.3 (to Boyet); but he also leaves II.1.39 in the mouth of a '*Lor*.', leaves the stage directions at the head of II.1 and IV.1 intact, and removes none of the references to the lords from the dialogue. To make the text coherent, the editor must move against what seems to be the thrust of authorial intention. Unable to rewrite Q–F dialogue, and recognizing the impossibility of cutting from the stage directions characters spoken to and speaking, he must follow Q – or, rather, he will (as at IV.1.3) reproduce the text which he believes stood in the foul papers. A theatre director, by contrast, should feel free to cut and rewrite the dialogue so that the lords can be removed.

In this edition, spelling and punctuation of the text have been modernized in accordance with the principles of the series, speech prefixes have been made consistent and on occasion emended, and stage directions have been regularized and amplified where necessary. Q marks neither acts nor scenes: the act and scene divisions given in this edition are the traditional ones derived respectively from F (ignoring the use of '*Actus Quartus*' for the second time at the head of Act V) and from the practice of eighteenth-century editors.

The collations lists which follow are selective. Quotations

from Q and F are given in the original spelling, but 'long s' (ʃ) has been replaced by the modern letter form. The more interesting variants and emendations not discussed above are considered in the Commentary.

COLLATIONS

I

The following is a list of readings in the present text of *Love's Labour's Lost* taken from F in preference to Q. Corrections of obvious Q misprints in F are not included. Rejected Q readings appear to the right of the square brackets.

I.1.	282	KING] *Ber.*
II.1.	32	Importunes] Importuous
	44	of sovereign parts] of soueraigne peerelsse
	64	ROSALINE] 3. *Lad.*
	88	unpeopled] vnpeeled
	172	in] within
	199	You] O you
III.1.	17	thin-belly] thinbellies
	64	voluble] volable
	144	What] O what
IV.1.	6	On] Ore
IV.2.	30	indiscreet] indistreell
	84	likest] liklest
IV.3.	73	idolatry] ydotarie
	318	Subtle] Subtit
V.1.	94	importunate] important
	114	rendered] rended (F *misprints* 'rendred')
V.2.	17	a] *not in* Q
	80	stabbed] stable
	209	vouchsafe but] do but vouchsafe
	297	vailing] varling

V.2.   463 slight zany] sleight saine
         514 least] best
         563 this] his
         644 gilt] gift
         745 wholesome] holdsome
         773 the ambassadors] embassadours
         905 foul] full
         919 ARMADO] *not in* Q
         920 You that way; we this way] *not in* Q

2

The following is a list of readings in the present text taken from
Q where F offers an interesting alternative. Obvious misprints
and minor omissions in F are excluded, as are most sophistica-
tions of Q, such as 'on' for 'a'. Rejected F readings appear to
the right of the square brackets.

I.1.   72 but] and
            109 Climb o'er the house to unlock the little gate]
                That were to clymbe ore the house to vnlocke
                the gate
            130 *can*] shall
            156 other] others
            182 farborough] Tharborough
            214 sinplicity] simplicitie
278, 279, 280 damsel] Damosell (Q *reads* 'Demsel' *at line*
                278)
            301 till] vntill
I.2.   40 fitteth] fits
             48 do] *not in* F
             88 maculate] immaculate
            122 suffer him to] let him
            125 F *marks an* 'Exit' *for Dull*
            134 that] what

208

157 too] *not in* F

167 was Samson] *Sampson* was

II.1.   21 F *puts the speech prefix* 'Prin.' *here, in the middle of a speech given to the Princess as* 'Queen.'

65 if] as

80 FIRST LORD] (*Lord.*); Ma.

114–28 F *changes six of* Q's *seven* 'Ber.' *speech prefixes to* 'Boy.' *in this transposed exchange. See the Account of the Text, pages 243–4*

114 mine own] my owne (*altering* Q's 'my none')

119 fool] soule

168 I will] would I

175 fair] farther

177 shall we] we shall

184 an] if

189 on] a

220 did] doe

230 where] whence

231 point you] point out

III.1.   7 Master, will] Will

11 your feet] the feete

12 eyelids] eie

56 The] Thy

82–90 I will example . . . adding four] *not in* F

130 honour] honours

IV.1.   2 steep-up rising] (steepe vp rising); steepe vprising

14 and again] & then again

128 An] *not in* F

IV.2.   34 me] *not in* F

61 o'sorel] *O sorell*

99 loves thee not] *not in* F

152 before] being

IV.3.   36 *will*] wilt

83 in] of

166 to tune] tuning

IV.3.	172	caudle] Candle
	214	heaven show] heauen will shew
	216	were] are
V.1.	76	singuled] singled
V.2.	11	year] yeeres
	45	not so] *not in* F
	79	is] *not in* F
	139	mockery] mocking
	149	speaker's] keepers
	185	her on this] you on the
	220	we] you
	240	Take] Take you
	312	thither] *not in* F
	315	pecks] pickes
	316	God] *Ioue*
	324	kissed his hand away] kist away his hand
	334	due] dutie
	389	were] are
	433	not you] you not
	541	pick] pricke
	572	afeard] affraid
	579	faith] insooth
	648	Peace!] *not in* F
	659–60	When he breathed . . . a man] *not in* F
	692	bepray] pray
	733	too short] so short
	748	ear] ears
	777	this in our] these are our (Q *omits* 'in')
	793	the] their
	802	instance] instant
	829	thy] my
	873	year] yeares
	919–20	The words . . . Apollo] *printed as two lines of verse in* F, *divided after* 'Mercury'

Rejected emendations

The following is a selection of emendations proposed by scholars but not adopted in the present text. Rejected emendations appear to the right of the square brackets, separated by semi-colons when there is more than one of interest.

I.1.	23	oaths] oath
	106	shows] mirth; earth
	110	sit] set
	114	sworn] swore
	164	who] whom
	216	*vicegerent*] viceregent
	241	*minnow*] minion
	263	*vessel*] vassal
I.2.	13–14	epitheton] appellation
	158	words] wards
II.1.	44	of sovereign parts] of his sovereign peerless; a sovereign pearl
	76	voluble] valuable
III.1.	22–3	men of note – do you note me? – that] men of note – do you note men? – that; men of note – do you note – men that
	63	flee] fly
	184	field] file
	193	whitely] wightly
IV.1.	71	*see*] saw
	72	*see*] saw
IV.2.	31	see] set
	38	Dictima] Dictynna
	118	*sings heaven's*] sings in heaven's; sings the heaven's
IV.3.	1–2	*The King ... myself*] *printed as part of Berowne's prose speech in most editions*
	57	shop] slop
	115	*whom Jove*] whom e'en Jove
	120	fasting] lasting

IV.3.	144	Faith] A faith
	178	men like you, men] moon-like men, men
	253	school] stole; scowl; style; shield; suit; scroll; soul
	254	crest] best; dress
	266	Ethiops of their] Ethiops their
		sweet] swart
	312	head] heed
	334	loves] moves; joys
V.1.	51	last] third
	140	not] now
V.2.	67	pair-taunt-like] planet-like; pursuitant-like
	152	ne'er] e'er
	261	bullets] (*omitted*)
	273	They] O, they
	309	runs] run
	503	Pompey] Pompion
	585	*canus*] *canis*
	596	How] Now
	651	fight, yea] fight ye
	708	MOTE] BOYET (*taking the* Q *and* F *'Boy.' not to refer to the page*)
	732	humble] nimble
	747	double] dull; deaf
	749	badges] bodges
	758	straying] strange
	809	flatter] fetter
	853	dear] drear
	854	then] them
	907–8, 916–17	Tu-whit│Tu-who] Tu-whit,│Tu-whit, Tu-who; Tu-whit,│Tu-who, Tu-who

4

Emendations

The following readings in the present text differ from those of
Q and F. Most of these alterations were first made by eigh-

teenth-century editors. The rejected readings to the right of the square brackets are common to Q and F unless otherwise indicated. Differences between Q and F accidentals are ignored, the Q form being given.

	THE CHARACTERS IN THE PLAY] *this list is not in Q or F*	
I.1.	62	feast] fast
	104	an] any
	127	BEROWNE] *not in Q or F*
	131	This] *Ber.* This
	295	goodman's] good mans
I.2.	13–14	epitheton] apethaton Q; apathaton F
	139	DULL] *Clo.*
II.1.	39	Lord Longaville] *Longauill*
	40	MARIA] *1. Lady*
	53	MARIA] *Lad.* Q; *Lad. 1.* F
	56	KATHARINE] *2. Lad.*
	64	ROSALINE] *3. Lad.*
	114–28	*This editor has moved lines 114–28 from their Q and F position between lines 179 and 180 in order to replace the fifteen lines of Q and F dialogue which are printed in the Commentary to lines 114–28. See the Account of the Text, pages 243–4*
	125	*Non point*] *No poynt*
	145	On] One
	181	Katharine] *Rosalin*
	196	Rosaline] *Katherin*
	240	MARIA] *Lad.* Q; *Lad.Ro.* F
	241	KATHARINE] *Lad. 2.* Q; *Lad.Ma.* F
	242	ROSALINE] *Lad. 3.* Q; *Lad.2.* F
	243	MARIA] *Lad.* Q; *La.1.* F
	244	MARIA] *Lad.* Q; *Lad.2* F
III.1.	13	throat as if] throate, if
	14	through the nose] through: nose
	22–3	men of note – do you note me? – that] men of note: do you note men that

III.1.   25 penny] penne
          146 Why] O, why
          148 Stay] O stay
          170 And] O and
       170–75 And I . . . so magnificent] *printed as three long*
                and highly irregular verse lines in Q; more satis-
                factory in F
          187 clock] Cloake
          201 and] *not in Q or F*

IV.1.   3 FIRST LORD] (*this editor*); Forr. Q; Boy. F
          70 *anatomize*] annothanize
          76 *king's*] King
          131 it] *not in Q or F*
          137 pin] is in
          145 to th'one side] ath toothen side Q; ath to the
                side F
          149 a] *not in Q or F*

IV.2.   3–4 in *sanguis,* blood] sanguis in blood
           5 *caelum*] Celo
       12, 20 an awd grey doe] (*A. L. Rowse*); a haud credo
          29 of] *not in Q or F*
          36 Dictynna . . . Dictynna] *Dictisima . . . dictis-*
                ima
          41 raught] rought Q; wrought F
          52 call I] cald
          66 HOLOFERNES] *Nath.*
          70 *pia mater*] primater
          73 NATHANIEL] *Holo.*
          77 HOLOFERNES] *Nath.*
          79 *sapit*] sapis
          82 HOLOFERNES] *Nath.*
             Parson – *quasi* pierce-one] Person, *quasi*
                Person
          86 HOLOFERNES] *Nath.*
             Piercing] Of persing
          92 HOLOFERNES] *Nath.*

Fauste precor gelida quando pecus omne] *Facile precor gellida, quando pecas omnia*

96–7 *Venetia, Venetia,|Chi non ti vede, non ti pretia*] *vemchie, vencha, que non te unde, que non te perreche*

102 NATHANIEL] *Holo.*

103 HOLOFERNES] *Nath.*

105 NATHANIEL] *no speech prefix here in* Q *or* F

120 canzonet] canganet

121–7 Here are ... you] *given to 'Nath.' in* Q *and* F

130 HOLOFERNES] *Nath.*

133 writing] written

135 Sir Nathaniel, this] *Ped.* Sir *Holofernes,* this

145 NATHANIEL] *Holo.*

155 ben] bien

IV.3. 47 KING] *Long.*

106 *Wished*] (*from 'The Passionate Pilgrim'*); Wish Q *and* F

110 *thorn*] (*from 'England's Helicon'*); throne Q *and* F

153 coaches] couches

174 to] by

by] to

178 men like you, men] men like men

246 wood] word

257 and] *not in* Q *or* F

293 *After this line* Q *and* F *print a 23-line draft of lines 294–330. See the Commentary to line 293*

335 authors] authour

358 betime] be time

359 *Allons! Allons!*] Alone alone

V.1. 1 *quod*] *quid*

9 *hominem*] *hominum*

20 'dout' *sine* 'b'] dout fine

25 insanie] infamie

27 *bone*] *bene*

V.1.   28 *Bone? 'Bone'* for *'bene'*] Priscian a little] *Bome*
               boon for boon prescian, a litle

           31 *gaudeo*] gaudio

           56 venue] vene we

           65 *manu*] *vnū*

           76 preambulate] *preambulat*

           88 choice] chose

          114 assistance] assistants

          120 Joshua, yourself; this] *Iosua,* your selfe, my
               selfe, and this

          145 *Allons!*] Alone,

V.2.   28 cure] care,
               care] cure

           65 hests] deuice

           74 wantonness] wantons be

          122 to parley, court] to parlee, to court

          123 love-suit] Loue-feat

          148 her] his

          152 ne'er] ere

          216 (*assigned to Rosaline*)

          277 '*Non point*'] No poynt Q; No point F

          309 runs o'er the land] (*this editor*); runs ore land

          338 man] mad man Q; madman F

          373 My gentle sweet] gentle sweete

          374 wit] wits

          482 brave manage] braue nuage Q; braue manager
               F

          528 *de la guerra*] delaguar

          554 PRINCESS] *Lady.*

          668 The party is gone] *printed as a stage direction
               in Q and F*

        685–6 Stir them on, stir] stir them or stir

          777 in] *not in* Q *or* F

          811 hermit] herrite Q; euer F
               After this line Q *and* F *print a six-line draft of
               lines 826–60. See the Commentary to line 811*

          883 VER] *not in* Q *or* F

884–5 And lady-smocks ... yellow hue] *these lines
are reversed in Q and F*

901 HIEMS] *Winter.*

5

Stage directions

The stage directions of this edition are based on those of Q,
with reference to F on the few occasions when it differs from
the earlier text. Certain clarifications and regularizations have
been made; for example, at the beginning of V.2, where Q has
'*Enter the Ladyes*' and F the still more peremptory '*Enter Ladies*',
the names of the women have been substituted. Some directions
noting necessary bits of stage business have been added. The
list below includes a selection of interesting Q and F directions
altered in this edition and examples of radical editorial re-
modelling of Q and F directions. Differences between Q and F
accidentals are ignored, the Q form being given. All indications
of persons addressed ('*to Costard*', for example) and indications
of words spoken aside are editorial; they are not included in this
list.

I.1.   27, 32 *He signs*] *not in Q or F*

         119 *reading*] *not in Q or F*

         158 *He signs*] *not in Q or F*

         216 *reading*] *not in Q or F*

         294 *Exeunt King, Longaville, and Dumaine*] *not in
         Q or F*

I.2.   139 *Exeunt Dull and Jaquenetta*] *Exeunt.*

II.1.   o *Enter the Princess of France, Rosaline, Maria,
         and Katharine, with Boyet and two more
         attendant Lords*] *Enter the Princesse of Fraunce,
         with three attending Ladies and three Lordes.*

         36 *Exit Boyet*] *after line 35 in Q and F*

         89 *Enter the King, Berowne, Longaville, and
         Dumaine*] *after line 88 in Q and F*

         110 *She offers the King a paper*] *not in Q or F*

         113 *The King reads*] *not in Q or F*

		Berowne and Rosaline converse apart] not in Q or F
II.1.	128	*He leaves her*] Exit.
	179	*Exeunt King, Berowne, Longaville, and Dumaine*] Exit.
	182	*Enter Longaville*] not in Q or F
	208	*He tries to kiss her*] not in Q or F
III.1.	0	*Enter Armado and Mote*] Enter Braggart and his Boy. Q; Enter Broggart and Boy.	Song F
	3	*singing*] not in Q or F
	63	*Exit*] not in Q or F
	128	*giving Costard a letter*] not in Q or F
	129–30	*giving him a coin*] not in Q or F
	165	*He gives Costard a letter*] not in Q or F
		He gives him money] not in Q or F
IV.1.	0	*Enter the Princess, Rosaline, Maria, Katharine, Boyet and two more attendant Lords, and a Forester*] Enter the Princesse, a Forrester, her Ladyes, and her Lordes.
	18	*She gives him money*] not in Q or F
	57	*She takes the letter*] not in Q or F
	59	*He reads the superscript*] not in Q or F
	63	*reading*] Boyet reedes.
	108	*Exeunt all except Boyet, Rosaline, Maria, and Costard*] Exeunt. F (not in Q)
	129	*Exit Rosaline*] Exit. F (after line 127 in Q)
	140	*Exeunt Boyet and Maria*] not in Q or F
	149–50	*Shout within . . . Exit*] Exeunt. Shoot within. Q and F (after line 150)
IV.2.	0	*Enter Holofernes, Nathaniel, and Dull*] Enter Dull, Holofernes, the Pedant and Nathaniel.
	80	*with a letter*] not in Q or F
	99	*He sings*] not in Q or F
	105	*reading*] not in Q or F
	120	*He takes the letter*] not in Q or F
	130	*reading*] not in Q or F
IV.3	1	*reading*] not in Q or F

218

19 *with a paper*] not in Q or F

24 *reading*] not in Q or F

41 *with several papers*] not in Q or F

54 *Reading*] not in Q or F

55 *He tears the paper*] not in Q or F

57–8 *taking another paper ... Reading*] He reades the Sonnet. Q *and* F (*after* 'shall go:')

74 *with a paper*] not in Q or F

75 *He stands aside*] not in Q or F

99 *reading*] Dumaine reades his Sonnet.

125, 129, *advancing*] not in Q or F
149

186 *with a letter*] not in Q or F

197 *Berowne tears the letter*] not in Q or F

201 *gathering up the pieces*] not in Q or F

275 *showing his shoe*] not in Q or F

359 *Exeunt King, Longaville, and Dumaine*] not in Q or F

362 *Exit*] Exeunt. F (*not in* Q)

V.1.   15 *He draws out his table-book*] Draw-out his Table-booke.

29 *Enter Armado, Mote, and Costard*] Enter Bragart, Boy.

V.2.   156 *A trumpet sounds*] Sound Trom. Q; Sound. F

157 *Enter blackamoors with music, Mote with a speech, and the King and the rest of the lords disguised like Russians and visored*] Enter Black-moores with musicke, the Boy with a speach, and the rest of the Lordes disguysed.

160 *The ladies turn their backs to him*] after line 161 in Q and F

214 *Instruments strike up*] not in Q or F

229, 237, *They converse apart*] not in Q or F
241, 255

309 *Enter the King, Berowne, Longaville, and Dumaine, having shed their disguises*] Enter the King and the rest.

V.2. 336 *Enter the Princess, Rosaline, Maria, and Kath-arine, having unmasked and exchanged favours, with Boyet*] *Enter the Ladies.*

521 *Armado and the King converse apart*] *not in* Q *or* F

528 *He gives the King a paper*] *not in* Q *or* F

530–31 *Consulting the paper*] *not in* Q *or* F

533 *Reading*] *not in* Q *or* F

576 *Nathaniel retires*] Q *and* F *put 'Exit Curat.' after line 582*

584 *as presenter*] *not in* Q *or* F

590 *Mote retires*] *Exit Boy.*

627 *Holofernes retires*] *not in* Q *or* F

662 *Berowne steps forth and whispers to Costard*] *Berowne steps foorth.*

811 *The King and the Princess converse apart*] *not in* Q *or* F

821, 825 *They converse apart*] *not in* Q *or* F